Emergency Management for Healthcare Leaders

The modern healthcare landscape is rife with an array of potential emergencies, from natural disasters to public health crises, cybersecurity threats to mass casualty incidents.

This book provides healthcare leaders with a multifaceted approach to emergency management that encompasses prevention, preparedness, response, and recovery. The book is designed to empower healthcare executives, administrators, and upcoming healthcare leaders with the knowledge, tools, and strategies necessary to navigate the complex challenges of emergency management within the healthcare environment. As healthcare leaders grapple with the unprecedented challenges of our times, this book provides a roadmap for their journey. It is a roadmap rooted in the belief that healthcare leaders hold the key to resilience and hope in moments of adversity. With limited resources in the current market on the topic of emergency management for healthcare leaders, this book delves into the principles of disaster preparedness, risk assessment, crisis communication, resource allocation, and recovery planning. Moreover, the authors explore case studies and real-world examples to illustrate successful strategies and lessons learned from past emergencies impacting hospital operations.

Whether you are a seasoned veteran or a rising star in healthcare leadership, this guide is tailored to help build and strengthen the capacity to lead during times of crisis for any healthcare leader. The hope is that this book will serve as a beacon of knowledge and guidance, helping all healthcare leaders and the emergency managers who work alongside them to become more effective and resilient, capable of steering an organization through challenging times with grace, precision, and compassion, thereby playing a pivotal role in ensuring the safety and well-being of the patients, staff, and the communities they serve.

Emergency Management for Healthcare Leaders

Navigating Crisis from Chaos to Control

Kimberly Bailey and Thomas Crawford

Routledge
Taylor & Francis Group
A PRODUCTIVITY PRESS BOOK

Designed cover image: T&F

First published 2025
by Routledge
605 Third Avenue, New York, NY 10158

and by Routledge
4 Park Square, Milton Park, Abingdon, Oxon, OX14 4RN

Routledge is an imprint of the Taylor & Francis Group, an informa business

ISBN: 9781032867915 (hbk)
ISBN: 9781032867908 (pbk)
ISBN: 9781003529194 (ebk)

DOI: 10.4324/9781003529194

Typeset in Adobe Garamond
by Deanta Global Publishing Services, Chennai, India

Dedications from Kimberly Bailey

This book is a tribute to my family and all of the individuals and professionals who have influenced my path in healthcare and emergency management. To my loved ones – Brad, Maycie, Ben, Olivia, Mom, and Dad – this book symbolizes the connection we share. Your constant support, patience, and motivation have been the bedrock on which I've crafted this work. Thank you for being the cornerstone of my existence and for accompanying me on this journey. To all the unsung heroes within the South Carolina Emergency Management Family who work tirelessly to protect our community's health and wellbeing during crises; your dedication is truly inspiring. This book is a tribute to you – the leaders in Emergency Management throughout South Carolina and across America – who face challenges, with bravery, endurance, and an unwavering sense of responsibility. Finally, a heartfelt thank you goes out to Dr. Tom Crawford for your guidance, wisdom, and unwavering support that has propelled us on this journey. You are a true beacon of leadership and my trusted ally in our shared mission to safeguard the wellbeing of our patients and the communities that we serve. Thank you for your invaluable contributions to this endeavor and for always believing in me without fail.

Dedications from Thomas Crawford

I would like to dedicate this book to the two most influential women in my life – my wife Danielle Crawford and my mother Cherly Sweet – I thank you both for your support, guidance, and your unwavering belief in me. It means more than you will ever know.

Contents

About the Authors

Kimberly Bailey holds a master's degree in emergency management and Homeland Security from Arizona State University and a bachelor's degree in English. She is a South Carolina State Certified Emergency Manager and a Certified Emergency Management Accreditation Program Assessor/ Accreditation Manager, among other certifications, including former Nationally Registered Paramedic and Certified Healthcare Simulation Educator.

Currently, Kimberly serves as the System Executive Director of Emergency Management for the Medical University of South Carolina (MUSC) Health System. MUSC Health is a prominent academic medical center operating more than 1,600 beds across all hospitals and facilities. Kimberly's role at MUSC Health involves coordinating emergency management standards, collaborating with various agencies, managing emergency operations centers, and leading projects such as the development of the High-Risk Infectious Disease Unit. Previously, she held significant roles including Academic Associate for Arizona State's Emergency Management and Homeland Security Program, South Carolina Department of Health Emerging Infectious Disease Planner, and the Bureau of Public Health Preparedness Training and Exercise Manager for the South Carolina Department of Health (formerly known as the South Carolina Department of Health and Environmental Control).

Kimberly served on the executive leadership team of the South Carolina Emergency Management Association (SCEMA), including a role as Treasurer from 2020 to 2023. In this capacity, she played a pivotal role in guiding the association's strategic direction and financial oversight. Kimberly's contributions reflect her deep commitment to advancing the field of emergency management and fostering collaborative relationships among those professionals and all stakeholders. Kimberly has contributed to numerous publications and articles on operational communications and simulation scenarios in emergency medical services. She has presented at various conferences and summits on topics related to emergency management and healthcare preparedness. Her extensive experience in emergency management and her role in shaping preparedness strategies highlight her expertise and dedication to improving healthcare emergency responses.

Thomas Crawford is a seasoned integrated healthcare (hospitals and physician practices) executive (President/CEO/COO) and decorated collegiate educator (four excellence in teaching awards from the University of Florida) that has consistently delivered collaborative accomplishments within health systems, rural and metropolitan hospitals, and physician practices. He has a track record of exceptional proven successes developing system-wide strategic initiatives that contributed to enhanced market positioning, consistent bottom-line profitability/growth, and advanced clinical and financial performance. Additionally, Dr. Crawford has consistently elevated physician and employee engagement by partnering to drive best-in-class operational efficiencies while focusing on enhancing the quality and safety of the care delivered. Lastly, Dr. Crawford's leadership efforts have been recognized locally, regionally, and nationally via numerous awards and honors – as a Marlon Fitzwater Medallion recipient to, most recently, being named 1 of Becker's 75 Health System COOs to Know in 2023 and 1 of 60 Academic COOs to Know in 2024.

Preface

Greetings to all leaders and readers of *Emergency Management for Healthcare Leaders: Navigating Crisis from Chaos to Control*. This valuable book aims to equip all healthcare leaders, hospital emergency managers, and future leaders with the knowledge, tools, and strategies needed to tackle the challenges of emergency management in the healthcare sector. As healthcare leaders confront the difficulties of our environment, this guide serves as a valuable compass for their journey. It is founded on the belief that healthcare leaders play a role in fostering resilience and optimism during emergency times.

In a time marked by transformations and uncertainties, emphasizing the necessity of an emergency management framework for every hospital or healthcare system is paramount. Emergency management can be likened to a tapestry woven with various threads symbolizing the components that contribute to its overall strength and efficacy. Each thread – ranging from preparedness and mitigation to response and recovery – interweaves with others, forming a fabric designed to endure the pressures of crises. The participation of stakeholders such as government bodies, first responders, and community members adds depth and diversity to this tapestry, showcasing the effort essential for effective emergency management. At its core lie healthcare facilities and hospitals, whose threads serve as the foundation for emergency response and recovery efforts.

Without the contributions of healthcare providers in delivering care, assessing patients, and offering assistance, the entire system would fall apart, leaving neighborhoods exposed and defenseless. The resources that healthcare organizations contribute to the fabric ensure that the system can react promptly and efficiently to any emergency, strengthening the resilience and flexibility of emergency management. Essentially, the fabric of emergency management demonstrates how combining elements and working together leads to a sturdy framework capable of safeguarding and supporting communities during challenging times.

Healthcare professionals carry a responsibility to safeguard, treat, and preserve lives during times of hardship. In this capacity, they encounter obstacles that require a blend of foresight, expertise, and unwavering resolve. This publication by a group of specialists in emergency management and healthcare serves as an example of the knowledge from those devoted to their communities.

The contemporary healthcare arena is filled with crises ranging from natural calamities to public health emergencies, cyber threats to incidents involving multiple casualties. This publication offers an approach to emergency management covering prevention, readiness, response strategies, and recovery measures.

Let's dive into the fundamentals of preparing for disasters, evaluating risks, communicating during crises, allocating resources, and planning for recovery. Additionally, we'll examine examples and real-life scenarios to demonstrate strategies and valuable lessons learned from previous emergencies.

Whether you're a healthcare professional or a rising star in a leadership role, this book is designed to support you in developing and enhancing your ability to lead during times of crisis. The goal is for this manual to be a source of knowledge and guidance, assisting you in becoming a resilient healthcare leader who can navigate your organization through tough times with poise, accuracy, and empathy. By sharpening your emergency management skills, you can play a role in ensuring the safety and well-being of your patients, staff, and the communities you serve.

The various sections of this book were authored by experts in healthcare and emergency management fields who cover all aspects of healthcare emergency preparedness. They present practical case studies, insights into emerging trends and innovations, as well as a forward-looking perspective. Beyond that, it stands as a tribute to the determination of healthcare leaders and emergency responders, showcasing their ability to adapt, learn from challenges, and continuously improve in the face of significant obstacles.

As you start reading this book, we suggest approaching the content with a willingness to learn and a commitment to implementing the concepts in your healthcare environment. Together we will delve into the art and science of managing healthcare emergencies, aiming to enhance the well-being of those, under your care.

Within this book, we will explore aspects of healthcare emergency management in depth. Topics will include preparedness principles, the significance of risk assessment, effective crisis communication strategies, resource allocation tactics, and detailed recovery planning. Through real-life examples and practical guidance, we aim to provide you with the knowledge and expertise needed to lead during times of crisis.

Throughout the chapters, we will offer you tools and insights to become a resilient and empathetic healthcare leader when facing adversity. Navigating the path forward poses obstacles, yet equipped with readiness, understanding, and perseverance you can guide your team through the terrain of crisis response, safeguarding the welfare and security of those under your care.

Foreword

Several years ago, I was invited to take part in a conference that studied high reliability in healthcare organizations. The purpose of the convocation was to better understand how hospitals, physician groups, and health systems achieve the concept of high reliability – which is a state of consistent high performance in a high-risk environment, despite the potential for complex challenges.

At this discussion, there were many different types of healthcare organizations. Some were national or regional in scope, while others were small rural community clinics. The commonality was that each organization had achieved high reliability in at least one domain. For some, it was service, and their patient satisfaction scores were consistently extraordinary. For others, it was a culture of safety achieved through the application of just cultural principles. Some organizations had a focus on patient harm, and their zero-harm performance was tremendous. And finally, a few organizations had a degree of performance in their revenue cycle that was quite enviable.

As the conference continued, I began to take more notice of organizations that had high reliability in more than one domain. This is when I first noted a concept I like to call the oyster method of high performance in healthcare. It changed my approach to organizational performance.

This methodology revolves around a "performance nidus" and "performance nacre." Like a bit of dirt or sand in an oyster that irritates and stimulates a reaction in that oyster, so too does a "performance nidus" cause organizations to react in a similar positive and beautiful manner. This time, instead of a magnificent oyster being produced, organizational high performance is the result. And like the oyster, this reaction can be used as a stimulant to do it again and again but in different parts of the organization.

A "performance nidus" may start in patient satisfaction, but the learnings are transferable. Just like the nacre laid down by an oyster doesn't matter on the nature of the original irritant, high-performance organizations develop their own nacre consisting of enhanced response to change, better processes, hardwiring best practices, improved accountability, higher-level leadership, and constant communication. The best organizations learn to lay down this high-performance framework in one area and then move on to other key areas, creating a high-performance learning organization.

The takeaway was that repeatedly highly reliable healthcare organizations all start the journey somewhere – it might be first in patient service. Or it could be safety, or maybe even in a more esoteric part of that organization.

At the Medical University of South Carolina (MUSC) health system, having been a witness on the front lines for almost 25 years, one of our "performance niduses" is storm weather planning, now expanded to emergency management.

MUSC, an academic health system that serves the quaternary health needs of much of South Carolina, is headquartered in Charleston. This city sits on a peninsula affected by three types of flooding – storm surge, tides, and rain. These intermix along with wind to produce an interminable number of variables that must be weighed when preparing for a storm while maintaining the patient care needs of South Carolinians. Sitting on the coast of the Atlantic in the path of storms that originate far away, this part of the continent experiences a heavy share of tropical events. While the disruptive nature of hurricanes is familiar to many people, we have come to appreciate how heavy rainstorms, a wind event, or even the rare ice storm will dislocate patient care if we don't plan, communicate, implement, adjust, reassess, and repeat.

The authors have been on the front lines of organizational emergency management for over a decade. While they have developed and perfected healthcare emergency management responses, the wise reader will see the "performance nacre" that can be used throughout healthcare to lift and sustain the highest levels of organizational performance.

Patrick J Cawley, MD

Acknowledgments

We would like to extend our heartfelt thanks to the entire team at Routledge and Productivity Press, whose support and commitment have been invaluable throughout this journey. A special note of gratitude goes to our editor, Kristine Rynne Mednansky, whose dedication, keen insight, and expertise have been instrumental in shaping and bringing this book to life. Her guidance and encouragement have made all the difference in ensuring that our vision was realized on every page. Most importantly, we extend our deepest gratitude to our colleagues in healthcare and the field of emergency management across the state of South Carolina and especially those listed below who each contributed to this book in their own special way. Their expertise and guidance have been invaluable in shaping this work. We would like to give very special thanks to the following contributors: Kim Stenson, Mario Formisano, Sam Hodge, Lary "Rocky" Tucker, Jamie Blair, and Tom McNeil.

Contributor Bios

Patrick J. Cawley, MD, MBA – Foreword

Patrick J. Cawley is the Chief Executive Officer of MUSC Health and Executive Vice President for Health Affairs of the Medical University of South Carolina. In this role, he oversees all clinical matters as they relate to MUSC. During his leadership, MUSC has significantly expanded its clinical enterprise with a new Children's Hospital, a regional health network, multiple ambulatory sites, development of additional clinical affiliates, and numerous novel joint ventures. Additionally, MUSC has become a national leader in telehealth and has continued as South Carolina's #1 hospital/health system per US News and World Report. Under Dr. Cawley's leadership, MUSC continues to receive numerous quality awards across all domains of quality: safety, effectiveness, efficiency, equity, timeliness, and patient centeredness.

Previously, he served as the Chief Medical Officer of MUSC Medical Center. In that role he was responsible for the quality and safety of all patient care programs as well as direct oversight of clinical service lines. He has led MUSC's improvement transformation in quality and patient safety, which was recognized by the University Health system Consortium in 2007 and again in 2012 by awarding the coveted Rising Star honor to MUSC.

Dr. Cawley is a Certified Physician Executive through the American College of Physician Executives and a Fellow of the American College of Healthcare Executives. He is a Fellow in the Liberty Fellowship Program and a member of the Aspen Global Leadership Network. He has been named one of America's Best Doctors®. He has also been awarded the Master of Hospital Medicine from the Society of Hospital Medicine.

Dr. Cawley is a Past-President of the Society of Hospital Medicine. He is actively involved in leadership roles in the American Hospital Association, the South Carolina Hospital Association, America's Essential Hospitals, Vizient, and the healthcare collaborative, Initiant. Dr. Cawley graduated from the University of Scranton. He earned his medical degree from Georgetown University before completing an internal medicine residency at Duke University. He holds a Master of Business Administration from the University of Massachusetts-Amherst. He is board certified in internal medicine with focused recognition in hospital medicine.

Kim Stenson – Quote/Interview Influence Chapter 2

Kim Stenson was named Director of the South Carolina Emergency Management Division of the Adjutant General's Office in June 2013. Under his direction, the Division provides oversight and coordination for emergency and disaster consequence management planning, and response and recovery operations for the State of South Carolina. Mr. Stenson is also responsible for coordination with emergency managers at the local and national levels. Prior to joining SCEMD in 1998, Mr. Stenson served as an infantry officer in the U.S. Army. While in the Army, he served in a variety of assignments in the United States, Europe, Asia, and the Middle East including combat service during the First Gulf War. Following his retirement from the U.S. Army, Mr. Stenson joined SCEMD, where he served successively as the Manager, Natural Hazards Plans; Chief, Preparedness; Chief, Preparedness and Recovery; and Chief of Staff, an appointment in 2008. He has led the Division's responses to major events, most notably for the Ice Storm in 2014, the October 2015 heavy rains and severe flooding incident, Hurricane Matthew in 2016, Hurricane Irma in 2017, Hurricane Florence in 2018, Hurricane Dorian in 2019, Severe Storms in 2020, COVID-19 Pandemic from 2020 to 2023, and Hurricane Ian in 2022. Mr. Stenson received a Bachelor of Arts in Political Science from Washington and Lee University in 1975 and a Master of Arts in history from Norwich University in 1987. He currently serves as Chairman of the State Emergency Response Commission, Chairman of the Public Health Emergency Plan Committee, Vice-Chairman of the Firefighter Mobilization Committee, and is a member of the Homeland Security Advisory Committee.

Mr. Stenson's military awards and decorations include the Bronze Star Medal and the Combat Infantry Badge. In 2016, he was awarded the Order of the Palmetto, South Carolina's highest civilian honor, by Governor Nikki Haley.

Mario Formisano – Contributor, Chapter 5

Mario Formisano has served as Dorchester County's Deputy County Administrator for Public Safety since July 1, 2021. In this role, he assists the County Administrator in implementing County policies as established by the County Council to promote the public safety and welfare of county residents, businesses, and visitors. Formisano provides coordinated leadership to the Consolidated Dispatch Center, Emergency Management, Emergency Medical Services, Fire Rescue, and Public Information Office; he also serves as a liaison to the County Sheriff and Coroner. From 2011 to 2021, Formisano served as Dorchester County's Director of Emergency Management, where he helped manage six federally declared disasters. He has more than fifteen years in public service, working for the South Carolina Emergency Management Division as a Regional Emergency Manager and was part of the disaster services team with the Summit County Chapter of the American Red Cross in Akron, Ohio. Formisano is an Active Member of the South Carolina Association of Counties, South Carolina City County Management Association, and South Carolina Emergency Management Association (Past President). He holds an Associate of Applied Science in Fire Protection Technology and a Bachelor of Science in Emergency Management from the University of Akron and a Master of Public Administration from the College of Charleston. He is a native of Northeast Ohio but has been called the Lowcountry home since 2007.

Sam Hodge – Contributor, Chapter 9

Sam Hodge serves as the Director of Emergency Management for Horry County in Conway, South Carolina. He formerly served as a Battalion Chief with Midway Fire Rescue in Pawley's Island, where he spent most of those 20 years in Emergency Services. During his career at Midway Fire Rescue, Mr. Hodge served in all ranks, starting as a Firefighter Paramedic, progressing through the ranks to Lieutenant, and then to the position of Battalion Chief. During this time, he was honored with the following awards: Community Service, Meritorious Service, Officer of the Year, and the South Carolina Meritorious Action Directly Resulting in the Saving of Life award. He served as President of the South Carolina Emergency Management Association (SCEMA) and was named South Carolina Emergency Management Director of the Year in 2011 and 2013. Mr. Hodge currently serves on the Executive Committee for the Pee Dee Healthcare Coalition, among other local, regional, and state committees. Mr. Hodge oversaw five Presidential Declared disasters during his last six years as a Director of Georgetown County Emergency Management before he retired from Georgetown County in September 2019 with over 30 years of service. After he retired from Georgetown County, he served as the Director of Emergency Management and Safety at Conway Medical Center in Conway, South Carolina, before joining the Horry County Team. Mr. Hodge resides in Murrells Inlet with his wife, Tonya, and has four children.

Rocky Tucker – Contributor, Chapter 8

Larry "Rocky" Tucker was introduced to the Incident Command System as a wildland firefighter with the North Carolina Forest Service and the South Carolina Forestry Commission in the 1990s. As an officer in the South Carolina Army National Guard, he was directly involved with disaster relief to local communities during Hurricane events ranging from Hurricane Hugo response in 1989 to Hurricane Floyd in 1999. Rocky began his formal career in Ēmergency Management with the South Carolina Emergency Management Division following historical flooding throughout the state in 2015. Building off two decades of experience in crisis consequence management, he served as a Regional Emergency Manager assisting county and municipal governments in the development of Emergency Management programs focused on the fundamentals of preparedness, response, and recovery. Over a seven-year period with SCEMD, Rocky spent countless hours in county Emergency Operations Centers either in response to disasters ranging from hurricanes and tornadoes to unseasonable snowstorms. He is recognized throughout South Carolina as a training expert with emphasis on building practical exercise solutions focused on community needs. Rocky currently works for MUSC Health as a Division Emergency Manager. In this role he brings a knowledge of emergency management principles and real-world experience to the healthcare community in which he serves.

Jamie Blair – Contributor, Chapter 8

Jamie Blair is a seasoned Emergency Management and Emergency/Disaster Medical Specialist with extensive real-world deployment experience. Notably, he served as the Logistics Section Chief for a FEMA Type I Incident Management Team during Hurricane Ike in 2008 and the Haiti Earthquake in 2010, where he provided critical logistical support to over 2,000 U.S. federal medical responders in the field. His expertise extends to college-level instruction, state-level exercise development, and leading public health logistical responses, including the COVID-19 pandemic in South Carolina. Mr. Blair has held significant roles, including Logistics Manager for the South Carolina Emergency Management Division and Director of the Public Health Preparedness Program for the South Carolina Department of Health and Environmental Control. He currently applies his expertise in the private sector, managing business continuity programs for AgFirst Farm Credit Bank, and teaches graduate-level Emergency Management courses at Southern New Hampshire University. Mr. Blair is a Certified Emergency Manager (CEM) through the International Association of Emergency Managers and a Certified Business Continuity Professional (CBCP) through Disaster Recovery Institute International.

Tom McNeil – Contributor, Chapters 3 and 5

Thomas McNeal is the Director of Emergency Management for Dorchester County, South Carolina, serving since December of 2021. His responsibilities include advising the County Administrator, Senior Leaders of key stakeholder agencies, and Senior Elected Officials in all matters of Emergency Management and Homeland Security Preparedness and Response Operations. He is also responsible for management of office staff, their programs and projects, and serves in a leadership role during large scale emergencies. Tom has experience at all levels of incident management and has deployed to several major disasters around the country most notably serving as the Planning Section Chief in the Emergency Operations Center during the Baltimore Riots, and in his own leadership position through response and recovery operations during a local Howard County Flood Emergency where an entire town in Maryland was destroyed. Tom joined the U.S. Army after high school serving as an Airborne Infantry Soldier in a Long-Range Surveillance Company. He left the military as a Non-Commissioned Officer and moved to Topeka, Kansas, where he attended Washburn University achieving a BS in Criminal Justice. Tom worked in Corrections before joining the Topeka Police Department where he served as a member of the Response Team (SWAT) and the Crises Negotiation Unit among other things. He got his first taste of emergency management deploying to Mississippi for Hurricane Katrina which had a life- and career-changing effect on him and led to his current career pathway. He became a member of the State of Kansas Incident Management Team and had the opportunity to deploy in leadership roles to several major disasters. Tom eventually left law enforcement and the State of Kansas to return to his roots in the State of Maryland where he transitioned to a new full-time role as an Emergency Manager. He served with the Howard County, Maryland Office of Emergency Management for nine years as the Deputy Director, then spent another four years as the Director of Security, Emergency Preparedness, and Response for the Howard County Public School System where he oversaw Security, Emergency Management, and Risk Management. Tom has a degree in Criminal Justice from Washburn University, is a graduate of the Executive Leaders Program at the Naval Post Graduate School, Center for Homeland Defense and Security, and is a Certified Emergency Manager through the International Association of Emergency Management.

Chapter 1

The Call

Thomas Crawford

I'm awoken by the sound of the health system's paging application on my cell phone – it's a distinct and, frankly annoying, alarm. I roll over and look at the clock – it's 1:47 a.m. The message is succinct and to the point: IAT (Incident Assessment Team) call at 2:00 a.m. I call into the IAT meeting, and there are numerous voices talking over each other. "I want to hear from the Administrator on Call (AOC)," I state authoritatively. "And I only want to hear about the problem, the impact and the plan." The AOC lets the group know that the problem is that a behavioral health patient got ahold of a chemical-based fire extinguisher and discharged it on the unit. The impact was that the floor of behavioral health patients would need to be evacuated, and the plan was to temporarily relocate them to another part of the psychiatric hospital. We worked through logistics with our overriding imperatives being patient and employee safety – any other issue could be addressed the following morning. The meeting ended with a good plan in place, so I went back to bed, hoping I would be able to get some additional sleep before my workday began.

Still tired from the night before, I walk into a conference room to interview a potential member of our leadership team. The discussion goes well, with the candidate providing me with thoughtful answers to my questions. "Do you have any questions for me?" I ask as the time allotted for the interview expires. "What keeps you up at night?" *This is ironic,* I thought to myself. Nevertheless, I have been asked this question numerous times before and my reply never changes, "The call," I answer in response. I always receive a puzzled look from the professional on the other side of the table, so I continue to elaborate. "It's the inevitable call that is associated with an event that the organization has to immediately respond to." Some of the examples I provide transform the candidates' look of concern into a palpable feeling of uneasiness. "Fires, flooding, violence, gun violence, bomb threats, patient elopement, infrastructure failures, unplanned information system downtime, to name a few." The list isn't exhaustive and only scratches the surface of what can happen despite hazard vulnerability analyses and attempts at mitigating potential issues before they occur.

Far too many organizations don't understand the risks associated with their operations, and when "the call" comes, they and their care team members feel ill-equipped to handle the scenarios that could impact our care team members and/or the patients we're here to serve. Consider the following:

DOI: 10.4324/9781003529194-1

- Health Facility Fires – According to the U.S. Fire Administration, "For each year from 2014 to 2016, an estimated 5,800 medical facility fires were reported to fire departments in the United States. It is estimated that these fires caused 5 deaths, 150 injuries, and $56 million in property loss per year."[1]
- Natural Disasters –- Per the research of Abdus et al., the total recorded number of natural catastrophes grew from 33 in 1960 to 441 disasters in 2000. Since 1960, there have been more than 11,000 recorded disasters, with flooding being five times more prevalent than other events.[2]
- Workplace Violence – Per the US Bureau of Labor Statistics, "the all-worker incidence rate for nonfatal occupational injuries and illnesses involving days away from work resulting from intentional injury by another person in the private healthcare and social assistance industry was 10.4 per 10,000 full-time workers, compared to the all-worker incidence rate of 2.1. The healthcare and social service industries experience the highest rates of injuries caused by workplace violence and are 5 times as likely to suffer a workplace violence injury than workers overall."[3]
- Sentinel Events – According to the Joint Commission, there were 1,441 sentinel events that occurred in 2022, more than double the amount reported in 2020.[4]
- Cyber Attacks – Per an article published in the *Chief Healthcare Executive,* 106,000,000 people were impacted by health-related cyber attacks, and it was forecasted that the number of impacted healthcare entities would balloon to over 500+ in 2023.[5]

Again, the afore-referenced list is not exhaustive; it was meant to highlight the need to catalog potential hazards, put mitigation plans in place, and to train your care team members who could find themselves running a healthcare emergency operations center (HEOC) and coordinating the response when the unforeseen occurs. Far too many times, in the healthcare industry, we underestimate the potential for unplanned significant impacts on our operations and place individuals into situations where they may not have the experience, training, or ability to manage through the chaos that inevitably ensues. This was well documented in the aftermath of Hurricane Katrina and has plagued other health systems around the country.

Why? It is multifactorial. Some organizations do not invest the time in simulating responses to highly probable events and/or the training required for their care team members to have the wealth of knowledge needed to mitigate/eliminate threats to an organization's operations. The need for training was underscored by a study by Balut et al. that surveyed 4,026 VA employees who reported they wanted/needed additional training on the emergency management of natural disasters (61%), the pandemic (63%), and man-made disasters (68%). [6]

I remember vividly being one of those individuals that needed additional training. I was a 25-year-old first-time manager working at a rural hospital that used out-of-the-box HICS (hospital incident command system) templates to run their emergency operations. Within this context, I knew where to report if paged; however, it was explained to me that I would fulfill the role assigned to me and would be provided with a job outline once assigned – so my role, as with my colleagues, was undetermined until I arrived on the scene. I vividly remember my pager going off on a snowy and icy Saturday afternoon; it was a mass casualty motor vehicle accident that overwhelmed our local resources. Note – I didn't find this out via an Incident Assessment Team call (because we didn't have one); I found out what I would be walking into from a colleague who called me as I was preparing to leave my house.

The main entryway to the hospital, on a Saturday, was also the entryway for the Emergency Department (ED). However, this was not a normal Saturday, I noted to myself, based on the quantity of cars that were in the ED parking lot. I walked through the sliding doors, and the ED waiting area was overwhelmed with patients waiting to be seen and several individuals who were trying to get an update on their loved ones. I caught the nurse manager, who was coming out to provide an update to the saturated waiting room, "Where did we establish the HEOC?" I questioned. "What HEOC?" she snapped back and added, "The AOC (administrator on call) isn't here yet!" "What can I do to help?" I asked. "I need a social worker," she replied with a hurried and frustrated tone. I was expecting a job sheet that provided me with an overview of my role and expectations. I never received one. "Come with me," she stated as she motioned me into the ED treatment area. She pulled me aside and started providing me with the context in a lowered voice. "There was a terrible accident on the highway this morning, multiple deaths. We have five-year old boy who was unhurt; however, his mother, stepfather, and brother all died in the accident." "I need you to sit with him and try and find his father, grandparents, anyone that can take care of him." "Does he know that his family members died?" I asked. "No," was the reply as she led me to the consult room where the little boy was waiting.

I find myself looking into the concerned face of a very sweet little boy. "Hi, my name's Tom," I let him know after entering the room. The little boy told me his name and quickly asked me, "Where's my mommy?" I had no response and felt very unprepared for the role I was filling. "Are you hungry?" I asked, attempting to quickly change the subject. He nodded his head yes. "How about I take you to the cafeteria, and I'll buy you whatever you want to eat." He smiled and nodded his head in approval. After getting him his macaroni and cheese and a soda, we went back to my office where I was able to piece together, with the little boy's help, the name of his birth father and potentially the state he lived in. "Do you like cartoons?" I asked. "Yes," he replied, smiling through his soda mustache. I brought the little boy across the hall to the medical staff lounge and tuned the TV to a cartoon station. "If you need anything, I'm right across the hall."

On that gray and miserable day, I made what is, over 25 years later, still the toughest call of my career. After much searching, I found the father's phone number, and with a knot in my stomach, I gave him a call. "Mr. Smith (name changed to provide anonymity), my name is Tom Crawford and I'm very sorry, but I have horrible news for you." I went on to tell him that his ex-wife, her husband, and his older son had all passed away in a terrible multi-vehicle car accident. Through the sobs – his and mine – I was able to give him the address to the hospital, and I promised that I would keep his young son safe until he arrived. We both agreed that I would not deliver the news about his family's passing and that the father would talk to him after he arrived.

There has got to be a better way to handle these emergent situations, I thought to myself after I turned the child over to his father. I walked back upstairs to the ED, and it was still chaotic with too few resources to handle the volume of critically injured patients. The good news is, there is a better way to mitigate and transform a chaotic environment into a controlled response that provides any healthcare entity with the knowledge and constructs required to effectively manage and learn from the unforeseen. That's the premise of this text: to provide the framework for the infrastructure and knowledge required to ensure you have trained individuals ready to respond when needed.

Case in point, a seasoned Administrator who was taking her last week of call before retiring. She was known to have the "black cloud" follow her, meaning every time we had a significant flooding event, she was the AOC. I saw her walking down the main hospital hallway, "Last week of call, is it going to flood?" I stated with a smile. "It's going to be sunny and in the 70s all week … there will be no flooding!" she replied. Then a little after 1:00 pm on a Thursday, the paging application on my cellphone started beeping. The message stated that there would be an IAT meeting at 1:15 pm. I jumped on the call and Brenda was in control as the AOC. She walked everyone through the problem – water main break on the fifth floor of our ambulatory care facility, the impact – significant retained water on the fifth floor and water intrusion on floors four and three, and the plan – quickly determine how many physicians we could relocate to unimpacted floors and for those that we could not provide exam rooms to, call their patients and offer to reschedule them later in the day (post clean-up) or, at their discretion, another day/time that would be more convenient for them.

I made my way to the HEOC, in part to compliment the team on a great response to the water main break and in part to give Brenda a hard time about a flood occurring without a rain cloud in the sky. Much to my chagrin, Brenda wasn't in the HEOC; she had left one of her counterparts in charge and went to assess the damage and the cleanup efforts. Undeterred, I made my way to our ambulatory care facility to look for Brenda. I found her on the fifth floor; she was assisting with the clean-up. She looked up as I approached her, and I quickly stated, "No worries, it's sunny and 70." Brenda smiled and retorted, "Go away, Tom Crawford, we have this under control." In truth, they did have the situation under control, and they did not need me. Why? Because we have an emergency preparedness infrastructure that focuses on mitigation, planning, operating, and recovering. Additionally, we invest a significant amount of time and effort into training. Although we cannot train for every potential issue that could occur, we can risk-stratify based on event probability and conduct tabletop exercises to ensure that our team is prepared and well-versed on how to respond.

Unfortunately, in healthcare, "the call" is inevitable; however, you can reduce the variability in responses by playing to your strengths, cataloging potential issues and risk stratifying them, and then training a select few individuals who will be in the call rotation on how to respond. It's not about going through the motions to appease the Joint Commission; on the contrary, it's about ensuring a perpetual state of readiness that underscores the safety of our care team members and patients as always paramount. Based on this simple yet overriding imperative, the same amount of effort and scrutiny that we place upon ensuring that we have a competent workforce at the bedside should be applied to ensuring we have well-trained and competent individuals taking call. It is not about having a large pool of people to decrease the call burden; rather, it's about ensuring you have a small seasoned and well-trained group that will benefit from the experiences that come with managing unplanned events.

When the call occurs will your AOC and emergency management team be prepared? Or will they feel like early careerist that was asked to be a social worker with zero training and experience? Remember, the call is inevitable.

The Bibliography section reflects the source information for the concepts and frameworks described in this chapter.

Bibliography

1. Federal Emergency Management Agency (FEMA). (n.d.). *Data snapshot: Medical facility fires*. https://www.fema.gov
2. Salam, A., Wireko, A. A., Jiffry, R., Ng, J. C., Patel, H., Zahid, M. J., Mehta, A., Huang, H., Abdul-Rahman, T., & Isik, A. (2023). The impact of natural disasters on healthcare and surgical services in low- and middle-income countries. *Ann Med Surg (Lond).*, 85(8), 3774–3777. https://doi.org/10.1097/MS9.0000000000001041
3. U.S. Bureau of Labor Statistics. (2018). *Workplace violence in healthcare, 2018*. https://www.bls.gov

4. The Joint Commission. (2023). *Sentinel event data CY2023 annual summary.* https://www.jointcommission.org
5. Chief Healthcare Executive. (2023). *Healthcare cyberattacks have affected more than 100 million people in 2023.* https://www.chiefhealthcareexecutive.com
6. Balut, M. D., Der-Martirosian, C., & Dobalian, A. (2022). Disaster preparedness training needs of healthcare workers at the US Department of Veterans Affairs. *South Med J.*, 115(2), 158–163. https://doi.org/10.14423/SMJ.0000000000001358

Chapter 2

The Imperative of Emergency Management in Healthcare

Kimberly Bailey

In Charleston, South Carolina, the sun shone brightly on a late summer afternoon in September 2019. Our historic city was bustling with tourists and residents enjoying the warm weather, but beneath the surface, a sense of unease lingered. Hurricane Dorian, a powerful and unpredictable storm, was approaching the East Coast, and its path was somewhat uncertain. For me, this was a familiar yet nerve-wracking scenario. My office (located in the heart of the hospital and chosen specifically because it has no windows) was filled with open emergency plans, maps, and emergency communication devices. My role as the hospital's emergency manager was clear: ensure readiness for any emergency, and a hurricane posed a significant threat. As Hurricane Dorian intensified over warm Atlantic waters, reaching Category 4 strength on August 30th, tension grew. Like many emergency managers anywhere along the east coast from Florida to New York at that time, I was glued to weather reports and briefings from the National Hurricane Center and the National Weather Service among other favorite weather partners of any good emergency manager. The storm had already wrought devastation in the Bahamas, and now it was tracking perilously close to the east coast, specifically the South Carolina coast. I prayed the forecasts we were getting from the amazing teams who produced them for us would prove accurate and the storm would stay offshore. Convening an emergency meeting with the hospital's leadership team, I reviewed our hurricane preparedness checklists and plans. These documents covered everything from patient evacuation protocols to ensuring backup power supplies. "We need to implement our hurricane protocols immediately. Our primary goal is to ensure the safety of our patients, staff, and facility. Let's go through our checklist," I emphasized. The team, seasoned by past hurricane experiences, sprang into action. Clinical teams prepared to move patients from vulnerable areas to safer parts of the state if needed. The facilities team secured windows and doors, checked generators, and ensured ample fuel reserves. Communication lines with state and local emergency services, as well as neighboring hospitals, were rigorously tested and confirmed. Despite the urgency in our actions, a sense of calm prevailed among hospital leadership and our experienced team.

 DOI: 10.4324/9781003529194-2

While the situation was serious and demanding, there were moments of camaraderie and light-heartedness in the Hospital Emergency Operations Center (HEOC). Amid the flurry of calls and coordination meetings, there were instances of shared laughter and humor, often sparked by anecdotes or moments of relief amidst the tension. These light-hearted exchanges helped maintain morale and a positive atmosphere despite the challenges posed by the severe weather. Additionally, the HEOC was well-prepared to sustain its operations, including provisions of homemade snacks and refreshments. Sometimes it looked like an elementary school bake sale from the 80's in there. The prepared snacks not only ensured that staff remained energized and focused but also provided a brief respite during intense periods of activity. The combination of focused professionalism and moments of joviality underscored the resilience and teamwork within the HEOC. It reflected a balanced approach to managing emergencies, acknowledging the seriousness of the situation while also supporting the well-being of those working tirelessly to ensure the safety and welfare of our patients and staff. We moved through the hospital, checking on preparations and offering words of encouragement. Around midnight, Hurricane Dorian, a Category 4 storm at that time, reached its closest point to Charleston, less than 45 miles offshore. Rain lashed against the windows, and the power briefly flickered before the generators kicked in. Inside, the hallways hummed with coordinated activity, running smoothly and according to our plan. As Hurricane Dorian approached, the intensity of the storm was palpable even within the corridors of the hospital. Despite being nowhere near an exit to the outside, I could feel the powerful gusts of wind sweeping down the hallways as I rounded on our care team members. The air seemed charged with the storm's energy, carrying with it a hint of moisture and the distant roar of the wind outside. It was as if the building itself was breathing in rhythm with the storm, the subtle vibrations and echoes of each gust reverberating through the walls. The sensation was both eerie and awe-inspiring, a visceral reminder of nature's immense power just beyond the hospital's sturdy confines. It was a reminder that even within the safety of the building, we were intimately connected to the forces of nature raging just outside our windows. The city endured strong winds and heavy rain from Dorian, but the hospital, though shaken, remained operational and secure. Throughout the night, I stayed vigilant, monitoring the situation and coordinating with my team and local authorities. As dawn broke on September 5th, the worst of the storm had passed. We had weathered the outer bands of Hurricane Dorian with minimal damage, as the eye of the storm did in fact remain offshore as predicted. Thanks to the leadership of the hospital and the tireless dedication of our staff, patients continued receiving uninterrupted care. In the days following, we conducted debriefings to review our response and identify areas for improvement. Our commitment to detail and continuous improvement ensured the hospital would be even better prepared for future emergencies. This story is mine, but not mine alone. It is experienced by countless emergency managers in similar crises across the country every day, and it underscores the vital role of preparation, leadership, and teamwork in managing disasters. Each experience with such formidable storms like Hurricane Dorian, or any other hazard reaffirms the importance of readiness and resilience in safeguarding lives and ensuring continuity of care.

–Kim Bailey

This chapter lays the groundwork for you to gain an understanding of the crucial roles healthcare leaders and hospital emergency managers play in handling emergencies and why selecting a leader is vital for an emergency management program in a hospital or healthcare system. We will delve into the importance of preparing for, responding to, and recovering from emergencies within the healthcare industry.

In the field of healthcare leadership, the primary focus is on providing top-notch care, enhancing outcomes, and managing operational challenges. Despite the evolving nature of healthcare, one constant remains: the occurrences of emergencies, disasters, and crises. These unexpected events, like disasters, public health crises, or other critical incidents, can disrupt well-established healthcare systems. Being ready with a trained team to effectively handle such situations is crucial for a hospital's readiness. The role of a healthcare leader is diverse. It requires dedication to patient and community welfare, a pursuit of delivering exceptional care, and an ability to navigate through the complex and often turbulent waters of emergency management. The significance of this duty cannot be emphasized enough as it is during crises that leadership in healthcare truly stands out. Let's start by recognizing the reasons why healthcare leaders should give importance to emergency management. Emergencies are inherently unpredictable. Natural disasters like earthquakes, tornadoes, and floods can occur without warning. Public health emergencies, such as pandemics or disease outbreaks, can emerge unexpectedly. Even events caused by humans, like cyber attacks or mass casualties, can happen suddenly, requiring healthcare systems and their leaders to react efficiently. It is crucial to ensure the operation of infrastructure, such as healthcare facilities, after any disaster or emergency. A robust emergency management program is vital for your organization. Local emergencies or large-scale disasters can present challenges for a single hospital or even an entire healthcare system in a region or state. To deliver services to the communities served by hospitals, we depend on internal and external resources and functions (such as electricity, fuel, water, food supplies, medical supplies, supply chains, communication routes, environmental resources, sterilization resources, etc.), each forming part of a complex interconnected system. Losing any operation or function could greatly impact healthcare service delivery during emergencies or major disasters when demand is high.

You may be asking yourself, what exactly does an emergency manager do and why is having one essential for your hospital? As a leader in healthcare, you're likely familiar with the role of emergency responders. We often witness ambulances, police cars, and fire trucks rushing by in our lives, indicating their response to some form of emergency. Many TV shows aim to depict the experiences of emergency responders. An emergency manager is not an emergency responder, so it may come as a surprise that an emergency manager typically doesn't directly respond to emergency scenes like first responders do. While emergency management and emergency response are interconnected concepts, they involve different phases and aspects of addressing emergencies and disasters. In the realm of emergencies or disasters, the emergency management department or emergency manager at your hospital serves as the conductor during a symphony performance. Just as a conductor guides a group of musicians to create music, emergency managers coordinate responses involving various agencies and stakeholders to navigate through crisis chaos. This role is extremely vital and often overlooked in the healthcare setting. Using the orchestra analogy, the conductor symbolizes the emergency manager or team leading each section with precision and unity. In times of crisis, different groups such as internal hospital departments, external law enforcement, fire departments, medical teams, and volunteer organizations each have important roles to play. It is similar to how a conductor directs an orchestra using gestures and cues, just as emergency management communicates through protocols and coordination channels. They make sure that everyone knows when to act, when to pause, and when to adjust their pace based on the situation – like how responders adapt during emergencies. The sheet music acts as a guide for the musicians, outlining the plan for the performance. Similarly, an emergency management plan sets out the steps and procedures to be followed in a crisis, serving as a roadmap for response efforts. Just as a successful symphony requires practice and teamwork among musicians, effective emergency management relies on training, preparedness, and cooperation among response organizations. When everyone does their part and follows the lead of those in charge, it leads to a coordinated response that lessens the impact of the crisis and aids in community recovery. The functions and duties of an Emergency Management Department in a hospital or healthcare system are quite similar to those of an Emergency Management Department in a city, county, or state. Every Emergency Management Department should have the authorized responsibility to oversee the process of coordinating, preparing for executing, and minimizing the impact of emergencies or disasters. Emergency Management involves planning and resource coordination for an efficient response to emergencies or disasters.

On the other hand, emergency responders concentrate on actions to address the initial effects of an emergency or disaster. Response activities focus on short-term measures needed to save lives, safeguard property, and fulfill needs, including search and rescue operations, prehospital medical care, and urgent evacuations. Only a small part of an emergency manager's role involves response activities. Nonetheless, both emergency management and emergency response play roles in emergency preparedness and disaster management. We will delve deeper into the distinctions between management and response and why they are significant in Chapter 6.

During disasters, like earthquakes, hurricanes, tornadoes, and volcanic eruptions, as well as other potential threats such as utility failures or terrorist activities, there is often a sudden surge in patients seeking medical care. This increased demand can overwhelm healthcare facilities, posing challenges for hospitals in managing the influx of patients. This situation can strain resources and staff and even lead to infrastructure failures. Staff shortages may arise, essential supplies could become scarce, or utilities may stop working. Emergency managers understand that simply following regulations and ensuring integrity during building construction may not be sufficient to prevent disruptions during disaster events like earthquakes, due to various factors affecting overall functionality – including external resource availability. That is why it is crucial for your organization to plan and prepare for all kinds of emergencies and disasters under the guidance of hospital emergency managers.

In the healthcare sector, every day presents a high-stakes scenario where lives are on the line. In emergencies, these stakes are raised further. The decisions taken by healthcare leaders and hospital emergency managers can literally mean life-or-death situations for patients and communities. People depend on the expertise of these leaders to navigate these situations successfully. The ability of healthcare facilities to deliver effective care is crucial for well-being and any interruptions in normal operations can pose serious risks. When hospitals or healthcare systems encounter issues, lives may be in jeopardy.

One primary reason is the delay in accessing care during emergencies. It is like an out-of-place note in an otherwise harmonious orchestra performance. Just as one out-of-sync instrument can disrupt the music's flow, operational disruptions in healthcare systems can cause delays for patients needing medical attention. In emergency management orchestration, the conductor aims to maintain coordination among response entities. However, when operational disruptions like infrastructure damage, communication breakdowns, or resource shortages occur, it is akin to an interruption in the music's rhythm. For individuals requiring care, these delays can be especially harmful. Picture a violinist suddenly losing their sheet music during a performance – the resulting chaos reflects the anxiety felt by those seeking help during a crisis.

When a musician arrives late, it can disrupt the group's performance. Similarly, delays in receiving treatment can worsen patients' conditions and lead to more severe outcomes. For instance, someone having a heart attack or serious injury might suffer harm if they don't get medical help promptly. After a disaster or mass casualty event, making sure people can access care quickly becomes a priority for healthcare leaders and local emergency agencies. To prevent delays in care, they may set up facilities, use different communication methods, organize transportation for patients, and send medical supplies and staff where they are most needed. By providing timely access to care which is crucial in emergencies, responders aim to coordinate the response, reduce the negative health effects, and guide individuals and communities toward recovery.

During emergencies, shortages of resources can pose challenges for healthcare systems by limiting their ability to provide medical care. These shortages include supplies, medications, and equipment needed to diagnose, treat, and manage health conditions. When a disaster occurs or there are a number of people injured, the sudden increase in the need for supplies can quickly deplete what is already available. Damage to buildings, disrupted delivery systems, and overwhelmed hospitals make it hard for healthcare workers to get what they need to provide care. Not having supplies has serious effects on how patients are treated. If there are not enough supplies, healthcare workers may have to decide who gets treatment first or limit what they can do, which could mean patients do not get the best care and their outcomes are not as good. For example, not having equipment like ventilators or defibrillators can make it harder to save the lives of people who are critically ill. Additionally, not having the medications and pharmaceutical supplies that are required can be very dangerous for patients with long-term conditions or sudden illnesses. For instance, not having medicines like insulin for people with diabetes or antibiotics for infections can lead to health problems worsening and causing more serious outcomes. When resources are scarce it affects how well healthcare systems can deal with emergencies and continue to care for people's needs. Hospitals might struggle to obtain supplies when they are already being rapidly depleted due to high demand. To manage resource shortages, emergency plans should focus on how resources are divided, where they come from, and how they are distributed.

Prioritizing the distribution of resources according to needs; finding ways to save resources; and collaborating with government bodies, non-governmental organizations (NGOs), and private organizations to acquire resources are essential steps. Being prepared by stocking up on supplies and forming partnerships with nearby areas for assistance and regularly evaluating available resources and requirements all contribute to strengthening your ability to respond effectively to emergencies. During emergencies such as natural disasters, pandemics, or mass casualty incidents, healthcare providers face challenges in ensuring they have the resources to deliver timely and high-quality care to patients. The surge in numbers puts a strain on the workforce, leading to staffing shortages and increased workloads. This can result in fatigue among healthcare workers, impacting patient care quality and supervision. In critical care areas like emergency departments and ICUs, hospitals may struggle to maintain levels of care due to a lack of skilled personnel, such as doctors, nurses, and support staff. These shortages can cause delays in treatment and suboptimal patient outcomes. The pressure on the remaining staff increases as they are given the responsibility of handling a larger number of patients with varied medical needs often in difficult circumstances like limited resources and physical fatigue. This situation can result in heightened stress and reduced morale among healthcare workers, making it more challenging to deliver high-quality care during emergencies. To tackle staffing shortages in times of crisis, healthcare facilities and emergency management agencies implement various strategies to strengthen workforce capacity and support healthcare providers. Hospital leadership and emergency managers can collaborate with external partners to bring in healthcare personnel from within the facility, neighboring institutions, or external agencies to boost staffing levels during peak demand periods. Many states have procedures for recruiting trained volunteers, including retired healthcare professionals, medical students, and community members with skills to provide assistance with care and support services. Emergency managers should be knowledgeable about these programs and know how to seek assistance from these organizations. A robust hospital emergency management program may have established procedures for providing training and support to healthcare workers to broaden their scope of practice and enhance their ability to fulfill roles and responsibilities as required during emergencies. By taking measures to address staffing shortages and implementing support strategies for healthcare workers, emergency management initiatives aim to ensure care delivery, minimize the impact of workforce challenges, and guarantee that patients receive the necessary medical attention of high-quality during times of crisis.

In times of emergency, operational disturbances such as power outages or infrastructure damage can lead to the disruption of healthcare services, much like an abrupt pause in a crucial symphonic performance. These disruptions affect procedures and services such as surgeries, intensive care, and diagnostic tests, which are crucial for diagnosing and treating patients with urgent medical requirements. In the coordination of healthcare provision, interruptions to services can have severe outcomes akin to an unexpected silence in the midst of a crescendo. Patients in need of interventions such as lifesaving surgeries or critical care treatments may face a lack of access to these essential services, putting their lives at immediate risk. The suspension of surgeries due to power outages or infrastructure issues resembles a conductor suddenly stopping in the middle of a piece, disrupting the harmony and leaving instruments silent. Similarly, healthcare facilities may be compelled to postpone planned surgeries or procedures, compromising the treatment of patients with conditions or urgent medical needs. In intensive care units (ICUs), disruptions in services such as ventilator support or lifesaving treatments can pose grave risks to patients relying on these measures to sustain their vital functions. Just as a sudden halt in music can unsettle listeners, the interruption of services in ICUs leaves patients exposed and urgently requiring interventions to safeguard their well-being. Diagnostic procedures, crucial for identifying and managing conditions, could also be affected by disturbances during emergencies. Without access to tools or facilities, healthcare providers may face challenges in accurately assessing the situation.

A patient's condition may not be promptly assessed, leading to delays in diagnosis and treatment decisions that could worsen health outcomes. To prevent the disruption of services during emergencies, healthcare facilities and emergency managers can collaborate with departments within hospitals to implement various strategies ensuring continuous care and patient safety.

Emergency management teams can partner with facilities to set up power generators and systems for electricity supply during power failures. This enables healthcare facilities to sustain services and uphold patient care. Installing systems and infrastructure helps mitigate the impact of damage to facilities or equipment, ensuring continued operation of vital services during emergencies. A robust emergency management program will create contingency plans and protocols to assist healthcare providers in managing disruptions and maintaining essential services. This includes guidelines for prioritizing patient care and efficiently allocating resources. Collaboration with emergency management agencies, utility companies, and other stakeholders is crucial for coordinating response efforts, addressing infrastructure challenges, and minimizing disruptions to critical healthcare services. By recognizing the risks associated with service interruptions during emergencies and implementing measures to address these challenges, healthcare facilities and emergency managers aim to maintain continuity of care while safeguarding patients requiring medical attention.

During emergencies, getting help on time can be difficult due to transportation issues, which act as barriers to receiving care. Hospitals in areas of flood-prone zones are well aware of these challenges. Natural disasters or major incidents can disrupt transportation systems, making roads impassable and hindering access to healthcare facilities for patients in need. The chaos that ensues during emergencies is like a conductor struggling to keep tempo in an orchestra, with movement disrupted and the path to safety filled with obstacles. Patients needing attention may face delays or being stranded on their way to hospitals, increasing the urgency of their medical needs and putting their health at risk. Time is critical in situations where every minute matters greatly. Patients arriving at hospitals in poor condition due to transport delays may suffer adverse outcomes as delayed interventions are less effective and complications become more likely. When roads are blocked, bridges damaged, or evacuation routes compromised, reaching healthcare facilities becomes a daunting task. In hard-to-reach areas, the challenges posed by transportation have a significant impact, especially where healthcare access is already limited. Emergencies in these regions worsen existing transportation issues, making it more challenging to deliver prompt medical assistance to those in need. To tackle these transportation obstacles during emergencies, leaders in healthcare and hospital emergency management should employ strategies to facilitate patient movement and ensure access to services.

Hospital emergency managers can arrange for the deployment of emergency vehicles such as ambulances, helicopters, and high-water rescue vehicles that are crucial for navigating through impassable roads and transporting patients to healthcare facilities. Collaborating with state transportation authorities and agencies can help identify routes, clear obstacles, and prioritize the passage of emergency vehicles to streamline patient transport to medical centers. Additionally, hospital emergency managers can assist facilities in setting up units or field hospitals in impacted areas to offer onsite medical care for individuals facing challenges accessing traditional healthcare facilities due to transportation constraints. This effort can be complemented by utilizing telemedicine technology for consultations, patient triage, and initiating treatment interventions for those unable to physically reach healthcare settings. When it comes to tackling transportation challenges during emergencies and putting in place plans to help patients get to where they need to be, emergency management agencies and healthcare providers work together to ensure that people requiring medical attention can receive timely care, no matter the hurdles they face on their path to recovery.

Communication plays a vital role in emergency response, allowing healthcare leaders and emergency managers to exchange information, coordinate actions, and make well-informed decisions when faced with rapidly changing situations. When communication systems fail during disruptions, the impact can be significant, leading to misunderstandings, delays in decision-making, and a lack of coordination that puts outcomes at risk. In the dance of emergency response efforts, smooth communication coordinates the actions of healthcare teams like a conductor guides each section of an orchestra with precision and clarity. If communication falters, it is akin to stumbling upon a note that disrupts the harmony of the performance, causing confusion and disorder among responders. During disruptions such as power outages, infrastructure damage, or overwhelmed communication networks, healthcare providers may find it challenging to convey information effectively. Important details about conditions, treatment plans, and available resources could get lost in the confusion, hindering the delivery of appropriate care. Communication breakdowns can lead to misunderstandings and confusion when responders work independently without sharing information or coordinating effectively. Just as musicians playing out of harmony create noise, fragmented communication among healthcare teams can result in disjointed care delivery, putting safety and outcomes at risk. In emergencies, delays in decision-making often result from communication failures. When there are no communication channels or established procedures for sharing information, healthcare providers may make ill-informed choices, negatively impacting patient care. A lack of teamwork and collaboration between healthcare teams and external organizations worsens the challenges caused by communication breakdowns. Without a strategy for emergency response and a shared understanding of roles and responsibilities, resources might not be utilized efficiently, efforts could be duplicated, and crucial needs might remain unmet. In times of emergencies, it is crucial for healthcare leaders and emergency managers to establish strategies to improve communication resilience and effectiveness, reducing the impact of breakdowns in communication. We will delve deeper into the significance of communication in Chapter 7 and learn how focusing on communication and taking steps to tackle communication issues can help healthcare facilities and emergency response agencies strengthen their ability to respond, enhance patient outcomes, and protect the well-being of those affected by emergencies.

Healthcare leaders bear ethical and liability responsibilities for ensuring the safety and welfare of those under their care. Failure to prepare for or respond to emergencies can lead to repercussions affecting an organization's standing and trust within the community. Understanding a hospital's ethical duty during a disaster is essential for reasons. Disasters be they human caused or natural, create complex challenges that can strain the resources and capabilities of healthcare institutions. Addressing ethical considerations helps steer healthcare professionals and organizations toward decisions that prioritize well-being, uphold moral values, and meet legal obligations. There are several reasons why it's vital to take into account legal and ethical responsibilities during disasters; one primary reason is patient-focused care.

Patient-focused care is at the core of legal guidelines that govern healthcare delivery in times of crisis where resources are limited, and decisions must be made quickly. This approach underscores the significance of honoring patients' autonomy, dignity, and preferences while also placing their wellbeing and best interests at the forefront. In situations like disasters or mass casualty events, upholding a commitment to patient-centered care becomes more crucial due to the chaos and urgency that can challenge these principles. Central to patient-centered care is the understanding that individuals seeking help are active participants in their own health journey, not just passive recipients of treatment. It recognizes their right to information, involvement in decision-making processes, and being treated with respect regardless of circumstances. This aspect gains importance during emergencies when patients may be feeling heightened levels of fear, anxiety, and vulnerability. By prioritizing patients' rights and welfare, healthcare providers can ensure that decisions made during a crisis are ethically sound and rooted in values like compassion and empathy. This entails giving precedence to patients' needs over logistical factors even amid challenges such as limited resources or overwhelming demand for medical services.

Patient-centered care extends to an approach that addresses the emotional and psychosocial needs of patients in times of crisis. This involves not only administering treatment but also providing emotional support, facilitating communication with family members, and honoring cultural and religious customs. By considering the individual, healthcare professionals can help alleviate distress, support recovery, and improve the care experience amidst challenges. Legal and ethical guidelines act as compasses for healthcare providers, reminding them of their responsibility to uphold rights and dignity even in difficult situations. These guidelines stress the significance of informed consent, confidentiality, and respecting autonomy to ensure that decisions made during emergencies are ethically sound and meet standards. Patient-centered care remains a tenet of healthcare delivery in demanding circumstances. By prioritizing rights, well-being, and preferences healthcare providers can maintain practices, build trust with patients, and deliver empathetic care that honors the intrinsic value of every individual regardless of the circumstances.

Ensuring quality healthcare remains an aspect of medical practice highlighting healthcare providers' unwavering dedication to providing excellent care to each patient, even in challenging times. This principle holds significance during crises or situations with numbers of casualties, where the demand for medical services may surpass available resources, presenting additional obstacles in delivering care. Legal and ethical standards act as guiding principles for healthcare professionals, delineating their duties and responsibilities to uphold quality care standards in difficult scenarios. These standards underscore the significance of prioritizing patient safety, respecting dignity, and following evidence-based practices irrespective of the circumstances at hand. Amidst a crisis, healthcare providers are expected to uphold care standards by striving to offer the best possible care within the given resources and conditions. This involves assessing needs, determining care priorities, and thoughtfully allocating resources to maximize benefits for a population. Adhering to care standards during emergencies necessitates healthcare providers' use of judgment, creativity, and adaptability in tailoring their practices according to changing needs and situational constraints.

In times of crises, healthcare workers may need to prioritize patients based on the severity of their conditions, find solutions to address resource shortages, and work closely with diverse teams to improve patient outcomes. While responding to disasters can mean deviating from daily standard procedures, healthcare providers are still expected to follow principles such as avoiding harm and promoting fairness. This involves focusing on treatments that can help patients reduce harm and ensuring everyone has access to care regardless of their backgrounds. Legal and ethical frameworks exist to hold healthcare providers accountable for their decisions and actions during emergencies. They include ways to monitor care quality and processes for addressing concerns or complaints about deviations from established norms. Upholding duties and ethical obligations is crucial for healthcare providers in maintaining care standards during disasters. By following ethical guidelines, they aim to provide care based on evidence that puts patient well-being first and upholds professional integrity even in challenging circumstances. Equality and fairness play roles in healthcare practices by emphasizing fair treatment for all individuals regardless of their social status, race, or other demographic factors.

This principle is especially important in times of disasters or mass casualties where it is crucial to distribute resources based on ethical standards. Ethical guidelines emphasize the need to uphold justice and equality, ensuring that healthcare access is determined by necessity rather than social status. In disaster response, this means prioritizing urgency over factors like wealth or social connections. Fairness in emergency situations requires healthcare providers to acknowledge and assist populations who may struggle to access care during crises, such as those from low-income backgrounds, minorities, immigrants, older adults, and individuals with disabilities. Making resource allocation decisions involves considering values and involving the community in transparent decision-making processes that aim for the greatest benefit for all while addressing the specific needs of disadvantaged groups. Ethical guidelines offer direction to healthcare providers and decision-makers when dealing with the complexities of resource allocation in emergencies. Concepts like utilitarianism, which aims to maximize benefits and minimize harm, and distributive justice, which focuses on fairness in resource distribution, can guide decision-making processes to ensure ethical and fair resource allocation. In disaster response, equity and fairness go beyond resources to address broader social and structural factors influencing health outcomes. This involves tackling disparities in healthcare access, economic gaps, and barriers to health equity during emergencies and in health overall. Prioritizing equity and fairness in disaster response is crucial for upholding standards, advocating for justice, and ensuring that the most vulnerable individuals receive necessary care during crises. By emphasizing equity, emergency response efforts become more effective while also fostering community resilience and solidarity in times of crisis. Upholding consent and clear communication are aspects of ethical healthcare practices that empower patients to make autonomous decisions about their care, even amidst emergencies or disasters.

Healthcare professionals have a duty to ensure that patients give consent for procedures, showing respect, for their right to make decisions and making sure they understand the risks, benefits, and options related to the treatments or procedures being offered. Informed consent goes beyond following the law; it shows a commitment to patient-centered care by honoring patients' independence and dignity. This principle remains important in emergencies, where quick decisions may be necessary and usual procedures may need to be adjusted. While getting written consent might not always be possible during emergencies, healthcare providers should still communicate effectively with patients and their families, making sure they grasp what is being suggested as well as any potential risks or uncertainties. Communication with patients and families is vital during crises, connecting healthcare professionals with those needing care. This involves not only explaining treatments and procedures but also addressing patients' worries, fears, and preferences in a caring and culturally sensitive way. In times of crisis, patients may feel more stressed, anxious, and uncertain, highlighting the importance of empathetic communication.

Healthcare professionals should aim to communicate effectively with patients and their families using language that's easy to understand, free from technical terms, and respectful of different cultures. They may need to use interpreters or language services to bridge any communication gaps, along with offering written materials or visual aids to support explanations. Healthcare providers should ensure that patients and their families feel comfortable asking questions, seeking clarification and sharing their preferences about their treatment. In cases where getting consent is not feasible due to the patient's condition or urgency of the situation, healthcare providers should still try their best to involve patients in decision making as much as possible. This might involve consulting with decision makers like family members or legal guardians and taking into account the patient's wishes and values when deciding on treatments.

During emergencies, providers and organizations might enjoy safeguards and protections, but there is still a concern with liability for medical malpractice or negligence. Healthcare providers may face risks of actions related to alleged mistakes or oversights in patient care, especially when working in conditions of limited resources or overwhelming demand. It is crucial for healthcare organizations to keep records of the care provided, follow established protocols and standards of practice, and prioritize safety to reduce the chances of facing legal consequences. Laws related to emergency response, disaster immunity, and Samaritan laws are put in place to shield healthcare providers and volunteers from liability when offering care during emergencies. Emergency response laws can temporarily waive regulations to facilitate a swift disaster response. These laws may simplify licensing processes, permit the use of treatments, or grant immunity from liability for healthcare providers acting in good faith within their duties during emergencies. Disaster response immunity laws aim to protect healthcare providers and entities engaged in disaster relief efforts from liability for their well-intentioned actions in providing care or aid during emergencies. The purpose of these laws is to inspire healthcare professionals to volunteer their services during disasters without the fear of repercussions for their contributions. Good Samaritan laws offer protection to individuals who help those in need during emergencies or accidents. These laws typically protect bystanders from liability for negligence when aiding with good intentions and no expectation of reward, encouraging people to step in during emergencies to save lives or prevent further harm. In addition to these safeguards, healthcare institutions should also secure liability insurance to minimize financial risks linked to potential legal claims or lawsuits arising from disaster response efforts. The insurance should be customized based on the organization's requirements and risks, covering aspects such as malpractice, general liability, and professional liability. Despite the challenges presented by disaster response scenarios that may require deviations from procedures, healthcare professionals must uphold standards and ensure that patients' rights are upheld, even in the most difficult situations. By emphasizing consent and clear communication, healthcare providers can maintain the trust and confidence of patients and their families, promoting a culture of respect, dignity, and collaboration in delivering care amidst emergency situations. Hospital leaders and emergency managers need to be mindful of their obligations and liabilities during disasters while also being aware of the protections accessible to them. By managing considerations and implementing appropriate risk management strategies, healthcare organizations can fulfill their responsibility of providing care during emergencies while protecting the rights and welfare of patients, staff members, and volunteers.

Legal and moral obligations go beyond the aftermath of disasters. Following a disaster, healthcare facilities could be held responsible for their choices and actions. Upholding standards and abiding by laws contribute to accountability in the aftermath of disasters. Considering ethical responsibilities in times of disaster is crucial for guiding healthcare decision-making, safeguarding rights, ensuring fairness in distributing resources, and upholding public trust. Healthcare institutions must be equipped to address these issues to deliver compassionate care under challenging circumstances. Legal and ethical factors play a role in fostering collaboration and generating an emergency response with both internal and external partners. This ensures resource utilization while addressing the needs of affected individuals promptly and harmoniously.

Legal frameworks often promote collaboration among healthcare entities, emergency responders, and public health agencies during disasters. These regulations may mandate the establishment of agency coordination mechanisms, like emergency operations centers (EOCs) or incident command systems (ICS), to facilitate communication, decision making, and resource allocation during emergencies. Ethical considerations also highlight the significance of teamwork and cooperation in responding to disasters as it is acknowledged that no single organization or entity can effectively tackle the challenges brought by events on its own. Working together fosters synergy, resilience, and innovation, enabling a variety of stakeholders to combine their knowledge, resources, and capabilities to mount a response to emergencies. Successful collaboration in times of disaster requires clear lines of communication, defined roles and responsibilities, as well as mechanisms for sharing information and making decisions. It is crucial for these partnerships to be established in advance of any crisis. This responsibility primarily falls on the shoulders of the emergency managers for each organization. Tasks might involve setting up agreements like mutual aid pacts or memoranda of understanding (MOUs) documents to outline the duties and obligations of participating organizations while facilitating the exchange of resources and assistance. These frameworks uphold accountability and transparency in endeavors, ensuring that decision-making processes are just and inclusive. This could involve tools for oversight, engaging stakeholders, along with evaluations and assessments of response actions to pinpoint areas for enhancement and address any deficiencies or gaps in coordination efforts. Collaboration among healthcare providers, local emergency managers, first responders, and public health agencies extends not only during response but also includes training and preparedness activities, mitigation measures, and recovery endeavors.

Working to identify risks strengthens capabilities and creates response strategies stakeholders can use to improve the resilience of communities and reduce the impact of disasters on public health and safety. Besides requirements, ethical values like doing good, avoiding harm, and ensuring fairness emphasize the obligation to cooperate and harmonize actions to prevent harm and enhance the well-being of affected individuals. Cooperation nurtures unity, empathy, and mutual assistance, reinforcing the values and commitments that support healthcare practices. Ultimately, effective coordination and teamwork among healthcare providers, emergency responders, and public health agencies are crucial for delivering an efficient reaction to disasters. By utilizing their combined strengths and resources, stakeholders such as community emergency managers, hospitals, and others can boost community resilience, save lives, and lessen the effects of disasters on individuals or families as well as their own staff. The trust of the community in healthcare institutions and how they are perceived by the public are pivotal in disaster response endeavors. This impacts individuals' willingness to seek attention, adhere to public health recommendations, and back emergency response efforts. Upholding principles and legal responsibilities are vital for maintaining community trust in healthcare institutions during times when scrutiny is high. Core ethical values, like honesty, openness, and responsibility, play a role in establishing and upholding trust between healthcare professionals and the local communities they support. In times of crisis, healthcare organizations need to show their dedication to these values by their behaviors, choices, and communication plans to uphold trust that their conduct is guided by ethical considerations and aligned with the values and expectations of the community.

Ensuring transparency and ethical decision-making is crucial in building trust and confidence in healthcare organizations during times of crisis. It is important to communicate promptly with the public regarding the emergency situation and the actions being taken by all stakeholders to manage it and any potential risks involved. Transparency plays a role in establishing credibility, dispelling rumors, and empowering individuals to make informed choices about their health and safety. Adhering to obligations is also significant in shaping how healthcare institutions are perceived during disasters. Complying with laws related to patient privacy, informed consent, and emergency response is essential for upholding trust in the reliability of healthcare services. Failing to meet these standards can damage trustworthiness and credibility, resulting in a negative public image and backlash against healthcare facilities. Effective communication strategies are vital for managing perception during crises. Healthcare organizations should actively engage with the community, listen to their concerns, and address any queries or misunderstandings about emergency response efforts. Utilizing communication platforms like social media, community discussions, and traditional media outlets can help share accurate information transparently and keep the public informed about developments in an accessible manner.

When it comes to healthcare, the institution's actions are key in earning trust and confidence beyond words. Healthcare providers need to show their dedication to patient-focused care through their actions, choices, and interactions with patients and the community. This involves prioritizing patient needs, respecting their autonomy and dignity, and ensuring access to care for everyone, regardless of their background or situation. By upholding standards, meeting responsibilities, and making transparent and ethical decisions, healthcare institutions can build trust within the community and demonstrate their ability to effectively handle disasters. A positive public image boosts community resilience and encourages teamwork, cooperation, and backing for emergency response efforts – ultimately leading to better outcomes for all stakeholders and the community they serve.

In times of disasters or widespread emergencies, injuries or fatalities are often inevitable. The healthcare system typically plays a role in responding to these events within the community. As healthcare leaders, you have a part in enhancing community resilience, ensuring that healthcare services remain accessible and dependable even in challenging circumstances. It is essential for healthcare leaders to grasp the significance of emergency management and the pivotal role of selecting an emergency manager to oversee their organization's emergency preparedness program. Hospitals and healthcare systems are pivotal players in shaping community resilience after a crisis. Community resilience refers to how a community can get ready to respond to, and bounce back from challenging situations like disasters, public health emergencies, and other crises. The influence of hospitals and healthcare systems on community resilience is profound. By ensuring access to healthcare services, aiding in emergency responses, offering support, and collaborating with community partners, hospitals greatly contribute to a community's ability to endure and recover from disaster impacts. Building community resilience requires action with the participation of healthcare institutions being vital for a united response.

In October 2015, South Carolina went through a significant disaster event when Hurricane Joaquin swept past the East Coast more than 600 miles away from South Carolina's shore. It started in the evening with rain tapping against the windowpanes. As night transitioned into day, that gentle tapping transformed into a steady downpour. Emergency managers shared information throughout the state, and each call or message I received brought more concerning updates. This weather system caused record-breaking rainfall in the state (many of which were recently broken in August of 2024 with Hurricane Debby) with totals ranging from 15 to 20 inches and localized amounts exceeding 25 inches. Emergency managers statewide sprang into action by mobilizing teams, activating Emergency Operations centers, and collaborating with state authorities. The urgency of the situation was apparent to all as roads transformed into rivers and homes faced threats from rising waters, pushing the state to the brink of a disaster. Amidst evacuation efforts in low-lying areas led by emergency crews, emergency managers juggled phone calls, dispatched rescue teams, and provided reassurance to anxious citizens. We endeavored to maintain a sense of calm and take actions to serve as a beacon of hope amidst the chaos. Floodwaters inundated large portions of some towns, washed away roads, and compromised the stability of our transportation networks. The combination of rainfall, runoff water accumulation, along with aging drainage systems led to the failure of fifty dams regulated by the state. This disruption severely impacted travel routes and transportation systems, impeding emergency response operations while limiting access to affected areas. Many residents were caught off guard by rising floodwaters.

Thousands of people had to leave their homes due to rising floodwaters, leading to emergency shelters. Sadly, the flooding in South Carolina claimed the lives of 19 individuals. A section of Interstate 95, a route connecting the Southeast and Northeast regions, remained closed for days. The flood caused damage to houses and businesses, with structures being compromised and personal belongings destroyed by the inundating water. A power substation in Clarendon County and major water lines in Richland County were also severely affected. The breach in the Columbia Canal disrupted the city's water supply, leaving around 375,000 residents without access to drinking water for two weeks. The aftermath of the disaster left homeowners facing hardships as they tried to recover from the devastation. Displaced individuals and families, including hospital workers, grappled with uncertainty about when they could return and rebuild their lives. The agriculture industry suffered greatly due to the floods, causing damage to crops and affecting farmers and the wider agricultural community. The flooding caused harm to the environment with water sources and habitat destruction. Issues like sewage leaks, chemical spills, and debris pollution exacerbated these problems, posing risks to health and ecosystem health. The impact of the 2015 floods on South Carolina's healthcare system presented challenges for healthcare workers, emergency responders, and local residents. Floodwaters damaged hospital infrastructure such as buildings, equipment, and utilities, leading to disruptions in services like closures and patient relocations. To address water supply issues at hospitals due to flooding, firefighters and the National Guard transported large amounts of water using trucks and pumps. The flooded roads and bridges made it hard for patients, staff members, and emergency responders to access hospitals efficiently. This hindered care delivery and evacuation efforts in some instances. Hospitals faced an influx of patients seeking treatment for flood-related injuries or illnesses during this time. The surge in demand strained hospital resources, such as staff availability, bed capacity, and medical supplies, which made it challenging to provide care.

The rising floodwaters posed a health concern due to contamination from sewage, chemicals, and infectious agents. Hospitals across the state had to take steps to deal with diseases, injuries, and other health risks linked to the floods. This involved offering vaccinations, checkups, and treatment services to those affected. The flooding also caused disruptions in transportation routes and supply chains, temporarily affecting hospitals' ability to obtain supplies, drugs, and equipment. Shortages or delays in accessing these resources could impact care both during and after the flood event. Addressing these challenges and ensuring that essential medical services continue uninterrupted required cooperation among healthcare institutions, government bodies, and community partners. With the damage caused by the floods, the people of South Carolina came together in a show of unity. Communities united, displaying strength in the face of adversity. Neighbors lent a helping hand as volunteers worked tirelessly to clean up and aid in recovery efforts, and support was offered to those affected. Emergency managers and first responders throughout the state dedicated themselves to coordinating recovery operations and ensuring that those impacted by the disaster received the assistance they needed to start. While the flood tested our resilience, it also brought us all together in a show of strength and solidarity. Reflecting on this event, emergency managers learned many lessons from this crisis. They understood that emergencies were bound to happen but believed that with preparation, determination, and a strong community bond, they could overcome any challenge thrown their way. This catastrophe highlighted how crucial community support and readiness are when facing hardship head-on and having the right people prepared for situations.

The unpredictable nature of emergencies presents obstacles for healthcare facilities and hospital operations. Having emergency plans in place is essential to address challenges and maintain high-quality healthcare services during crises. Consider this: if an emergency occurred at your facility tomorrow, how well prepared would your healthcare system be? How effective is your emergency preparedness program? How do you assess its proficiency? It is crucial to have a grasp of emergency management fundamentals and establish an emergency preparedness program for your hospital or healthcare organization. It is vital to create an emergency management program for your hospital or healthcare facility. Selecting the emergency manager is a step in this process, and you will find guidance on how to make that choice in the next chapter.

No matter how well we plan and prepare, it is impossible to anticipate every aspect of an emergency. Despite our efforts to predict obstacles and create thorough response plans, unexpected factors and unique situations will always come up. Emergencies are unpredictable by nature, influenced by behaviors and environmental conditions that vary widely, making it impossible for any plan to cover every scenario. This uncertainty emphasizes the importance of being flexible and adaptable in emergency preparedness. While detailed planning is essential, fostering a culture of resilience and readiness is just as important for teams to respond effectively to events. Acknowledging that some variables are beyond our control encourages a flexible approach to emergency management, enabling organizations to navigate real-world crises with agility and creativity.

> *Amidst the challenges posed by the COVID 19 pandemic collaborating with more than 50 state agencies and organizations exposed us to the complexities of handling a crisis of this magnitude. We encountered tasks including setting up alternative care facilities and managing large scale distribution of protective equipment across the state putting our emergency management frameworks to the test. Close collaboration with hospitals and healthcare providers played a crucial role in our response efforts during this time. This experience underscored the importance of cooperation between state emergency management agencies, counties and healthcare systems across our state.*

It's crucial for hospitals to actively participate in hazard reduction and emergency preparedness making sure they are fully incorporated into response plans. By strengthening these collaborations and fine tuning our methods we can improve our capacity to handle crises and provide assistance to the communities we serve. -Kim Stenson, Director, South Carolina Emergency Management Division

The Bibliography section reflects the source information for the concepts and frameworks described in this chapter.

Bibliography

1. Centers for Medicare & Medicaid Services. (2023). *Emergency preparedness requirements for Medicare and Medicaid participating providers and suppliers.* https://www.cms.gov/medicare/provider-enrollment-and-certification/emergency-preparedness
2. Commission on Accreditation of Rehabilitation Facilities. (2023). *CARF accreditation.* https://www.carf.org/
3. Federal Emergency Management Agency. (2019). *National response framework* (5th ed.). https://www.fema.gov/media-library/assets/documents/117791
4. Federal Emergency Management Agency. (2021). *Developing and maintaining emergency operations plans; Comprehensive Preparedness Guide (CPG) 101* (Version 3.0). https://www.fema.gov/media-library/assets/documents/25970
5. Federal Emergency Management Agency. (2021). *Incident command system resources.* https://www.fema.gov/what-we-do/emergency-management/incident-command-system
6. Federal Emergency Management Agency. (2022). *Community preparedness and response.* https://www.fema.gov/what-we-do/community-preparedness
7. Federal Emergency Management Agency. (2022). *National incident management system* (3rd ed.). https://www.fema.gov/media-library/assets/documents/26328
8. National Committee for Quality Assurance. (2023). *Accreditation and certification.* https://www.ncqa.org/
9. The Joint Commission. (2023). *Standards for hospital accreditation.* https://www.jointcommission.org/standards/

Chapter 3

Foundations of Healthcare Emergency Management

Kimberly Bailey/Thomas McNeil

> *The impact of a large emergency or disaster can be far reaching and impact the ability of a medical facility to properly function or to even cease to operate. When that situation occurs, it is imperative that the healthcare leaders understand the function of emergency management, and how following the response and recovery process outlined in the basic concepts of emergency management will help them be more resilient as an organization and to return to full functionality with less effort, cost, and time. As leaders, we know how important it is to have a working understanding of how the departments and functions we manage operate to better guide and evaluate them. Emergency management, as a process, is typically very foreign to most clinical leaders. It is more typical than not, for leaders to struggle through the management of a large emergency or disaster because they are not following a set plan, or they have not taken the time to practice leading their team through the steps outlined in the plan. Healthcare leaders and hospital emergency managers should strive to enhance their knowledge on how emergency management works to best follow the proven concepts and to learn to trust the process.*
>
> **~Thomas McNeal**

In Chapter 2, we discussed the importance of healthcare emergency management and the crucial role played by healthcare leaders in preparing for, responding to, and recovering from emergencies. Moving on to Chapter 3, we will now explore the principles that underpin healthcare emergency management. These core concepts serve as the foundation on which effective emergency management strategies are developed. Having a grasp of these basics is essential for ensuring that healthcare leaders and hospital emergency managers are well prepared to navigate the challenges they may encounter.

Throughout this chapter, we will delve deeper into the aspects of emergency management, equipping you with the knowledge and resources needed to establish a foundation in healthcare emergency management. By grasping these principles, you will be better positioned to assess an emergency situation and guide your organization through the ever-changing landscape of

DOI: 10.4324/9781003529194-3

healthcare emergency management. Our exploration begins with an overview of the National Response Framework (NRF). The NRF is a US Government document that outlines how the country responds to disasters and emergencies. This framework is particularly relevant to the healthcare sector as it offers a collaborative approach to handling emergencies at a level that promotes coordination, communication, and interoperability, across different industries, including healthcare organizations.

The NRF is crucial for the healthcare sector to understand for many reasons. The NRF sets up a unified structure for handling national incidents, making sure that response actions are well-organized, united, and cooperative across different sectors and agencies, including healthcare. The NRF promotes interoperability and collaboration among organizations, which is vital for the healthcare field as it often requires coordination with public health agencies, emergency responders, and other healthcare entities to meet varied community needs during disasters. By outlining roles and responsibilities for government levels, agencies, and organizations involved in emergency response, the NRF aids hospitals, clinics, and other healthcare providers in understanding their functions within the broader response initiative. It also offers guidance on resource management, such as identifying, assigning, and deploying resources during emergencies. Efficient resource management is crucial for the healthcare industry to ensure access to supplies, personnel, and equipment. Effective communication plays a role during emergencies; hence, the NRF underscores the significance of communication and information sharing. This is particularly important in the field of healthcare, where the exchange of information with response agencies, public health departments, and the public is crucial. The NRF integrates the Incident Command System (ICS) as a method for managing incidents that assists healthcare facilities in establishing an organizational structure. This fosters better collaboration among healthcare entities and response agencies. The NRF also recognizes the significance of all sectors, including healthcare, in enhancing community resilience. Healthcare facilities are essential for community well-being, and their involvement in the NRF ensures participation in initiatives to strengthen community resilience before, during, and after emergencies. By emphasizing training and drills, the NRF ensures that response personnel are well prepared for coordinated actions during crises. In the healthcare sector, this entails training healthcare professionals and conducting drills to assess emergency response plans. By aligning emergency response efforts with existing laws, regulations, and authorities, the NRF establishes a framework that facilitates compliance for healthcare facilities. Embracing a "whole community" approach acknowledges that all segments of society – including healthcare – contribute to emergency responses. Involving the healthcare sector as part of this community approach leads to a comprehensive and efficient disaster response.

Emergency management programs in healthcare like those in cities, counties, or states follow a process with four key phases: Mitigation, preparedness, response, and recovery. Each phase plays a vital role in effectively managing emergencies within the healthcare sector. These phases involve actions and considerations that bolster the resilience and efficiency of healthcare systems and facilities when faced with crises. The seamless integration of these phases is crucial for disaster preparedness and response in healthcare. By doing so, healthcare facilities can meet needs during emergencies while also proactively minimizing risks and strengthening their long-term resilience.

In the stage known as the mitigation phase, efforts are made to prevent or minimize the impact of emergencies. This involves tasks like evaluating risks, identifying hazards, and implementing measures to reduce the hospital or healthcare system's vulnerability. Mitigation also encompasses steps taken to avert or lessen the severity of disasters and emergencies' potential consequences. Within the healthcare sector, mitigation activities may involve recognizing infrastructure enhancements to fortify a facility against hazards like hurricanes. It could also mean designing hospitals to withstand earthquakes or floods, enforcing infection control measures to halt disease spread, and formulating emergency plans to ensure services during crises. Healthcare leaders and emergency managers need to identify and tackle risks in order to mitigate future emergency impacts effectively.

The subsequent phase is known as the preparedness phase, which concentrates on activities that improve the healthcare industry's capacity to respond efficiently during emergencies. This includes creating and regularly updating emergency response strategies, conducting training sessions and drills for healthcare personnel, establishing communication procedures, and ensuring access to resources and supplies. Healthcare facilities need to be ready to handle emergencies, like disasters and disease outbreaks. Preparedness involves planning, training, and allocating resources to ensure that healthcare organizations can respond effectively in times of crisis. Leaders and emergency managers play a role in creating emergency plans, conducting drills and exercises, and ensuring that staff are well prepared for their roles. For instance, a healthcare facility regularly runs drills and engages in training activities to make sure staff know emergency response procedures, communication protocols, and how to use evacuation or emergency equipment in situations.

When an emergency occurs, the response phase kicks in. Healthcare leaders and emergency managers take charge of decision-making during this phase by coordinating resources, providing guidance, and making decisions to meet the needs of patients and the community. Response actions in the healthcare sector involve putting plans into action to address the effects of emergencies. This includes activating incident command structures, mobilizing personnel, setting up triage areas, delivering care, and collaborating with other healthcare facilities as well as emergency responders or stakeholders. Effective response measures are vital for saving lives and reducing the impact of the emergency on the community. Effective communication and quick decision-making are crucial at this stage. For instance, when a populated community is hit by a tornado, a hospital springs into action by activating its incident command system, setting up a triage area, providing care to injured patients and working closely with stakeholders and public health agencies to ensure care.

The final phase, known as the recovery phase, focuses on bringing back the healthcare system and community to a state of normalcy or a "new normal" post an emergency. Recovery efforts kick off from the start of the event. In healthcare settings, recovery involves tasks like rescheduling patient appointments, reopening services, repairing damaged facilities, addressing long-term health effects, offering medical support to those impacted by the disaster, and assessing the response to pinpoint areas for improvement in handling future emergencies. Recovery may be an extended process aimed at reinstating healthcare operations and stabilizing the community. Healthcare leaders and emergency managers play roles in evaluating the emergency's impact, providing assistance to those leading efforts in rebuilding infrastructure, and resuming routine healthcare services.

When a healthcare facility is hit by a flood, the recovery process involves rebuilding infrastructure, replacing equipment, caring for patients affected by the flood, and using lessons learned to improve resilience. The National Incident Management System (NIMS) and the Incident Command System (ICS) are connected frameworks that aim to improve the management and coordination of emergency response efforts. NIMS acts as a system for handling incidents, with ICS playing a role within NIMS. The ICS is a management system used by emergency responders and organizations to coordinate response activities during incidents, emergencies, or disasters. The effectiveness of hospitals in implementing ICS into their response framework can vary depending on factors like readiness, training programs, leadership backing, and the unique challenges posed by incidents. Many hospitals have acknowledged the advantages of ICS and have taken steps to integrate some form of it into their emergency response plan. Having some kind of structure in place is essential for the response, as it offers an efficient framework for managing emergencies and disasters.

Many hospitals and healthcare systems find it challenging to implement an ICS due to the need for extensive staff training in secondary roles and retention of information primarily used during rare emergency situations. Some hospital emergency managers opt to adjust the ICS to suit their organization's needs by modifying this structure and using a combination of tools included in the NRF and ICS components, as we will explore in depth in Chapter 6. The use of an ICS framework with modified adjustments, such as policy groups and/or ESF structure, may better fit your organization while still offering a scalable structure for organizing personnel, facilities, equipment, and communication in a systematic and coordinated way. Any ICS is designed to be versatile across incidents, promoting interoperability and coordination among entities involved in emergency responses. It is extensively utilized in emergency management and response, with many healthcare professionals being trained in its principles. Implementing ICS into a hospital's emergency plans ensures that hospital leaders are well versed in the system, leading to effective responses during real incidents. An established ICS is vital for hospitals and healthcare systems as it offers an adaptable and coordinated approach to emergency management. By embracing ICS principles, healthcare organizations can improve their capacity to respond effectively to emergencies, ultimately enhancing outcomes and community resilience.

To better align with hospital operations, hospital leaders and emergency managers may consider adapting the NIMS ICS. This involves making modifications tailored to address the challenges and priorities of healthcare environments. Hospitals can enhance their use of ICS by integrating expertise throughout the command structure to ensure decisions closely align with patient care needs and clinical workflows.

During emergencies, hospitals use facilities like triage areas, surge capacity units, and command centers within medical communication systems to improve their response efforts. They set goals to prioritize safety, continuity of care, and facility resilience within the broader Incident Command System (ICS) framework. Working closely with agencies like health departments, EMS, and law enforcement is made easier through established ICS protocols.

Regular training sessions and drills tailored to healthcare scenarios help hospital staff understand ICS principles and test structures during simulations. Efficient information management through health information systems and electronic medical records enables data sharing among incident command personnel and healthcare providers in a timely manner. Protocols for resource management are also enhanced to tackle the challenges of sourcing, distributing, and using supplies and equipment in emergencies. By making these adjustments, hospitals improve their emergency response capabilities for organized, effective, and patient-focused care during crises. The main objective of any ICS structure is to boost the efficiency, effectiveness, and safety of incident management activities by establishing a defined setup, with clear roles and responsibilities assigned. In healthcare settings, it is crucial for all team members involved in emergency responses to work in a unified manner. Having a standardized approach ensures collaboration among different departments and professionals during crises. Unity of command helps avoid confusion and promotes a coordinated response, whether its within one hospital facility or several across an entire healthcare system that may be dealing with multiple issues. An established ICS establishes a hierarchy that is vital for making quick decisions and effective communication. In healthcare scenarios where swift actions are key, a defined chain of command minimizes confusion and ensures tasks are completed efficiently. This structured setup fosters a decision-making process and coordination by outlining roles and responsibilities during emergencies.

The principle of span of control in ICS sets up ratios between supervisors and subordinates, ensuring that supervisors can effectively oversee a number of subordinates. This promotes communication and decision-making, allowing ICS to adjust its size as needed for situations, whether it is a small local incident or a large-scale disaster.

ICS uses a common language and established communication procedures, which help stakeholders from different agencies and fields understand each other, leading to smoother information flow both within the healthcare system and across different agencies. This boosts communication effectiveness during emergencies. ICS also offers a method for managing resources such as personnel, equipment, and supplies. In healthcare settings where having the resources is crucial for patient care, effective resource management through a structured process that follows ICS principles ensures that resources are deployed appropriately when needed. It involves identifying, ordering, dispatching, tracking, and recovering resources to maintain accountability and clear lines of responsibility throughout the response process. By ensuring there is an organized and collaborative approach, hospital leaders and emergency managers can enhance the safety of both patients and staff in times of emergencies.

A crucial element of every hospital readiness plan is the Emergency Operations Plan (EOP). This detailed document lays out how the hospital will handle emergencies and disasters, serving as a guide for healthcare leaders and emergency managers. It outlines the roles of stakeholders, communication strategies, resource management tactics, and more. A robust EOP is a necessary tool for navigating crises in healthcare organizations. Typically crafted by the hospital's emergency manager with input from internal and external partners, the main goal is to create a framework for coordinating responses during emergencies to safeguard lives, assets, and the surroundings. Depending on an organization's nature and potential risks involved, additional plans such as continuity of operations plans (COOP) to ensure functions continue amidst disruptions, hazard-specific plans for incidents like floods or chemical spills, accommodating staff during a disaster event, mass casualty plans, and crisis communications plans detailing information dissemination protocols may complement an EOP in the form of additional standalone plans, or annexes or attachments to the EOP.

In addition, organizations may create plans for managing resources to handle the distribution and monitoring of supplies and personnel, establish agreements for aid to enhance collaboration with parties, and implement training sessions and drills to equip staff for their roles during emergencies. These collective strategies contribute to an emergency preparedness and response approach, ensuring that an organization can effectively address potential threats and incidents. By combining these plans, healthcare institutions and governmental bodies can develop a framework for emergency management to deal with a spectrum of potential crises.

A sample group of stakeholders who should review and provide feedback on the hospital's Emergency Operations Plan (EOP) or accompanying plans could include (but is not limited to) the Hospitals Chief Operating Officer (COO), leaders from critical operational areas within the hospital, local emergency responders, municipal or county emergency officials, healthcare coalition partners, as well as regional or state response collaborators. Different formats can be utilized in crafting an EOP. For instance, a hospital emergency manager might draft an EOP outlining the approach to handling emergencies while also developing a plan focused on addressing a specific issue or risk such as a Hurricane Response Plan or an Evacuation Plan.

Emergency management professionals often turn to resources from agencies like ASPR, FEMA, CDC, or similar organizations when crafting emergency plans. It is common for these professionals to share examples of plans or planning formats with colleagues as well. An example of a format that might be used for an Emergency Operations Plan (EOP) or a supporting plan can be found in the FEMA document titled "Developing and Maintaining Emergency Operations Plans; Comprehensive Preparedness Guide (CPG) 101," dated September 2021, Version 3.0.*

Creating an EOP and supporting plans is part of a hospital or healthcare system's strategy to ensure the safety of patients, staff, and the community during emergencies. These plans serve as a roadmap for preparedness, response, recovery, and mitigation efforts, assisting healthcare facilities in navigating challenging situations.

For hospitals and healthcare systems, having an EOP is essential for many reasons. It promotes preparedness by helping facilities get ready for emergencies such as disasters, disease outbreaks, mass casualty incidents, and unforeseen events. With a plan in place, hospitals can ensure that staff are trained appropriately, resources are allocated effectively, and response actions are well coordinated. Efficient coordination of resources is another aspect addressed by these plans. During healthcare emergencies, it is crucial for hospital departments and external organizations to work together. An Emergency Operations Plan (EOP) details the responsibilities of individuals and groups to ensure communication and coordination, especially when multiple facilities are involved within the same healthcare system. The focus of any healthcare institution is to deliver effective patient care with safety as the top priority. The EOP plays a role in safeguarding patients during emergencies by establishing procedures for evacuation, staying put, medical care, and other necessary actions. Regular training and exercises based on the EOP enhance staff preparedness and awareness of emergency protocols. This training equips healthcare workers with the knowledge needed to respond promptly and efficiently in crisis situations, minimizing errors and enhancing safety for both patients and staff. In times of emergency, there may be a demand for resources like supplies, personnel, and equipment. The EOP offers guidelines on how these resources should be distributed to address needs promptly. Many healthcare facilities are required by regulatory authorities to create and implement an EOP. An equipped healthcare center also boosts the confidence of the community, knowing that the hospital has a strategy in place to manage emergencies. This can reassure the other stakeholders, building trust and backing. Lastly, ongoing enhancement is accomplished by reviewing and updating the EOP, enabling healthcare systems and hospitals to integrate insights from emergencies and evolving best practices, ensuring that the plan stays relevant and efficient in the long run.

Leaders in healthcare and emergency preparedness should have an understanding of the regulations that apply to their healthcare environment. They must work towards staying compliant as these regulations greatly influence how hospitals and healthcare systems handle emergencies. These rules are put in place to ensure that healthcare institutions are ready for events. They establish guidelines and expectations for readiness, response, and recovery efforts, ensuring that healthcare facilities are well prepared to manage emergencies. Regulatory and accreditation requirements play a role in how hospitals and healthcare systems approach emergency management in various ways. Adhering to these requirements is crucial as many areas have laws or regulations requiring healthcare facilities to create and maintain emergency plans. These documents outline what is needed for readiness, response, recovery, and mitigation actions. Compliance with these regulations is vital to avoid penalties and keep the facility's operating license intact.

Accreditation criteria are another element that a well-written EOP can support. Various respected accreditation organizations ensure that hospitals meet standards of quality and safety. The Joint Commission (JC) stands out as one of the recognized accrediting bodies in the United

* Federal Emergency Management Agency. (2021). *Developing and maintaining emergency operations plans; Comprehensive Preparedness Guide (CPG) 101* (Version 3.0). https://www.fema.gov/media-library/assets/documents/25970

States, setting demanding standards for healthcare institutions. Likewise, the National Committee for Quality Assurance (NCQA) focuses on enhancing healthcare quality through accreditation processes and performance evaluation. Many important organizations are responsible for accrediting rehabilitation facilities and programs. For instance, the Commission on Accreditation of Rehabilitation Facilities (CARF) is one organization. Internationally, the International Society for Quality in Health Care (ISQua) accredits health and social care organizations across the globe. In Canada, Accreditation Canada offers accreditation services to healthcare organizations to enhance safety and care quality. DNV GL Healthcare, a foundation, also provides accreditation services based on the National Integrated Accreditation for Healthcare Organizations (NIAHO) standards, which incorporate ISO 9001 quality management principles. Additionally, the Healthcare Facilities Accreditation Program (HFAP) focuses on accrediting hospitals and healthcare facilities with an emphasis on safety and quality enhancement. The Center for Improvement in Healthcare Quality (CIHQ) focuses on providing accreditation services that prioritize compliance and performance improvement. These organizations are instrumental in ensuring that hospitals follow standards and continuously strive for excellence in healthcare delivery. Regulatory bodies and accreditation entities often mandate hospitals to create Emergency Operations Plans (EOPs). These plans should encompass elements such as risk assessment, communication strategies, resource allocation, staff training, and collaboration with agencies. While specific requirements may differ among entities, the key focus remains on having a documented and efficient plan in place. Emergency management requirements are typically included in accreditation standards.

Established emergency management programs, with accreditation from bodies like the Emergency Management Accreditation Program (EMAP) can bring many advantages for hospitals or healthcare systems. The accreditation of a hospital's emergency management program offers benefits, including validation, enhanced patient safety, regulatory adherence, community trust, and access to resources. It serves as a validation of the hospital's dedication to excellence in emergency management by showcasing its compliance with or surpassing industry-recognized benchmarks. This reinforces confidence among patients, staff, and the community in the hospital's commitment to quality care during emergencies. Once established, ongoing compliance with these standards is essential for hospitals to obtain and uphold their status, creating an environment of perpetual preparedness for the organization. Accreditation and regulation ensure that hospitals meet criteria concerning emergency management to ensure safety for patients and staff. Accredited hospitals are generally more prepared to handle emergencies through trained personnel, established communication channels, and tested emergency protocols. The rigorous assessments involved in the accreditation process help pinpoint areas for enhancement leading to a coordinated response strategy.

Community trust and confidence are strengthened by accreditation, which serves as an indication of a hospital's dedication to maintaining high-quality standards and ensuring safety. This builds trust among the community, patients, and stakeholders making them more inclined to choose a healthcare provider with accreditation. Accreditation criteria often include measures for managing risks during emergencies, assisting hospitals in identifying risks, evaluating them, and taking steps to reduce their impact or prevent events from occurring. Accreditation can also facilitate access to funding and resources since some funding sources, insurers, and government programs may give preference or require healthcare providers to hold accreditation. The accreditation process involves evaluation and enhancement efforts that encourage hospitals to update their emergency management plans in response to evolving threats. By incorporating lessons learned from exercise activities and real-world events into their plans, hospitals ensure improvements in their emergency preparedness capabilities. Hospitals are required to maintain records of training sessions, drills, and actual emergency responses to meet documentation and reporting standards. Regulatory bodies may inspect these records to evaluate compliance.

It is essential for hospitals to continuously improve their Emergency Operations Plans by incorporating insights gained from drills, real emergencies, and changing healthcare landscape as part of accreditation frameworks. The primary focus is on safety and maintaining care continuity during emergencies. Hospitals must have plans in place for evacuation and medical treatment, ensuring essential services are preserved to meet regulatory requirements and enhance comprehensive emergency readiness. Adhering to these standards not only fulfills obligations, but also strengthens the safety and resilience of healthcare facilities in effectively responding to unforeseen circumstances. Emphasizing structured emergency management practices plays a role in safeguarding both patients and healthcare providers.

Successful management of healthcare emergencies heavily relies on collaborating with agencies and organizations. Healthcare leaders need to build relationships with state and federal emergency management agencies, as well as other healthcare providers and community groups, to improve preparedness efforts. Collaboration between entities provides key advantages for healthcare facilities and systems. Sharing resources among organizations enhances their capabilities by pooling staff, equipment, supplies, and facilities to increase their response capacity during large-scale incidents. Collaboration also involves leveraging knowledge from fields of emergency management like public health, law enforcement, EMS, and disaster response to ensure a well-rounded approach to responding. Working together on planning leads to emergency plans that address specific community needs and challenges while establishing communication channels for distributing crucial information quickly. By engaging with the community through efforts that involve stakeholders in preparedness activities and ensuring response plans align with community priorities, this method encourages efficient resource allocation, prevents duplication of efforts, and follows legal requirements related to emergency readiness. Participating in training exercises and drills enhances coordination among agencies by allowing them to refine their roles, identify areas needing improvement, and adjust strategies based on changing circumstances. In the end, inter-agency collaboration empowers healthcare institutions to effectively navigate emergency situations while protecting community well-being through unified and resilient responses.

In order for hospitals and healthcare systems to effectively incorporate these components, it is crucial for hospital leaders to focus on choosing an emergency manager who possesses a grasp of emergency management principles. This ensures the creation and execution of emergency plans, adherence to regulations, and capable leadership during emergency situations.

The Bibliography section reflects the source information for the concepts and frameworks described in this chapter.

Bibliography

1. Centers for Disease Control and Prevention. (2020). *Emergency preparedness and response.* https://www.cdc.gov/cpr/index.htm
2. Centers for Disease Control and Prevention. (2021). *Public health emergency management phases.* https://www.cdc.gov/phpr/what-we-do/ph-emergency-management-phases.htm
3. Centers for Medicare & Medicaid Services. (2023). *Emergency preparedness requirements for Medicare and Medicaid participating providers and suppliers.* https://www.cms.gov/medicare/provider-enrollment-and-certification/emergency-preparedness
4. Commission on Accreditation of Rehabilitation Facilities. (2023). *CARF accreditation.* https://www.carf.org/

5. Federal Emergency Management Agency. (2019). *National response framework* (5th ed.). https://www.fema.gov/media-library/assets/documents/117791
6. Federal Emergency Management Agency. (2021). *Incident command system resources.* https://www.fema.gov/what-we-do/emergency-management/incident-command-system
7. Federal Emergency Management Agency. (2022). *Community preparedness and response.* https://www.fema.gov/what-we-do/community-preparedness
8. Federal Emergency Management Agency. (2022). *National incident management system* (3rd ed.). https://www.fema.gov/media-library/assets/documents/26328
9. National Committee for Quality Assurance. (2023). *Accreditation and certification.* https://www.ncqa.org/
10. The Joint Commission. (2023). *Standards for hospital accreditation.* https://www.jointcommission.org/standards/

Chapter 4

Selecting an Emergency Manager for Your Organization

Kimberly Bailey/Thomas Crawford

On far too many occasions and, frankly, at too many healthcare institutions, emergency management is not seen as an essential role and becomes "other duties as assigned." Based on this approach, the four essential elements of emergency preparedness – mitigation, preparation, response/operations, and recovery – are limited. I have worked in organizations that appointed the ED Nurse Manager or the Facilities Manager as the Emergency Manager and it simply didn't work. Why? Because their fulltime roles limited their individual ability to concentrate on mitigating known issues, ensuring those on call were properly trained and equipped with the knowledge and skills required to effectively manage "events" and our organizational learning opportunities were stunted by not formally conducting hotwashes (post event assessments designed to capture what went well and what needed to improve).

Case in point, early in my career I worked at a facility that lost connectivity to its HIS (hospital information system or electronic medical record) for three days. The Emergency Manager was the Director of Facilities, who quickly set up a Hospital Emergency Operations Center (HEOC) and declared that every clinical area would need to operationalize their downtime procedures. Unfortunately, the downtime procedures were never reviewed or tested and after updating our HIS with multiple upgrades our downtime protocols were outdated and rendered useless. The result? Care could have been compromised and the hospital could not recreate more than 50% of its chargeable patient transactions. I always found it ironic that the lost revenue would have more than covered the cost of a seasoned Emergency Manager that would have ensured we mitigated the known risk by reviewing the plans (annually and after upgrades), testing downtime protocols and ensuring our care team members knew exactly how to operationalize them if a real event occurred.

Before selecting an Emergency Manager, dedicate the time and resources required to ensure your organization has mitigated known issues and is prepared to answer the call when it

DOI: 10.4324/9781003529194-4

occurs. How? Ensure that emergency management is more than other duties as assigned and you'll quickly realize that a seasoned healthcare emergency manager will save you time, resources and – potentially – lives.

-Tom Crawford

In Chapter 3, we delved into the aspects of healthcare emergency management and why understanding these concepts is crucial for healthcare leaders and emergency managers. Moving on to Chapter 4, we will explore the significance of selecting an emergency manager to oversee your organization. We will outline what qualities to seek and which ones to avoid in the selection process, along with providing some questions to help you pick the suitable candidate.

Following Hurricane Katrina in August 2005, Memorial Medical Center in New Orleans, Louisiana, faced a crisis. The Category 5 hurricane caused flooding and city-wide damage, leading to power outages, infrastructure destruction, and a significant humanitarian crisis. It was later revealed that when Hurricane Katrina hit, Memorial Medical Center was unprepared for the enormity of the disaster. Situated in an area of the city prone to flooding, the hospital quickly became overwhelmed by floodwaters, isolating it from all access points and disabling critical services. Delayed responses, ineffective communication practices, and mismanagement of resources exacerbated the tragedy. In the aftermath of these events, various healthcare professionals came under scrutiny for their decisions made during the crisis. Both the hospital's administration and its emergency manager faced criticism in opinion as well as legal proceedings.

The mishandling of the situation has significantly harmed the reputation of Memorial Medical Center and shaken trust in the healthcare system's ability to manage emergencies. Instances like this serve as a reminder of the outcomes that can result when hospital leaders and emergency managers are unprepared. They highlight the role of leadership in emergency management and stress the importance of having a capable emergency manager who can develop robust plans for preparedness and response within the organization. So, how do you go about selecting the emergency manager for your organization?

Emergency management essentially functions as project management for large-scale disasters (and your day-to-day dumpster fires). While corporate-level project management and emergency management have different objectives and contexts, they share the same principles and methodologies. It's crucial to bear this in mind when assessing emergency managers for your organization; seek out many of the same qualities you would expect from a strong project manager.

Emergency managers may have many different backgrounds, with no one size fits all degree for this field. Although many start their careers in emergency response, *emergency management* encompasses a spectrum from preparedness and mitigation to response and recovery. It entails planning, coordination, and integration of activities aimed at bolstering resilience and minimizing disaster impacts.

Emergency management is a process that involves addressing all aspects of an emergency situation. It includes guidance, collaboration with stakeholders, and a comprehensive approach to handling emergencies before, during, and after they occur. This may involve tasks such as creating an Emergency Operations Plan (EOP), participating in Local Emergency Planning Committee (LEPC) meetings, and managing the Hospital Emergency Operations Center (HEOC).

Emergency response pertains specifically to the actions taken during and after an emergency to meet needs and minimize the impact. Whether dealing with a car accident, heart attack, or house fire, it focuses on decision making, coordination among responders and agencies, and effective crisis management. Responders are typically trained in fields like firefighting or law enforcement rather than holding dual roles as emergency managers. While emergency management and emergency response have many interconnected concepts within the emergency framework, they serve distinct roles in handling crises effectively. When selecting an emergency manager for a healthcare facility or hospital system, understanding these nuances is crucial for evaluating candidates' qualifications. To this point, some candidates may also confuse the duties related to responding to emergencies with those linked to emergency management when applying for a job.

A proficient emergency manager excels in an autonomous work setting but might seek other opportunities if micromanaged. It is crucial to have an emergency manager who is dependable and capable of working with minimal supervision. Autonomy plays a role for many reasons, but primarily it enables them to establish connections freely. Effective emergency management hinges on collaborating with partners such as government agencies, nonprofits, healthcare providers, and private sector entities. By participating in meetings involving many stakeholders, hospital emergency managers gain valuable insights into plans and decisions made by other organizations. This allows them to offer input from the hospital's standpoint, which is often overlooked but vital for community planning and response. These interactions ensure that all involved parties, including the hospital's leaders and staff, are well prepared and can collaborate seamlessly during emergencies. Regular face-to-face engagements help foster trust and strong relationships with all stakeholders for the benefit of the hospital's emergency preparedness.

When searching for someone to fill the role of an emergency manager, it is important to evaluate the candidates' people skills, including how well they can collaborate and their ability to communicate effectively in crisis situations.

During the progression, it is advisable to explore the connections and assess the candidate's familiarity with local stakeholders. This becomes particularly crucial if the candidate hails from a region outside of where your facility is located. For instance, consider an emergency manager residing in California who is interviewing for a role at a Tennessee hospital. Such an individual would likely face a learning curve and require more time to adjust compared to a candidate from Tennessee, where there is a good chance existing relationships are already in place. It is not about dismissing the California candidate; rather, it is about recognizing that they may need time to build relationships with stakeholders in the area before being fully effective. With dedication and skill, any adept emergency manager should be able to manage this process within a few months, so if the candidate from another area feels like a better fit for your organization, hire them.

As a healthcare leader, you are likely establishing connections with community leaders by participating in City or County Council meetings, engaging with state legislators, and collaborating with executives in your network to exchange information and sometimes strategize together. Your network of leaders will also share updates with you and seek information from you in times of disasters or emergencies. Elected officials at all levels of government rely on their jurisdiction's emergency managers to gather real-time information during emergencies or disasters and provide them with updates as situations unfold. Granting your emergency manager the autonomy to collect this information by managing their schedule, attending external meetings, and participating in relevant events will ensure that you also have the necessary data when needed. A competent emergency manager will actively support your organization and ensure its involvement in the planning stages for stakeholder organizations who may be creating plans that can impact your facility. These relationships will later translate into information exchange during events, something that is essential for healthcare leaders. While higher-level executives might not always possess the hands-on awareness that emergency managers have during emergencies, the responsibility of an emergency manager is to acquire the information needed for making informed decisions that impact hospital operations.

Healthcare leaders who underestimate the importance of autonomy may mistakenly assume that emergency managers have little to do during times of non-disaster. However, the truth is quite the opposite. As we've previously discussed, emergency managers play a role in important tasks during non-emergency times to ensure readiness, adaptability, and efficient response when emergencies do arise. Leaders who comprehend these duties are more likely to recognize the significance of emergency managers when there's no crisis at hand. If a leader perceives an emergency manager as having little to do in the absence of a crisis, they might think about assigning additional responsibilities, which could lead to adverse outcomes. Giving tasks (like roles in the areas of facilities, quality control, or security for example) to the emergency manager can scatter their focus and take away from their main duties concerning emergency management and readiness. This could leave the organization unprepared to handle crises when they occur or create large gaps in preparedness training. Balancing multiple responsibilities can result in heightened stress and exhaustion for the emergency manager. Dealing with emergencies is already a demanding job. It is crucial that you have faith in the emergency manager you bring on board for your organization and that there is trust between both parties. You are forming a unified team with a shared goal of safeguarding the organization.

There will be occasions when you spend periods of time preparing for an event, and you may be facing decisions that require quick thinking to prevent worsening situations. Sometimes there won't even be time to plan for an event. It is crucial for your emergency manager to have the ability to make sound decisions even in the absence of clear leadership, as some choices may have legal implications down the line. Emergency managers are professionals with expertise in disaster response and management. Their autonomy allows them to apply their knowledge effectively. During emergencies, situations can shift rapidly, necessitating responses. Autonomous emergency managers can adapt strategies and tactics on the fly to address evolving threats.

Emergency managers can attain degrees, certifications, or credentials showcasing their expertise and qualifications in emergency management. Hospital emergency managers form a specialized group and may possess additional certifications demonstrating proficiency in healthcare or hospital emergency management and their ability to tackle healthcare-specific challenges. It is worth noting that the relevance and recognition of certifications may vary and are often as valuable as formal education in the field of emergency management.

The ideal candidate may not possess a formal or traditional degree, so it is important to draft the job description with some flexibility and base the decision on the organization's specific needs and the role of emergency management. Many emergency managers engage in training and obtain certifications to stay up to date with emerging best practices and technologies, even without a formal degree. Some emergency managers may hold certifications to showcase their expertise in specific aspects of the field. Ongoing professional development and participation in training programs play a role in staying current in this ever-evolving field.

An emergency manager with vision and strategic planning skills is essential to ensure that the healthcare facility is well prepared for a variety of emergencies. This involves creating emergency plans, conducting risk assessments, and coordinating exercises and training sessions. Evaluating the qualities of an emergency manager during the selection process is vital for healthcare leaders to ensure that the chosen individual can effectively handle the complexities and challenges of emergency situations. The right emergency manager can significantly improve a healthcare facility's readiness, response, and recovery capabilities, ultimately safeguarding the welfare of patients, staff, and the broader community. Having a desire to foster relationships and collaborate is a very important characteristic to consider when choosing an emergency manager. Emergency managers who excel in their roles are known for their collaborative nature. They are recognized for their willingness to share plans and information. An emergency manager's inability to collaborate or reluctance to network can have negative effects on the organization and may not be well received within the emergency management community they are part of. In emergency management, a diverse array of resources such as personnel, equipment, and supplies are often required. Collaboration and networking empower emergency managers to establish connections with agencies, organizations, and community partners, enhancing access to these resources during crises. The practice of collaboration and networking facilitates the exchange of information among stakeholders and agencies, particularly vital for hospitals and healthcare systems. Failure to collaborate could lead to information channels resulting in miscommunication, redundant efforts, and a fragmented response. Effective emergency response necessitates coordination among entities, including government bodies, nonprofit organizations, and community groups. An emergency manager lacking in collaboration skills may find it challenging to harmonize efforts effectively, leading to a disjointed response that compromises efficiency. Collaboration enables emergency managers to leverage the experiences and expertise of others in refining their approach to managing emergencies. Networking within and outside the hospital setting offers opportunities to engage in training activities, exchange best practices, and gather insights from the achievements and obstacles experienced by colleagues. An emergency manager who shuns collaboration could miss out on learning experiences. Working together with partners is crucial for establishing trust and credibility. A solitary emergency manager might be viewed as distant or unresponsive, diminishing trust and potentially impeding community collaboration with the hospital in times of crisis. Emergency scenarios are fluid, and collaborative networks offer adaptability and flexibility, enabling emergency managers to tweak strategies based on new information and evolving circumstances. In times of crisis, having a support network is vital for mobilizing resources, volunteers, and extra personnel. An isolated emergency manager may face difficulties in mobilizing support, which could delay response efforts within the hospital or healthcare system. Collaboration is also crucial for conducting risk assessments since various agencies and organizations bring diverse perspectives and expertise to the table. An emergency manager operating in isolation might overlook risks or vulnerabilities, resulting in inadequate planning and readiness. Some regulations and accreditation standards mandate collaboration among entities for compliance. Emergency managers who do not collaborate run the risk of not meeting these requirements, resulting in regulatory challenges. It is important to involve stakeholders in the selection process, including healthcare administrators, department heads, and representatives from emergency management agencies or Healthcare Coalition partners (including other local hospitals) with whom the emergency manager will work closely.

When hiring an emergency manager for a hospital or healthcare system, it is essential to prioritize personality traits that greatly influence their effectiveness in handling high-pressure situations. Among these traits, maintaining calmness and composure during such scenarios emerges as critical. This quality allows the emergency manager to make sound decisions without feeling overwhelmed by the urgency of the situation, which is crucial for maintaining control and achieving the best possible outcomes. Being able to act decisively is also key for an emergency manager. Emergencies often demand decision-making with limited information available. A competent emergency manager needs to be able to make well-thought-out decisions to swiftly reduce the impact of an emergency. This quick decision-making ensures that necessary steps are taken promptly, potentially saving lives and resources. Integrity and ethical judgment are of utmost importance. Transparency and honesty are essential for fostering trust with team members, patients, and the community at large.

Leadership skills are essential for any hospital emergency manager even if they don't have subordinates. Strong leaders inspire confidence, motivate their teams, and create a guided environment for staff. This is especially important if you have multiple facilities in your healthcare system. An emergency manager with strong leadership qualities will be more effective and will be able to assist their team during crises, guaranteeing a coordinated and efficient response. Decision-making guided by principles ensures that actions align with standards and serve the best interests of all stakeholders. When they are willing to take ownership of decisions and actions, they will build trust and respect within the team, which is crucial for a successful emergency management program and overall hospital preparedness.

The ability to provide clear communication is another trait to look for. Being able to convey emergency information in a comprehensive manner is vital during emergencies when misunderstandings can have consequences. An emergency manager must ensure that instructions are clearly understood and followed accurately. In addition, effective communication in emergency management involves listening to others, understanding their concerns, and incorporating feedback into the response strategy. This two-way communication creates an environment where everyone is well informed and aligned with the emergency response plan. Attention to detail plays a role in managing emergencies.

Emergency managers typically prioritize planning due to the nature of their responsibilities and the critical importance of preparedness in crisis management. They often rely on checklists, plans, and data collection to ensure effective planning and execution. A meticulous approach to resource allocation and procedural implementation is vital for an emergency response. Emergency managers must possess skills to manage multiple tasks simultaneously to maintain order and prioritize effectively. This ensures that all aspects of the emergency receive attention. Creative problem-solving is another strong attribute for an emergency manager to possess. Emergencies can bring about challenges that may not have immediate solutions. It is essential for emergency managers to think creatively and devise approaches to address these challenges. Analytical skills are critical for assessing situations and determining the most appropriate course of action during emergencies. The capability to adjust quickly to changing circumstances and new information is essential. Flexibility enables emergency managers to modify strategies as necessary in response to evolving challenges. Embracing new ideas and approaches fosters enhancement and more effective responses to future emergencies. Resilience, the capacity to endure prolonged stress and setbacks, is vital for emergency managers to navigate long hours and tough conditions while maintaining their effectiveness. Perseverance, characterized by determination to overcome obstacles and persist through challenges, plays a role in ensuring that all required actions are taken to handle and resolve emergencies.

When choosing an emergency manager for a healthcare system, it is imperative to prioritize these character traits. These qualities help identify individuals who possess expertise and also exhibit the personal attributes needed for effective leadership during crises. Together, these traits contribute to an empathetic approach to emergency management that safeguards the safety and well-being of patients staff members, and the wider community. By focusing on these characteristics during the selection process, healthcare leaders can improve their organization's readiness and response capabilities, ultimately protecting their institution from a variety of crises.

Selecting an emergency manager for a healthcare environment involves a process with several steps and considerations. Initially, it is crucial to define the requirements and duties of the position to fit the unique needs of the healthcare facility. This entails specifying the qualifications, experience, and expertise in emergency management. The subsequent step involves creating a recruitment plan that attracts a range of candidates through different channels and professional networks. Crafting a recruitment strategy for hiring an emergency manager in healthcare involves utilizing organizations, platforms, and professional networks to attract diverse candidates. Some key entities that play a role in this process are:

- American College of Healthcare Executives (ACHE): This association offers networking opportunities and professional growth prospects for healthcare executives specializing in emergency management.
- Association of Healthcare Emergency Preparedness Professionals (AHEPP): AHEPP focuses on advancing healthcare emergency management by providing access to professionals and recruitment resources.
- The International Association of Emergency Managers (IAEM) is an organization that supports professionals in emergency management across sectors, including healthcare. Its platform and community can be helpful for finding candidates.
- The National Emergency Management Association (NEMA) represents state directors in emergency management. It offers a network of experts in the field, which can be beneficial for recruitment efforts.
- Healthcare Information and Management Systems Society (HIMSS) focuses on the integration of healthcare and information technology, connecting professionals experienced in managing healthcare emergencies and crises.
- The Public Health Preparedness and Response Network (PHPRN) links health and emergency management professionals, providing a pool of candidates with skills.
- LinkedIn's professional network and job posting features are useful for reaching a range of candidates, including those with expertise in healthcare emergency management.

Attending conferences like the Annual Emergency Management Higher Education Symposium or the Preparedness Summit can help identify candidates through networking opportunities.

Collaborating with universities offering degrees or certifications in emergency management, health, or healthcare administration can give access to graduates and alumni with specialized training. Job boards and recruitment platforms, such as Indeed, Glassdoor, and specialty job sites like Careers in Government, can help attract a range of candidates.

When evaluating candidates, it is important to look beyond their skills and knowledge. Consider their personality traits and soft skills like leadership, communication, and problem-solving abilities. This can be done through interviews, judgment tests, and scenario-based assessments that replicate real-life emergency scenarios. Gathering feedback from stakeholders can offer insights into the candidate's suitability for the role. It is recommended to have an interview panel consisting of both staff and external stakeholders from the community the emergency manager will engage with. Conducting reference checks is essential to confirm performance and reliability.

The selection process should be comprehensive and systematic to find an emergency manager who not only meets requirements but also fits well with the organization's culture and values for an efficient response to emergencies. Clearly define the responsibilities and expectations of the emergency manager role within the healthcare system or facility they will serve.

When interviewing for the role, you can inquire about aspects such as developing emergency plans, organizing training sessions and drills, ensuring compliance with regulations, fostering collaboration among agencies, or serving as a link between the hospital and community partners. During the interview, you may ask questions like:

- *Can you share an instance where you were involved in creating an Emergency Operations Plan (EOP) or other emergency plans? It's crucial to confirm if the candidate was the author of the plan since most emergency managers seek input from others to ensure coverage for all stakeholders. When assessing the example provided, look for a plan that presents a framework outlining procedures and protocols for addressing different emergencies. The EOP should clearly define the hospital's command structure, assigning roles and responsibilities within the incident command system for leadership coordination. Additionally, it should incorporate recovery strategies aimed at restoring operations post emergency.*
- *Could you describe an exercise that you led and share a sample of an After-Action Report that you authored? You are interested in candidates with experience in developing exercises across levels, including discussion-based activities and full-scale simulations. There are certifications related to exercises that candidates can pursue, as outlined later in this section.*
- *Are you familiar with the regulations and standards set by your organization's accrediting body? It' is essential to ensure that candidates understand the requirements governing healthcare emergency management at your hospital. This includes being well-versed in the guidelines from accrediting bodies, state and Federal government agencies, and other relevant regulatory entities. Some applicants may be transitioning from a public emergency management role to a sector position within your organization. While they may need time to adapt to healthcare concepts and practices, their existing relationships at state or Federal levels could prove valuable during emergencies. The ability to leverage connections for obtaining resources is crucial for an emergency manager. A seasoned professional should be able to grasp hospital standards within a month and become proficient within a year.*
- *Which coalitions, committees, organizations, or external agencies do you believe are collaborators in this role if you are chosen? It's vital to find a candidate who recognizes the significance of networking in this position.*

The top candidate should be able to list examples of groups involved in emergency management with whom they commonly interact. For instance, all states have some sort of Healthcare Coalition. These coalitions typically receive funding for projects from grants. Hospital emergency managers who are familiar with these groups have a strong networking opportunity and sometimes the chance to apply for supplemental funding for hospital projects related to emergency management.

Given the challenges in healthcare environments, the ideal candidate should grasp healthcare-specific concepts like patient care continuity, medical response protocols, infection control, and the regulatory framework governing healthcare facilities. It is possible to learn most of these concepts, but an emergency manager without any healthcare background may have a steeper learning curve. Don't let this be a deterrent if you strongly believe that this individual is the best fit for your organization.

The following interview questions are crafted to help you assess the candidate's comprehension of the significance of networking in emergency management and their ability to foster and leverage relationships for preparedness, response, and recovery efforts.

- *Do you happen to know the emergency manager of the county where the hospital is situated? Have you developed a rapport with them? Alternatively, could you share some of the projects you've worked on together?*
- *Can you describe a scenario where networking and teamwork were crucial for the success of an emergency management project or response effort that you were part of?*

- *What is your approach to building and nurturing relationships with emergency management professionals, government entities, nonprofit organizations, and private businesses?*
- *From your perspective, how important is interagency collaboration in ensuring successful emergency management endeavors? Could you recount an experience where you had to collaborate with agencies or organizations towards a common objective?*
- *Emergency management often calls for engagement with a range of stakeholders. How do you go about forging partnerships and communicating effectively with individuals from different backgrounds, occupations, and levels of government?*
- *Could you share a situation when networking helped you access resources, expertise, or assistance during a crisis or disaster situation?*
- *How do you keep yourself updated on the advancements, practices, and innovations, in emergency management?*
- *Do you actively participate in groups, attend conferences, or take part in networking events to improve your knowledge and skills?*
- *How do you encourage collaboration among organizations and agencies with goals and priorities in emergency management?*
- *Tell me about your experiences with mutual aid agreements and partnerships. How do you ensure that these agreements benefit all parties involved effectively?*
- *In what ways do you approach establishing connections within the community and engaging with the public regarding emergency preparedness and response?*
- *Can you share a story where your networking and relationship-building skills were key in overcoming challenges or achieving an outcome?*

Think about the candidate's background in creating and running training programs and emergency exercises. A seasoned emergency manager will have examples of documents for planning and executing exercises. Many managers create long-term training and exercise plans to address all types of hazards. Having experience in organizing simulations and assessing healthcare staff performance during drills is advantageous. An emergency manager who is knowledgeable about exercise frameworks or holds a FEMA certification as a Master Exercise Planner brings exceptional value. The Homeland Security Exercise and Evaluation Program (HSEEP) is widely acknowledged as one of the frameworks for designing and assessing emergency management exercises in the United States, although there are others available. HSEEP aims to improve emergency readiness through practices for managing, designing, conducting, evaluating, and enhancing exercise programs.

For hospital emergency managers, it's essential to be well-versed in the exercise design process and grasp the significance of both the exercise and evaluation procedures. Using a framework ensures a standardized approach in creating, executing, and assessing exercises. Understanding HSEEP principles enables hospital emergency managers to align their exercises with a recognized methodology. These tools help hospital emergency managers gauge staff performance, pinpoint improvement areas, and enhance emergency response effectiveness – fostering a cycle of enhancement. Following each exercise, a comprehensive assessment is carried out to glean insights and identify ways for refinement. This iterative process empowers hospital emergency managers to continually elevate their emergency plans and response capabilities. Collaboration with many stakeholder agencies and organizations is common during exercises. Adhering to established guidelines allows hospital emergency managers to seamlessly integrate their facility's response capabilities, promoting better coordination and communication. Many accrediting bodies stipulate that healthcare facilities must conduct exercises as part of their readiness endeavors.

Hospital emergency managers who are well versed in HSEEP or a similar standardized exercise development process have an edge in meeting these requirements and ensuring compliance. Acquiring an understanding of exercise principles is beneficial for the growth of hospital emergency managers. It showcases a dedication to adhering to recognized standards and staying up to date on the trends in emergency management.

Having knowledge of the exercise and evaluation processes is crucial for hospital emergency managers to improve the efficiency of their emergency readiness initiatives. This approach offers a uniform method for creating and evaluating exercises, ultimately bolstering the resilience and preparedness of healthcare facilities. The following set of sample questions is designed to evaluate candidates' experience, skills, and strategies regarding training and exercises within the realm of emergency management. Seek candidates who exhibit a comprehension of the significance of training, realistic drills, and ongoing enhancements in emergency readiness and response.

- *(If not detailed on a resume) Do you hold any certifications related to exercise development? (Possessing FEMA certification as a Master Exercise Planner or a similar qualification would be advantageous)*
- *What is the extensive exercise you have been involved in? Could you describe your role during that scenario? (Look for instances involving exercise development, creation of situation manuals, exercise plans, or other documentation associated with exercise activities.)*
- *Have you ever created a Multiyear Training and Exercise Plan (MYTEP) or an Integrated Preparedness Plan (IPP)? If so, could I take a look at it? If you have conducted a Hazard Vulnerability Analysis as an example, we can compare it with the MYTEP or IPP to ensure that the training included relates to the HVA.*
- *How do you identify the training needs of personnel in the hospital and within the emergency management system?*
- *Have you introduced any specialized training initiatives? Could you provide an example?*
- *How do you assess the effectiveness of training programs and drills?*
- *Can you share a situation where insights from training directly impacted changes in emergency plans or procedures? Talk about your experience in collaborating on training and drills with agencies and organizations. How do you ensure there is a unified approach? How do you convey the significance of training and drills to stakeholders, including hospital leadership and staff? Have you been involved in creating or revising training programs to meet demands?*

Assessing a candidate's ability to adapt and adjust is vital for an emergency management role, where unforeseen circumstances are constantly changing and unpredictable.

Look for a candidate who shows flexibility, adaptability, and the ability to make decisions when things get tough. The candidate should be able to change plans and adjust priorities quickly based on what's happening at the time. Seek out candidates who have a history of being flexible, thinking fast, and solving problems effectively in changing environments. Here are some questions to see how well a candidate can handle pressure, adapt to changes, and learn from their experiences – qualities essential for an emergency manager dealing with situations.

- *Can you tell me about a time when you had to adapt to changes in an emergency management scenario? How did you manage it, and what was the result?*
- *Emergencies often call for decision-making. Can you share an instance where you had to make a decision under pressure? How did you ensure it was the right choice?*

- *Share a situation where you needed to modify an emergency response plan on short notice. What factors did you take into account? How did you communicate the changes with parties?*
- *In emergency management, unexpected challenges can pop up.*
- *Can you talk about a difficulty you encountered, how you dealt with it, and what lessons you took away from the situation?*
- *How do you organize tasks or duties when faced with a crisis? Could you give an example of a time when you had to balance priorities?*
- *During emergencies, cooperation with stakeholders is often necessary. Can you share an incident where you had to collaborate with individuals or organizations with differing goals or approaches? How did you manage those disparities?*
- *Tell me about a moment when you had to lead a team through a crisis or emergency. How did you steer your team members during that time?*
- *When resources are scarce in situations, can you describe an instance where you needed to optimize resources but still achieve successful results?*
- *Have there been occasions where you had to convey information to diverse audiences like the public, elected officials or other agencies? How did you ensure effective communication in a changing setting?*

Look for candidates who value learning and professional growth in the field of emergency management. Attending industry conferences to stay updated on practices and obtaining additional certifications are all positive signs. Most states have an Emergency Management Association or a similar organization where emergency managers gather to exchange knowledge, engage in exercises, and build connections. It is important that the candidate is actively involved in activities or professional development initiatives. There are conferences held across the United States for emergency managers. Many states host Emergency Management conferences, and the International Association of Emergency Managers (IAEM) organizes regional events and a major conference each year. Healthcare coalitions are also encouraged to support their members' attendance at preparedness-focused conferences.

During the interview process, you may inquire about conferences related to emergency management that the candidate has attended within the year or associations related to emergency management that the candidate is a part of. Evaluating the fit of an emergency manager within a hospital environment is essential to ensure they align with the institution's values, priorities, and unique challenges. Assess how well the candidate's values and approach match your healthcare system's culture. An emergency manager who comprehends and embraces the organization's values is more likely to integrate into the team.

When looking for candidates, it is important to find individuals with not technical expertise but also a strong understanding and respect for the intricacies of healthcare emergency management. Asking questions during interviews can help the interview team gauge the candidates' grasp of the hospital's culture, their background in healthcare emergency management, and their ability to fit well within a healthcare setting.

- *How do you see our hospital's mission aligning with your emergency management approach?*
- *When planning for emergency response, how do you prioritize safety and ensure continuity of care?*
- *Could you share a scenario where you had to juggle patient needs with emergency management strategies?*

- *Explain how you collaborate with hospital leadership, department heads, and different teams within the hospital. How do you build consensus and get support for emergency management initiatives?*
- *Balancing swift responses with challenges to healthcare settings like patient care and regulatory compliance can be tricky. How do you manage this balance?*
- *Ensuring that emergency plans meet healthcare regulations and accreditation standards is crucial. How do you guarantee compliance?*
- *Share instances where you've interacted with accreditation or regulatory bodies in the healthcare industry during your work experience.*
- *How do you handle communication in a healthcare setting during emergencies, taking into account the roles and duties of hospital staff?*
- *Are you well-versed in hospital operations such as processes, logistics, and managing the supply chain?*
- *Could you share your experience dealing with crisis intervention in healthcare environments, especially when it comes to addressing the emotional impacts of emergencies on both staff members and patients?*
- *In what ways do you tackle the challenges that come with managing emergencies related to diseases or public health crises within a hospital environment?*
- *How do you ensure you stay informed about trends and recommended practices in emergency management within the healthcare industry?*

Common Degrees and Certifications for Emergency Managers (not a comprehensive compilation):

- Doctoral Degree (Ph.D. or D.E.M.) in Emergency Management; Doctoral programs focusing on emergency management cater to individuals interested in conducting research contributing to academia or pursuing leadership positions within specialized areas of emergency management.
- Masters Degree in Emergency Management: Advanced degrees like a Master of Science or Master of Arts in Emergency Management provide knowledge and specialization. These programs typically involve coursework, research projects, and sometimes internships or practical training. Completing a master's degree in Public Administration (MPA) with a Focus on Emergency Management involves individuals opting for an MPA degree but specializing in emergency management. This offers an insight into administration specifically emphasizing emergency response and preparedness.
- Pursuing a Master's Degree in Homeland Security entails exploring topics concerning security, terrorism, and emergency management. These programs tend to attract individuals aspiring to take on leadership roles within the field of emergency management.
- Attaining a Master's Degree in Public Health (MPH) with an Emphasis on Emergency Preparedness equips students with an understanding of public health matters relating to emergencies and disasters.
- Opting for a Bachelor's Degree in Emergency Management is an option offered by universities focusing specifically on emergency management or closely related fields. These programs typically cover areas such as disaster preparedness, response strategies, recovery efforts, risk assessment techniques, and mitigation measures.
- Enrolling in a Bachelor's Degree program, in Homeland Security involves studying issues related to security, including emergency management practices, disaster response tactics, and safeguarding critical infrastructure.

- A Bachelor's Degree in Public Administration or Public Policy offers a foundation in governance, policy formation, and the functions of government agencies in handling emergencies.
- Those interested in emergency management for natural disasters may benefit from pursuing a Bachelor's Degree in Environmental Science or Environmental Management. These programs typically cover topics such as climate change, hazard assessment, and sustainable development.
- Individuals looking to specialize in emergency management within healthcare environments may find Bachelor's Degrees in Health Administration or Public Health relevant. These programs often include coursework on response healthcare emergency planning and public health policies.
- Pursuing a Bachelor's Degree in Geography or Geographic Information Systems (GIS) equips students with skills in mapping, spatial analysis, and data visualization crucial for understanding and addressing aspects of emergencies.
- The Certified Emergency Manager (CEM) designation provided by the International Association of Emergency Managers (IAEM) is widely recognized as one of the certifications in the field. It signifies a grasp of emergency management principles and competencies. Entry-level Emergency Manager (EEM), provided by IAEM, the EEM certification targets newcomers in the emergency management field, acting as a starting point for those aiming for the CEM certification.
- State Emergency Management Professional Certification (SEMP or State CEM): Certain states have their certification programs for emergency management professionals. These certifications, similar to CEM, cover skills such as planning, response coordination, and recovery efforts, showcasing a grasp of emergency management principles and skills.
- FEMA's Professional Development Series (PDS); FEMA offers a series of courses known as the Professional Development Series to lay a groundwork in emergency management. Completion of PDS is often seen as an asset for entry-level and mid-level positions in emergency management.
- Expert Exercise Practitioner (EEP): Offered by EMI, this certification focuses on individuals involved in creating, conducting, and assessing emergency exercises. It highlights proficiency in planning and executing drills and simulations.
- Accredited Hazardous Materials Supervisor (AHMS): IHMM offers this credential for professionals handling materials and waste. These certifications, like the Certified Business Continuity Professional (CBCP) and Certified Protection Professional (CPP), offer knowledge that can be applied in emergency situations. The CBCP certification from the Disaster Recovery Institute International (DRII) focuses on business continuity and can also benefit emergency managers dealing with continuity during crises. Similarly, the CPP certification from ASIS International covers a range of security aspects, including emergency management, making it suitable for professionals overseeing organizational security. The Certified Homeland Protection Professional (CHPP) certification by the National Sheriffs Association (NSA) is tailored for individuals in safety and security fields dealing with homeland security and emergency management. Additionally, the Certified Continuity Manager (CCM) certification administered by the International Consortium for Organizational Resilience (ICOR) targets professionals involved in business continuity, disaster recovery, and emergency management practices. Lastly, individuals holding Emergency Medical Technician (EMT) or Paramedic certifications bring medical response skills to emergency management roles in healthcare settings.

When choosing an emergency manager and evaluating their qualifications or certifications, it is crucial for hospital administrators to grasp their organization's requirements and the duties of the emergency manager. An emergency manager with a lack of experience could have an impact on a Level 1 Trauma center in a large city, whereas it might not be as relevant for a smaller facility. The number of hospitals or staff members supervised by the emergency manager or emergency management program director should also be considered when making this decision. By following these steps and taking these factors into consideration, healthcare leaders can choose an emergency manager or program director who is well prepared to improve the emergency readiness and response capabilities of the hospital or healthcare system.

The Bibliography section reflects the source information for the concepts and frameworks described in this chapter.

Bibliography

1. Centers for Disease Control and Prevention. (2020). *Emergency preparedness and response.* https://www.cdc.gov/cpr/index.htm
2. Centers for Disease Control and Prevention. (2021). *Public health emergency management phases.* https://www.cdc.gov/phpr/what-we-do/ph-emergency-management-phases.htm
3. Centers for Medicare & Medicaid Services. (2023). *Emergency preparedness requirements for Medicare and Medicaid participating providers and suppliers.* https://www.cms.gov/medicare/provider-enrollment-and-certification/emergency-preparedness
4. Commission on Accreditation of Rehabilitation Facilities. (2023). CARF accreditation. https://www.carf.org/
5. Federal Emergency Management Agency. (2019). *National response framework* (5th ed.). https://www.fema.gov/media-library/assets/documents/117791
6. Federal Emergency Management Agency. (2021). *Developing and maintaining emergency operations plans; Comprehensive Preparedness Guide (CPG) 101 (Version 3.0)* . https://www.fema.gov/media-library/assets/documents/25970
7. Federal Emergency Management Agency. (2021). *Incident command system resources.* https://www.fema.gov/what-we-do/emergency-management/incident-command-system
8. Federal Emergency Management Agency. (2022). *Community preparedness and response.* https://www.fema.gov/what-we-do/community-preparedness
9. Federal Emergency Management Agency. (2022). *National incident management system* (3rd ed.). https://www.fema.gov/media-library/assets/documents/26328
10. National Committee for Quality Assurance. (2023). *Accreditation and certification.* https://www.ncqa.org/
11. The Joint Commission. (2023). *Standards for hospital accreditation.* https://www.jointcommission.org/standards/

Chapter 5

Risk Assessment and Hazard Identification

Kimberly Bailey/Mario Formisano/Thomas McNeal

Howard County, Maryland, occasionally faces substantial snowstorms that can disrupt transportation networks for several days, necessitating extensive snow removal efforts. Even a few inches of snow can cause major issues, especially with smaller snowplows struggling to keep up, increasing the time needed to clear the roads. During severe snow events, smaller snowplows become ineffective, increasing the time needed for road clearance using the larger plows. Recognizing these risks, the county developed a comprehensive approach involving multiple departments to handle such emergencies better. During one particularly severe storm, I saw this approach in action. The Howard County Office of Emergency Management, Department of Human Services, Office of Aging, and County Health Department collaborated to create a Medical Triage and Transport Plan. This plan centralized all calls for medical assistance at a dedicated Medical Triage Desk within the County's Emergency Operations Center (EOC). Staffed by the Office of Aging and a Medical Officer from the Health Department, the desk was crucial in managing the situation. I remember a call for help from a citizen who relies on regular dialysis, couldn't get to her appointment due to the snow. The Medical Triage Desk quickly triaged her call and coordinated with her dialysis center. The staff's personal relationship with her through community programs provided her with much-needed reassurance, alleviating her anxiety about missing her treatment. This system not only ensured that she received the medical care she needed but also played a significant role in reducing the overall number of government-arranged medical transportation requests by an astounding 80%! With the County Health Officer directly coordinating urgent cases, fewer disruptions occurred to the snowplow routes, significantly improving road clearance times. The Medical Triage Desk also validated requests from physicians and medical staff, ensuring that only the most critical cases required cleared roads and transportation assistance from the county, allowing for effective resource allocation. The Medical Triage and Transport Plan demonstrated Howard County's commitment to comprehensive emergency management and community welfare. By ensuring timely medical assistance, reducing the strain on snow removal operations, providing psychological

DOI: 10.4324/9781003529194-5

support to vulnerable residents, and streamlining emergency responses, the county effectively mitigated the risks associated with severe snowstorms. The implementation of the Medical Triage and Transport Plan enhanced the efficiency and safety of medical responses during snow emergencies and demonstrated the county's commitment to comprehensive emergency management and community welfare. This initiative successfully mitigated the risks associated with severe snowstorms by ensuring timely medical assistance, reducing the strain on snow removal operations, providing psychological support to vulnerable residents, and streamlining emergency responses.

~Thomas McNeal

Effective management of healthcare emergencies starts with an understanding of the risks and dangers that healthcare institutions could encounter. In Chapter 5, we see in depth discussion on the process of assessing risks and identifying hazards, which forms the basis for emergency planning and readiness. By the conclusion of this chapter, you will have a comprehension of how vital risk assessment and hazard identification are in managing healthcare emergencies. This fundamental knowledge will empower you to take a stance towards readiness and make informed decisions regarding resource allocation and strategies to mitigate risks within your healthcare facility.

It is essential for healthcare leaders and emergency managers to recognize the importance of the risk assessment process and their responsibility in addressing threats. Contrary to belief, the initial step in risk assessment does not involve evaluating the infrastructure of the facility. Before examining infrastructure, it is crucial to define all risks that need evaluation. To achieve this, it is necessary to understand how emergency management fits into the entire operational structure rather than being limited to facilities management alone.

Many hospitals (I would argue the majority) have incorporated their emergency managers into specific departments such as facilities management or quality/risk areas. The thought process behind this is probably more traditional these days and left over from a time when hospital leaders believed that most emergencies at the hospital would be related to some kind of infrastructure issue (internal flood, utility failure, etc.). But today's world requires more of your emergency manager than just making sure your medical gases are topped off and generators will work in an emergency. There are significant benefits to separating emergency management from any specific department and creating a standalone Emergency Management Department within your organization that reports directly to an operating position or something similar in function. Emergency management covers a range of tasks, including preparing for, recovering from, and lessening the impacts of emergencies and disasters. It also involves creating policies and procedures related to these events. Placing the emergency manager in a specific department will limit their ability to effectively deal with these challenges. To handle emergency preparedness well, it is important for the emergency manager to work independently and have direct access to high-level leaders. Collaboration between departments is crucial in emergency management, involving coordination among areas like services, security, and public relations. Having the emergency manager separate from any department promotes this collaboration, making it easier to take a comprehensive approach to planning for emergencies and responding to them. The emergency manager should essentially be part of all major teams so that they can create emergency plans that are tailored to the hospital's diverse requirements.

During emergencies, effective communication and coordination are vital. Placing the emergency manager in a stand-alone department improves communication with hospital leadership, clinical units, and external organizations. This direct interaction ensures that emergency plans are closely aligned with the hospital's goals and strategies, enhancing response efficiency and patient safety, which are central to the hospital's mission. In times of crisis, having an emergency management department is crucial for putting patients at the forefront of emergency planning and response efforts. This ensures that the hospital's focus remains on delivering top-notch patient care during such situations.

Adhering to standards and meeting accreditation requirements emphasize the importance of embedding emergency management practices within healthcare frameworks. By aligning with healthcare regulations, emergency managers can effectively navigate evolving requirements, ultimately boosting the hospital's readiness and response capabilities. Effective emergency management relies on planning and thorough risk assessment. Placing the emergency manager outside of any other department offers a perspective on risks like infectious disease outbreaks or cyber threats, leading to proactive risk mitigation strategies across the hospital. By working and collaborating across fields, the emergency manager can effectively prioritize patient safety, improve communication and coordination, ensure compliance with regulations, and strategically manage risks to maintain the hospital's ability to handle emergencies. By separating the emergency management function from the facilities' department's chain of command, a thorough patient-focused and strategic approach to emergency preparedness and response in a hospital environment is ensured. This separation encourages collaboration, communication, and expertise that are vital for addressing the challenges that come with healthcare emergencies.

Having the emergency manager integrated into system operations will be key in supporting and reducing risks in various ways. Ideally the organization's emergency manager or director of emergency management should report directly to the Chief Operating Officer or an equivalent position. Including emergency management as part of the operations team allows for the identification and evaluation of potential risks across the entire organization. This integrated approach ensures a comprehensive, coordinated, and efficient response to emergencies that benefits both the organization and its communities. It aids in identifying hazards, vulnerabilities, and possible threats, which paves the way for mitigation strategies. Integrating emergency management into hospital operations brings advantages that help reduce risks and strengthen overall organizational resilience.

A patient-centered approach ensures that the hospital's emergency preparedness plans seamlessly align with its objective of providing high-quality healthcare during times of crisis. By incorporating emergency management into hospital operations, facilities can create plans and responses that cover staff, communication methods, medical procedures, and community involvement. This method allows hospitals to effectively handle emergencies affecting multiple departments simultaneously, ensuring a comprehensive response and action plan across all aspects of hospital activities. Collaborating across departments such as clinical, administrative, security, and communication is crucial for effective emergency management. Integrating emergency preparedness into hospital operations promotes a response system that improves communication and teamwork during crises. This collaborative effort is essential for maintaining services and creating continuity plans to minimize disruptions in care. Efficient allocation and management of resources play a vital role in emergency readiness. By embedding emergency management within hospital operations, leaders can strategically distribute resources, finances, and materials to support emergency responses. Proactive resource planning helps reduce the risk of shortages during crises, ensuring delivery of services while enhancing organizational resilience. The integration of emergency management into hospital activities facilitates continuous improvement efforts. Evaluating responses post event allows hospitals to assess effectiveness, identify areas for improvement, and update protocols accordingly.

This ongoing process guarantees that emergency plans stay up to date and efficient, minimizing the chances of using outdated strategies in crises. Healthcare organizations naturally prioritize compliance, often requiring emergency management as a mandate. By integrating emergency management practices into hospital operations, healthcare institutions ensure adherence to standards, fostering a culture focused on safety and readiness while reducing regulatory risks. Effective communication and public relations are crucial in emergencies, necessitating strategies to engage both external and internal stakeholders. Incorporating these practices into hospital operations allows for the creation of communication plans that cater to community, media, and organizational requirements. Timely and accurate communication helps prevent the spread of misinformation and supports response efforts. Ensuring alignment means that emergency management initiatives are in sync with the hospital's core mission, vision, and strategic objectives. By integrating emergency plans into all of the hospital's operations, leaders maintain consistency between emergency preparedness efforts and organizational goals, promoting a holistic approach to risk management and resilience building. Active community involvement is key in preparing for emergencies; it involves collaborating with partners and stakeholders. Removing emergency management from any one department and integrating it within hospital operations strengthens community ties and improves preparedness through outreach activities and educational programs that operational leaders are often involved with.

Managing risks is an aspect of emergency preparedness. Proactive planning and response strategies, integrated into hospital functions, help mitigate risks linked to disruptions, potential legal issues, and rising expenses. By giving priority to emergency readiness, hospitals safeguard their health while ensuring patient care during emergencies. The incorporation of emergency readiness into hospital operations strengthens resilience by focusing on patient-centered care, promoting planning and collaboration, optimizing resource allocation, and continuously improving. This approach involves ensuring compliance with regulations, enhancing communication tactics, aligning with objectives, involving the community, preparing staff members, and reducing risks. By adopting this strategy, hospitals are better equipped to handle emergencies while sustaining essential services to safeguard both patient well-being and organizational sustainability.

Risk assessment is a process for evaluating potential hazards, vulnerabilities, and the likelihood of adverse events in hospital and healthcare settings. It plays a role in risk management and disaster preparedness for hospitals and healthcare facilities. Through the evaluation of hazards, vulnerabilities, and the probability of adverse events occurring, hospitals can identify and prioritize risks that could impact patient safety, staff welfare, operational continuity, and overall organizational resilience.

By assessing hazards and risks specific to their environment, hospital leaders and emergency managers can pinpoint unique risks they face. Whether it be disasters, infectious disease outbreaks, technological breakdowns, or security breaches, understanding these threats allows hospitals to tailor their preparedness strategies accordingly. This targeted approach ensures the allocation of resources, with interventions directed at mitigating the critical risks.

Assessing the impact of identified risks is vital for hospitals to understand the severity of outcomes. By recognizing how risks could impact care staff operations and facility infrastructure, healthcare leaders can prioritize response efforts and allocate resources efficiently. This helps ensure that crucial functions continue to operate during emergencies, minimizing disruptions in care and sustaining healthcare services. Prioritizing risks based on their importance and the organization's capacity to handle them leads to a more effective approach in risk management. Hospitals and healthcare systems can create emergency plans and protocols that address vulnerabilities and weaknesses. Taking this approach not only improves readiness but also fosters a culture of safety both within and outside the organization. Regular risk assessments aid hospitals in complying with standards and accreditation requirements. Healthcare regulations often require risk management practices to uphold patient safety and organizational stability. By following these guidelines, hospitals demonstrate their dedication to providing high-quality care while reducing financial risks associated with noncompliance. Integrating risk assessment into hospital operations encourages continuous improvement. Assessing incidents post emergency allows hospitals to learn from events, identify areas for enhancement, and update response procedures accordingly. This continuous process strengthens the organization's ability to adapt and prepare for challenges.

Effective evaluation of risks plays a role in supporting decision-making processes. By aligning risk management efforts with the mission, vision, and strategic priorities of the hospital, healthcare leaders ensure that emergency preparedness initiatives are seamlessly integrated into the organization's overarching objectives. This alignment promotes a front in mitigating risks, thereby strengthening the hospital's ability to withstand challenges. An executed risk assessment fosters open communication among different departments and stakeholders. Involving administrative and support teams in the assessment process helps create a shared understanding of risks and instills a collective sense of responsibility to address them. This collaborative effort enhances the hospital's readiness to handle emergencies efficiently. Healthcare institutions must be adaptable to changing landscapes and emerging dangers. Regular risk assessments allow hospitals to stay abreast of evolving threats and modify their preparedness strategies accordingly. This flexibility ensures that hospitals can effectively navigate obstacles and uncertainties while maintaining resilience. Thorough risk assessment and hazard identification are essential components in equipping hospitals for emergencies. By recognizing and prioritizing risks, healthcare organizations can formulate emergency plans and response strategies that minimize the impact of disasters, safeguarding the well-being and continuity of care for patients, staff, as well as the broader community. Undertaking a risk assessment and pinpointing hazards are pivotal stages in managing healthcare emergencies.

Hospitals need to identify and classify risks to create emergency plans that prioritize the safety of patients, staff, and the continuity of operations. Initially, healthcare institutions must categorize dangers that could impact their functions. These dangers might involve disasters, outbreaks of diseases, failures in technology, breaches in security, and more. Understanding the nature of these risks enables hospitals to formulate preparedness strategies that tackle threats. After identification, prioritizing risks based on their significance and the organization's capacity to handle them ensures a method for risk reduction. Hospitals should evaluate the impact of identified risks by examining how they could influence patient care, staff operations, and facility infrastructure. This evaluation assists healthcare leaders in prioritizing response efforts, efficiently allocating resources to minimize disruptions during emergencies.

The development of an emergency plan necessitates teamwork and coordination across departments. Leaders within hospitals and emergency management should engage administrative and support teams in the risk assessment process. This collaborative approach encourages a shared understanding of risks as well as collective accountability for addressing them effectively. Successful risk assessment supports planning activities and decision-making processes.

By aligning risk management efforts with the hospital's core values and long-term objectives, healthcare leaders ensure that emergency preparedness measures are seamlessly woven into the organization's overarching mission. This alignment promotes a strategy for managing risks and strengthens the hospital's ability to bounce back from adversities. Conducting risk assessments helps hospitals adhere to industry regulations and maintain accreditation standards. Healthcare guidelines typically require risk management protocols to safeguard patient wellbeing and uphold stability. Adhering to these protocols showcases a dedication to delivering top-notch care while minimizing financial liabilities linked to noncompliance. Continuous enhancement plays a role in emergency response strategies. Through incident reviews, hospitals can glean insights from crisis situations, pinpoint areas for improvement, and refine response procedures accordingly. This ongoing process boosts the organization's adaptability and preparedness in tackling obstacles.

Sufficient readiness and immediate action during crises can help reduce vulnerabilities linked to operational interruptions and potential legal disputes while also lowering operational expenses for hospitals by incorporating emergency management strategies into their daily operations to safeguard their financial well-being. Assessing the risks involves analyzing dangers and vulnerabilities to determine how likely adverse events are to happen in a hospital or healthcare setting. This evaluation is crucial for identifying the risks that are specific to a healthcare institution. Focus on risks according to their importance and how well the organization can handle them. By performing an evaluation of risks in healthcare settings and emergency management scenarios, healthcare leaders can prioritize their resources and attention towards tackling the most significant dangers to improve the overall readiness of the organization. The frequency of risk evaluations in hospitals may differ depending on factors like regulatory obligations, shifts in the healthcare sector landscape, the nature of hospital activities, and emerging risks. Nevertheless, it is commonly advised for hospitals to carry out risk assessments on a regular basis and at least once a year to ensure continuous readiness and the ability to adjust to changing situations. Regulatory mandates often dictate how frequently hospitals must conduct risk assessments, highlighting the importance for healthcare officials and emergency coordinators to stay informed and adhere to the regulations established by healthcare entities.

When there are shifts in how a hospital runs, updates to facilities need to be completed, shifts in healthcare trends, new medical tools are brought in, when patient groups change, or when the hospital layout is altered, it might be a good idea to conduct risk assessments more often.

Hospitals need to assess risks considering new threats or hazards that may arise. This could involve infectious illnesses, new developments in local or global security environments, revised models for natural hazards, like flooding, and other variables that might affect the hospital's capacity to deliver care.

After events like major incidents or emergencies occur in a hospital setting, it is essential to perform a thorough assessment of the risks post event. This assessment aims to pinpoint areas for enhancement in the response protocols and aids in the revision of the emergency preparedness strategies of the hospital.

Continuous observation of the healthcare setting enables hospitals to detect emerging risks. Though not a risk assessment in its own right, consistent surveillance and monitoring help institutions stay updated on potential changes that might necessitate further scrutiny.

Some hospitals synchronize risk evaluations with their planning schedules, which helps incorporate risk management into the organization's broader strategic outlook and pinpoint possible risks that could impact long-term objectives. Hospitals could see advantages from working with local or national healthcare networks through collaborative efforts to engage in shared risk assessments with other healthcare providers to better grasp common risks and enhance overall readiness collectively.

Hospitals should be flexible and adaptive in their risk assessment methods by taking into account both evaluations and the necessity for more frequent assessments based on particular situations. Keeping risk assessments up to date helps healthcare institutions stay proactive in recognizing and managing risks to patient safety and operational efficiency while also enhancing overall resilience.

Healthcare institutions face risks that can be either natural or manmade in nature. There are many types of hazards that hospitals may encounter such as; Natural disasters such as earthquakes, floods, hurricanes, wildfires, severe weather events, and pandemics. These are the risks that healthcare facilities need to consider. It is crucial for healthcare facilities to understand the environmental factors that could make them vulnerable to these hazards. Human-created dangers consist of a range of risks, like cyber assaults, acts of terrorism well as industrial mishaps, and spills of hazardous materials, that healthcare leaders should keep in mind along with the necessary security measures to reduce their impact.

Emerging technologies in the healthcare sector, like state-of-the-art devices and digital health records, bring along certain risks of their own that need to be carefully managed to guarantee their safety and reliability as part of comprehensive risk evaluation procedures. Hospital emergency managers carry out various kinds of risk assessments to recognize and address possible threats to the hospital's operations and the well-being of patients and staff members.

By examining clinical information data sets, a person in charge of emergencies can acquire valuable insights into how emergencies affect the care of patients, the use of resources, and the general functioning of hospitals. Such data is crucial for improving plans for handling emergencies and fine-tuning strategies for response, as well as consistently enhancing the healthcare system's capacity to provide efficient and prompt care during critical situations. Healthcare leaders and emergency managers can use a variety of tools to evaluate and address risks systematically while focusing efforts to reduce them effectively and be ready to handle obstacles better, resulting in improved readiness and the ability to deliver quality care safely during emergencies.

One of the tools used is known as the Hazard Vulnerability Assessment or Analysis (HVA), which investigates natural disasters as well as hazards caused by technology or human activities. The HVA methodically examines past information and local hazard details to determine which risks should be given attention in terms of resources and planning efforts. For instance, a hospital situated near a coast might focus more on preparing for hurricanes and floods due to their location and previous storm occurrences, whereas a hospital in the center of the country may focus more on tornadoes or earthquakes as the primary natural disaster hazard.

Another important tool to consider is the Failure Modes and Effects Analysis (FMEA), which specifically looks at risks related to operations and processes. FMEA requires a team to pinpoint possible failure areas in a process, evaluate their consequences, and decide on steps to minimize these risks. Within the healthcare sector, FMEA proves valuable in reviewing procedures, machinery, or structural impacts. Examples could be utilizing a FMEA to analyze the risk when planning to upgrade or replace multiple Automatic Transfer Switches, or the roll out of a new medication delivery system to prevent mistakes and enhance patient well-being.

Enterprise Risk Management (ERM) involves an analysis of strategic, financial, operational, and compliance risks spanning the entire organization. By examining the interconnectedness of risks and their effects on the hospitals overarching goals, ERM supports top management in embedding risk management into strategic decision-making. For example, ERM can be applied to evaluate cybersecurity risks to prevent data breaches and uphold adherence.

After something goes wrong at a hospital and there's a risk of it happening again in the future (such as a medication error), a Root Cause Analysis (RCA) can be used to figure out why it happened in the first place and how to stop it from happening again next time.

In addition to these methods mentioned above, there is also a technique called a Strengths, Weaknesses, Opportunities, Threats (SWOT) Analysis, which evaluates the environmental risks faced by organizations or institutions such as hospitals. Leaders can use this tool to recognize their strengths and weaknesses, as well as opportunities and threats externally, to help them make decisions and pinpoint areas with potential risks or possibilities for growth.

The assessment of high-stakes risks, such as those impacting finances, can be done through Quantitative Risk Assessment (QRA). This approach assigns values to the likelihood and consequences of certain events to aid decision-making and resource distribution using statistical analysis and modeling techniques. For example, QRA could evaluate the risk tied to a significant equipment breakdown, which can help a hospital decide on investing in maintenance or insurance coverage.

Operational data play a role in evaluating risks that could affect the delivery of care effectively by providing details on staffing levels and resource availability within the facility on a day-to-day basis for emergency management purposes, at healthcare institutions to respond adequately to crises and ensure the smooth operation of essential services. A hospital emergency manager would appreciate having access to operational information like the number of beds available in different units and their occupancy rates during emergencies to plan an effective response strategy. Practical data on staffing levels, the presence of isolation rooms, and medical equipment inventory also help in assessing the hospital's capability to handle an increased patient load during crisis situations. This information plays a role in determining how patients are assigned to beds and resources are distributed based on bed availability. By analyzing operational data, an emergency manager can gain insights into the hospital's capacity, resource availability, and operational resilience during emergencies. This information is essential for developing and optimizing emergency response plans, ensuring efficient resource allocation, and maintaining continuity of essential services.

Analyzing information on incidents and negative occurrences offers valuable knowledge about the risks encountered by a healthcare system in the past. This historical data helps emergency coordinators comprehend weaknesses and areas that can be enhanced. For instance, examining data on incidents like power failures is essential for understanding the difficulties faced by the hospital, assessing the response's efficacy, and pinpointing areas that require enhancement. Essential information, such as when the power went out, the duration of the event, and why it happened, is crucial for a thorough assessment of the situation at the hospital and aids in making informed decisions regarding backup plans and resource distribution while refining communication tactics to enhance readiness for similar events in the future. Reviewing incidents post event and learning from them allows healthcare leaders and emergency managers to refine emergency strategies, protocols, and training procedures to better handle crises effectively.

Identifying risks plays a large role in healthcare emergency management procedures. To proactively spot clinical and operational risks, hospitals analyze past data and seek input from experienced leaders and emergency managers. Implementing measures early on enhances patient safety, care quality, and regulatory adherence. Recognizing threats also aids in strategically allocating resources during emergencies, enabling hospitals to uphold operational efficiency and continuity. Using data to inform decisions and predict outcomes, while regularly monitoring the situation at hand in healthcare settings, enables leaders to make informed choices and adjust to evolving situations effectively.

Data are essential in managing risks across areas like patient care safety and regulatory adherence in healthcare settings. In our current environment, AI systems heavily depend on data from patient safety issues and incidents to drive quality improvement efforts and prevent recurrence of events in the future. A blend of knowledge, along with administrative and operational proficiency, facilitates a thorough evaluation of potential risks. Collaborating across fields with healthcare professionals, hospital administrators, and risk management specialists ensures a comprehensive range of viewpoints are considered during the assessment of potential risks.

Ultimately, it is crucial to have a blend of data and knowledge for a thorough and successful evaluation of risks in healthcare setups. By merging information with operational and incident data, along with the perspectives of healthcare experts and risk management professionals, you can proactively pinpoint and address risks to ensure top-notch patient care, boost organizational adaptability, and instill trust among stakeholders in the healthcare system's readiness to manage crises and provide outstanding service. That is always the goal!

Chapter 6

Preparedness Planning

Kimberly Bailey/Thomas Crawford

I was recently watching Five Days at Memorial which highlights the challenges faced by a hospital immediately post Hurricane Katrina. One scene both resonated and, frankly, frightened me – the storm had passed; however, the levies breached, and New Orleans was beginning to flood. The scenario was particularly problematic for the hospital because their generator for emergency power was not elevated; on the contrary, it was ground level. Meaning, as soon as the flood waters began penetrating the building, the hospital would quickly be without power and those critically ill patients on ventilators, pumps, etc., would be without the equipment needed to sustain their lives.

Knowing the inevitable potential for harm to their patients and care team members, the Incident Commander pulled the emergency management binder – that held all the hospital's emergency plans – she quickly scanned the table of contents and located the tab for the evacuation plan; however, when she turned to that section of the binder – there was no evacuation plan.

Emergency management plans are living documents that provide instructions on how to effectively respond to various emergency operational scenarios. The plans are updated post events to capture what worked well and what needed to be improved and every Administrator on Call or potential Incident Commander are continually trained to ensure they have the fund of knowledge required to help safely navigate when not in normal operations. Why do we place an emphasis on planning and training? With lives in peril, you don't want to find yourself in a situation where you're uncomfortable managing the situation and your binder is empty.

Preparedness planning for hospitals and large healthcare systems is a critical component of maintaining healthcare delivery during emergencies. The unpredictable nature of crises, whether natural disasters, pandemics, or man-made incidents, necessitates a robust and comprehensive approach to planning.

~Tom Crawford

DOI: 10.4324/9781003529194-6

In Chapter 5, we delved into the process of evaluating risks and identifying hazards. Now, as we move on to Chapter 6, we shift our focus from recognizing dangers to the planning that serves as the foundation of healthcare emergency preparedness. By the conclusion of this chapter, healthcare leaders will understand the fundamentals of readiness planning. This knowledge will enable you to collaborate with your emergency manager in developing adaptable and efficient preparedness strategies to ensure that your healthcare facility is well prepared to handle a variety of emergencies.

This chapter discusses aspects of readiness planning, stressing the importance of emergency response procedures, thorough staff training, effective resource allocation, resilient infrastructure management, successful communication tactics, and cooperation with external partners.

Just as we outlined the disparities between emergency management and emergency response in Chapter 2, there are also distinctions between emergency management and emergency preparedness. While interconnected, they are concepts within the framework of managing emergencies. As you now understand, emergency management involves coordinating resources and procedures during and after an emergency event. It encompasses four phases: mitigation, preparedness, response, and recovery. Emergency management goes beyond readiness to include crisis response, resource deployment, and coordination among different agencies overseeing recovery efforts to restore normalcy. In essence, preparedness is about being proactive before a crisis strikes, while management involves handling all aspects of an emergency, from prevention to recovery.

No matter how well we plan and prepare, it is impossible to foresee every detail in an emergency. Preparedness involves planning and steps taken to be equipped for emergencies. This includes developing emergency plans, conducting exercises, gathering emergency supplies, and educating hospital leaders and staff on risks and appropriate responses. The aim of preparedness is to reduce the impact of disasters through anticipation and readiness. It is a process that follows a pattern known as the Preparedness Cycle – which comprises Planning, Organization and Equipping, Training and Exercise, and the Evaluating and Improving phases.

Emergency management can be compared to a rock being thrown into water. The initial impact of the rock hitting the water symbolizes the onset of a healthcare emergency, such as a mass casualty event, a severe disease outbreak, or a major system failure. The size and speed of the rock mirror the severity and urgency of the crisis, requiring immediate and decisive action. The splash and the first chaotic waves correspond to the hospital's immediate response. This includes activating the hospital's emergency operations plan, triaging incoming patients, and rapidly deploying medical staff to critical areas. Just as the waves spread quickly, the hospital must stabilize the situation, ensuring that life-saving treatments are administered and that resources are effectively managed. The ripples produced represent the cascading effects and concurrent events that occur following a critical incident. As the ripples expand outward, they signify the broader, more complex challenges that the hospital must address. Each ripple represents different aspects of the emergency, such as coordinating with external agencies, managing surge capacity, communicating with patients' families, and ensuring the continuity of care for all patients. These ripples also reflect the hospital's efforts to manage the ongoing crisis, including secondary impacts like staff fatigue, supply shortages, and the need for ongoing patient care.

Over time, the ripples in the water begin to fade, symbolizing the transition from crisis response to recovery within the hospital. The focus shifts to restoring normal operations, debriefing staff, and implementing lessons learned to improve future preparedness. Just as overlapping ripples from multiple rocks can create complex patterns, a hospital may face compounded challenges when multiple incidents occur simultaneously, such as a natural disaster combined with an influx of patients. Ultimately, emergency management in a hospital environment, like the ripples in water, involves addressing the immediate impacts of a crisis while simultaneously managing the broader, cascading effects, all with the goal of ensuring patient safety and returning to normal operations. Hospitals or large healthcare systems need to be prepared for the rock to be thrown in the water at any time.

In a hospital or healthcare setting, the initial phase of preparedness involves creating emergency response plans suited to situations like natural disasters, pandemics, or mass casualty incidents. This stage marks the beginning of readiness by setting up the framework for how the organization will handle emergencies. It involves identifying operations and resources, defining roles for staff, and establishing communication protocols within the hospital and with external partners. Effective planning ensures that all emergency response aspects are addressed, including patient care, logistics support, and public information sharing. Healthcare leaders and emergency teams collaborate during this phase to craft emergency plans and tactics. An essential part is developing response protocols covering scenarios like hurricanes, earthquakes, chemical spills, or active shooter incidents. These protocols should include evacuation strategies, shelter procedures, and communication plans for coordination and collaboration with agencies. They should also specify staff roles under incident command structures, along with decision-making processes. Hospital leaders and emergency managers should plan to address all hazards in their planning. For example, hospitals in hurricane-prone areas should have specific plans for the rapid evacuation of all patients pre storm. The strategies or guidelines developed by your organization should be documented, undergo reviews led by your emergency management team, and be shared with involved parties. These plans should be updated on a scheduled basis to incorporate new insights, technologies, and regulatory mandates. Many regulatory bodies require established policies around emergency preparedness. To meet this requirement, keep any policy related to emergency preparedness focused on the process of establishing the required plan, rather than including the actual plan as it stands in the policy. It is advisable for hospital leaders and emergency managers to avoid formalizing written emergency plans or operational procedures into formal policies to preserve the flexibility and adaptability needed during crises. Policies are typically documents that outline fixed rules and procedures the hospital states it will follow, which can hinder the ability to react promptly or pivot during the response with the evolving nature of emergencies. Emergency situations often pose challenges that demand real-time decision making and the freedom to deviate from established plans when necessary. By maintaining all your emergency plans as frameworks rather than rigid policies that may have legal implications if not followed, hospital leaders and emergency managers can easily modify their response strategies in real-time, adjust according to the specific circumstances of the emergency, and innovate as required. This approach facilitates coordination, mobilization of resources, and customized responses tailored to suit the needs of an emergency situation. This flexibility ensures that hospitals can incorporate insights gained from drills and actual incidents into their plans without undergoing policy revisions. Having structured plans is important, but it is equally crucial to keep them flexible. This allows for responses to the ever-changing challenges that can arise during emergencies or disasters affecting hospital operations.

Another key aspect of being prepared is organization and provision. Getting organized and equipped is vital for putting emergency plans into action. This phase involves arranging the hospital's emergency response teams and making sure they are well trained. It also includes acquiring and maintaining equipment like emergency response kits, protective gear, backup generators, and emergency communication devices. Hospitals need to ensure these resources are easily accessible and that staff know how to use them. Additionally, this phase includes establishing systems for managing resources such as tracking inventory and distributing supplies. With organization and proper equipment, hospitals can swiftly deploy resources and personnel during emergencies for an effective response.

The success of any emergency plan depends heavily on how prepared your staff is. Regular training sessions and practice drills are essential to ensure all team members know their roles well and can carry them out effectively under pressure. The hospital's emergency management program should incorporate many types of training methods, such as classroom sessions, practical drills, and interactive workshops or tabletop exercises. For instance, your emergency management team should be conducting disaster-focused exercises involving all hospital departments to enable staff to rehearse coordinated responses to events like mass casualties or disease outbreaks. These exercises should be followed by feedback sessions called after-action reviews to pinpoint areas for enhancement and reinforce the lessons learned. There are many examples of formatting for exercise documents that can be found through reputable resource banks at no cost.

Studying real-world instances of preparedness planning can offer insights and lessons. A significant learning opportunity arose on February 22, 2011, at 12:50 pm when a powerful 6.3 magnitude earthquake struck Christchurch in New Zealand's South Island. This event caused damage to infrastructure throughout the city, including its healthcare system. Multiple structures collapsed, water mains ruptured, sewer pipes were damaged, city streets and buildings were inundated with water, and power outages were widespread. The earthquake resulted in 185 fatalities and around 8,600 injuries. Christchurch Hospital suffered damage that severely impacted its operational ability following the quake. Structural deficiencies led to disruptions across the hospital campus; flooding occurred in building basements due to liquefaction, retaining walls failed, causing severe damage to sewage lines, and numerous parking facilities were deemed unsafe. Many medical facilities faced roof damage, separation of joint issues, and firewall damage. Similar to the rock-in-the-lake metaphor, each of these problems led to a chain of circumstances that temporarily affected the hospital's operations and services. Such incidents serve as a reminder for healthcare leaders and emergency managers to prioritize preparedness efforts by allocating resources to address risks and hazards.

Likewise, the COVID-19 pandemic emphasized the importance of planning as hospitals had to expand capacity, implement new infection control measures, and navigate supply chain disruptions. These real-life examples underscore the need for improvement in preparedness planning based on lessons learned from emergencies. Healthcare leaders can expect hospital emergency managers to coordinate exercises, functional drills, and full-scale simulations to evaluate readiness levels and pinpoint areas needing enhancement.

Ensuring that hospital staff are well trained and prepared to handle emergencies is crucial. Regular training sessions and drills help them understand their roles, practice skills, and gain confidence in responding. From exercises to full-scale drills, these activities simulate real-life scenarios to assess the hospital's readiness and response capabilities. By identifying weaknesses in plans, refining procedures, and enhancing coordination among departments and external agencies, staff can better prepare for emergencies. Continuous training also focuses on emerging threats like diseases or cybersecurity risks to keep the staff informed and ready. Through education and realistic simulations, hospital leaders and healthcare workers can be equipped to act efficiently during crises. Feedback from exercises plays a role in improving emergency response plans based on real-world experiences.

Healthcare administrators and emergency managers must ensure that there are communication channels in place for staff to raise any identified issues or suggest procedures to maintain as practices after training exercises or real-life incidents. Gathering feedback from all parties following an exercise or event is essential for hospitals to assess their emergency response efficiency and pinpoint areas needing improvement. Administering surveys or questionnaires to participants, including employees from various departments, first responders, and volunteers helps hospitals collect feedback. Questions may address topics such as role clarity, communication protocol effectiveness, resource adequacy, and overall satisfaction with the response. Leveraging technology platforms like digital surveys, digital feedback forms, or mobile applications can simplify the feedback collection process as well. These tools empower stakeholders to provide feedback if preferred, thereby boosting participation rates and encouraging candid responses.

Emergency managers can lead structured After-Action Reviews (AARs) or debriefing sessions after an incident. This allows participants to share their viewpoints by assembling stakeholders to review the entire response procedure. Convening these focus groups, comprising stakeholders like department leaders, emergency management team members, and frontline personnel, creates a platform for discussions. During these sessions, you can delve into parts of the response, gather feedback, and brainstorm constructive ideas for improvement. After-Action Reviews (AARs) focus on recognizing strategies, areas for enhancement, and key takeaways. They offer an evaluation of response efforts and assist hospitals in formulating action plans to address any identified shortcomings. These sessions may concentrate on scenarios or incidents from the exercise or event, prompting participants to reflect on their experiences and propose enhancements. It is crucial to integrate feedback into an improvement process to maintain readiness. By obtaining feedback from all parties through a multipronged approach, hospitals can gain comprehensive insights into their emergency response capabilities, pinpoint strengths and weaknesses, and bolster preparedness for future events. This continuous feedback cycle is vital in ensuring that hospitals continuously adapt their emergency response tactics to meet the changing demands of healthcare crises.

Efficient resource management also plays a role in preparedness planning. Hospitals need to uphold inventories of resources, medicines, and personal protective gear (PPE) to manage spikes in patient numbers during emergencies. The importance of this was starkly evident during the COVID-19 crisis when numerous healthcare systems encountered shortages of ventilators and PPE. Forward-thinking hospitals prioritize their readiness by forming partnerships with suppliers and creating backup plans to handle potential disruptions in the supply chain. They focus on maintaining and rotating stockpiles, collaborating with suppliers, and developing contingency strategies for any supply chain interruptions. Moreover, hospitals establish protocols for procuring and distributing resources during emergencies to ensure critical supplies are readily available when and where needed most. The significance of resource allocation and management will be further discussed in Chapter 8.

In Chapter 3 we delved into the Incident Command System (ICS), a framework used for emergency management where preparedness hinges on having a team at the ready. This team must be selected thoughtfully by healthcare leaders who should incorporate ICS and NIMS principles into their preparedness planning or adapt them to suit their organization better. Organizational emergency management leadership structures should aim for a coordinated response to crises by emphasizing the importance of a clear chain of command structure for effective coordination.

Different healthcare organizations may have varying structures for responding to events based on their size and complexity. No matter which structure you choose, all require an Incident Commander (IC) to kickstart the response efforts. The Hospital Incident Command System (HICS) approach and Emergency Support Functions (ESFs) approach offer distinct methods to emergency management and response within a hospital system, each with its own set of advantages and challenges.

Hospital Incident Command System (HICS) is a common hierarchical, role-based system specifically designed for hospitals, emphasizing a clear command structure with predefined roles such as Incident Commander, Operations, and Logistics. This structure ensures that everyone understands their responsibilities and allows for scalability depending on the incident's complexity.

While the HICS model provides a clear and organized framework for emergency management, it does have several disadvantages that can impact its effectiveness. One significant drawback is its rigidity, as the highly structured, hierarchical nature of HICS can be inflexible in dynamic or rapidly changing situations. This rigidity may slow down decision-making processes, particularly in complex incidents that require quick adaptation and cross-departmental collaboration. Additionally, HICS can be resource-intensive, requiring the activation of numerous roles and positions, even in incidents where a full command structure may not be necessary. This can place a strain on hospital personnel and resources, particularly in smaller facilities or during less severe incidents. In the HICS model, employees are assigned to HICS positions that they may only activate during rare emergency events, leading to a lack of familiarity and confidence when an incident actually occurs. This sporadic involvement can make it difficult for staff to fully understand their roles and responsibilities within the HICS structure, potentially leading to confusion or hesitation during a real emergency.

Sustaining the training required to keep staff proficient in their HICS roles is also resource intensive. Regular drills, exercises, and refresher courses are necessary to maintain readiness, but these activities can be time-consuming and may disrupt normal hospital operations. Additionally, staff turnover and the influx of new employees require continuous training efforts, which can strain the hospital's emergency management department, training resources, and budget. The need for ongoing education and practice to ensure that all staff are competent in their HICS roles adds to the overall burden of maintaining the system, particularly in environments where emergencies are infrequent. To that point, the challenge of training staff who only fill their roles on an occasional basis can be daunting for the emergency manager, who may have to provide additional just-in-time training at the onset of each event when they may have conflicting priorities. HICS can sometimes lead to role overlap and confusion, especially in large or multi-faceted incidents where responsibilities are not clearly delineated. This overlap can create challenges in communication and coordination, potentially leading to inefficiencies or gaps in the response. Another disadvantage is that HICS may not always align well with external partners who do not use the same system, complicating coordination efforts during incidents that involve multiple agencies or organizations. Lastly, the standardized nature of HICS, while beneficial for consistency, can limit the hospital's ability to customize the response to the specific needs of the situation, potentially reducing the overall effectiveness of the emergency.

In contrast, Emergency Support Functions (ESFs) are another option and a great way to organize and coordinate different aspects of an emergency response based on specific needs or tasks. Instead of assigning people to specific roles with fixed responsibilities, like in a traditional HICS, ESFs focus on getting the right resources and people together to handle specific functions during an emergency.

In a hospital setting, ESFs can be incorporated into the response by activating only the functions that are needed for a particular situation. For example, if there's a natural disaster, the hospital might activate *ESF 8: Health and Medical Services*, which would involve doctors, nurses, and other medical staff working together to treat patients, manage the influx of injured people, and coordinate with other hospitals. Another example could be *ESF 6: Mass Care*, where hospital resources might be used to set up temporary shelters, provide food and water, support the families of patients who are affected by the disaster, or even develop their own staff accommodations plan for staff who may need to stay at the hospital for an extended period of time.

If the incident affects the hospital's physical infrastructure, *ESF 3: Public Works and Engineering* might be activated, bringing in hospital engineers, maintenance teams, and external contractors to assess and repair damage to buildings or utilities. The hospital's response teams under each ESF would consist of personnel from various departments with the expertise needed to handle the specific function, working together to ensure that all aspects of the response are covered effectively. This approach allows the hospital to be flexible and efficient, using the right resources for the right tasks during an emergency. Hospitals can modify the names of Emergency Support Functions (ESFs) to better align with their internal operations while still maintaining consistency with the local, state, and federal ESFs. This approach allows hospitals to tailor the ESF framework to their specific needs and organizational structure, making it more intuitive for hospital staff, yet still ensuring effective coordination with external agencies during an emergency.

For example, *ESF 8: Public Health and Medical Services* could be renamed "Healthcare Operations and Patient Care" within the hospital. This name more accurately reflects the hospital's primary focus on patient care and clinical operations while still aligning with the broader ESF 8 category at the local, state, and federal levels. Similarly, *ESF 6: Mass Care* could be adapted to "Patient and Family Support Services," emphasizing the hospital's role in providing care, shelter, and support to both patients and their families during an emergency.

Another example might be *ESF 3: Public Works and Engineering*, which could be renamed "Infrastructure and Facility Management" in the hospital setting. This change highlights the hospital's responsibility for maintaining and repairing its physical infrastructure while still connecting to the broader ESF 3 framework that focuses on public works and engineering.

To ensure alignment with external agencies, hospitals can include references to the original ESF numbers or titles in their internal documents and training materials. For instance, the hospital's modified ESF names could be presented as "Healthcare Operations and Patient Care (ESF 8)" or "Infrastructure and Facility Management (ESF 3)," clearly linking the hospital's terminology to the established ESF structure. This approach allows hospitals to customize the ESF framework to better fit their operations while maintaining the necessary alignment for effective communication and coordination with external partners during emergencies.

ESFs are organized around functional areas rather than specific roles, focusing on tasks such as transportation, communications, or public health. This function-based approach offers greater flexibility, allowing hospitals to activate only the necessary functions for a particular incident. ESFs can enhance collaboration across departments and align more easily with external agencies, which also use the ESF structure. An ESF-structured response is advantageous for hospitals because it simplifies the emergency response process, requiring less training for staff and offering a more "out of the box" approach. Unlike traditional emergency management models that involve detailed, role-specific training, the ESF structure focuses on broad functional areas like healthcare operations, logistics, and communication. This means that instead of training staff to fill specific, predefined roles within a rigid command structure, they are prepared to contribute within their area of expertise as part of a larger functional group. With the ESF model, much of the detailed planning and coordination are handled by the hospital's emergency management program, which is responsible for ensuring that each ESF is ready to be activated and that the right resources and personnel are available. The emergency management team designs the response plans, identifies the necessary resources, and ensures alignment with external agencies. As a result, frontline staff can focus on their day-to-day responsibilities with minimal additional training, as their involvement in an emergency is based on their existing skills and duties.

This approach reduces the burden on staff, who may have limited time for extensive emergency response training, and allows them to step into their roles more naturally during an incident. The ESF framework also provides clear guidance and support, enabling staff to quickly understand what needs to be done in their functional area without needing to master a complex command system. Overall, the ESF structure makes emergency response more accessible and manageable for hospital personnel, while the emergency management team takes on the responsibility of ensuring that the overall response is well-coordinated and effective. However, the flexibility of ESFs can lead to potential gaps in leadership or confusion over responsibilities if the structure is not well understood.

If hospital leaders or emergency managers are looking for a new approach to the usual HICS construct and the facility is not very large, they may choose to simplify the response setup by concentrating on a smaller group of leaders instead of the complete set of official branch sections or ESFs. This central team would include decision makers who would gather during crises to evaluate consequences, talk about tactics, and prepare for what comes next. Rather than triggering all sections of the HICS, these individuals would convene at the HEOC where they would supervise the evolving circumstances and determine crucial actions. In county or state emergency response programs, Multiagency Coordination Groups (MAC Groups) are comprised of officials and representatives from agencies who collaborate to offer policy advice and make important decisions about resource allocation. In a hospital environment, this same concept would work in a manner uniting top-level executives, department leaders, and other essential staff members with the knowledge and power to make well-informed choices that steer the hospital's response actions. By using a more concentrated team, hospital leaders can help simplify how decisions are made and ensure that urgent matters are dealt with promptly and effectively. This method offers the advantage of more adaptable responses in emergency situations as the primary team can promptly come together and adjust to evolving scenarios without having to engage and organize numerous HICS divisions. This setup also promotes communication and teamwork among the hospital's leadership, ensuring that all operational aspects of the hospital are taken into account when making emergency-related decisions. In terms of and viewed as a whole perspective-wise, this different method has the potential to improve the hospital's capacity to handle intricate situations with efficiency, leading to a flexible and prompt system for handling emergencies effectively.

The choice between a HICS response model, an ESF response model, or a modified MAC group depends on the hospital's specific needs, resources, and resources and strength of the emergency management program or team. HICS provides a clear, familiar structure that ensures order and role clarity but may be less adaptable in complex situations. ESFs offer flexibility and a functional focus, which can improve efficiency and coordination, especially in multifaceted incidents, or for organizations with multiple facilities or regions, but may introduce challenges in training and leadership. Hospitals may benefit from a hybrid approach, combining elements of both HICS and ESFs to create a robust, adaptable emergency response system.

In all models, the IC holds the reins of command and control during emergency responses. In healthcare setups, the IC could be the COO or CMO, whereas larger institutions might designate an individual in emergency management for this pivotal role. The IC is responsible for making decisions, allocating resources, and liaising with parties when necessary. Your emergency manager can assist in deciding which of these models would benefit your organization. A simple organizational structure for a more formal HICS structure for a hospital might look something like this:

A simple organizational structure for an ESF structure for a hospital might look something like this:

IC or emergency manager leads planning meeting calls, and leaders from the following areas report out on status, barriers, and issues on each call.

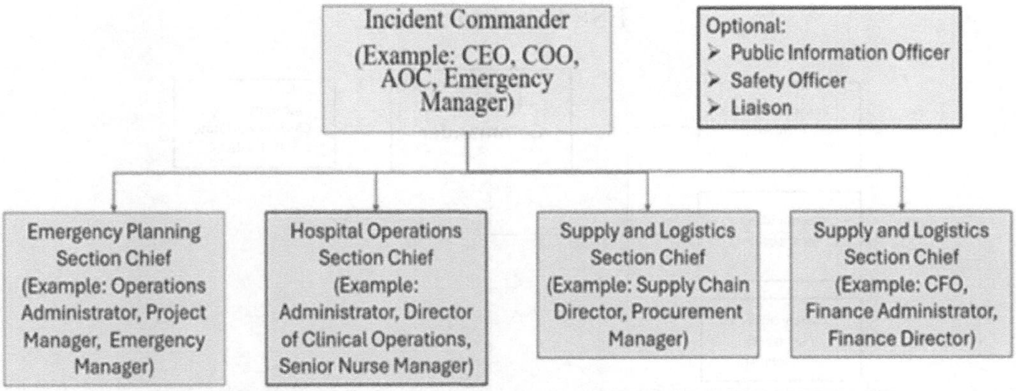

Figure 6.1 Chart of Incident Command Structure.

ESF 1: Transportation (Hospital)

- Purpose: Organize patients, staff, and medical supply transportation.
- Hospital Departments Involved: Logistics, Patient Transport Services, Ambulance Services.
- Tasks: Coordinate transfers between facilities, arrange emergency staff transportation, and ensure ambulance availability.

ESF 2: Communications (Hospital)

- Objective: Manage hospital communication systems internally and with partners.
- Hospital Departments Involved: IT, Telecommunications, Public Relations.
- Responsibilities: Maintain external communication channels, oversee emergency communication systems, and provide updates to staff and external agencies.

ESF 3: Infrastructure and Facility Management (Hospital)

- Focus Area: Supervise hospital infrastructure and utilities during emergencies.
- Hospital Departments Involved: Facilities Management, Engineering, Maintenance.
- Duties: Evaluate and repair hospital building damages, guarantee system functionality (electricity, water, HVAC), and collaborate with external contractors when necessary.

ESF 4: Firefighting and Safety (Hospital)

- Goal: Handle fire prevention measures and responses to incidents within the hospital premises, ensuring safety.
- Hospital Departments Involved: Security, Fire Safety, and Environmental Health and Safety are teams in the hospital setting.
- Responsibilities: Working closely with fire departments, ensuring the functionality of fire suppression systems and conducting safety inspections across the hospital premises.

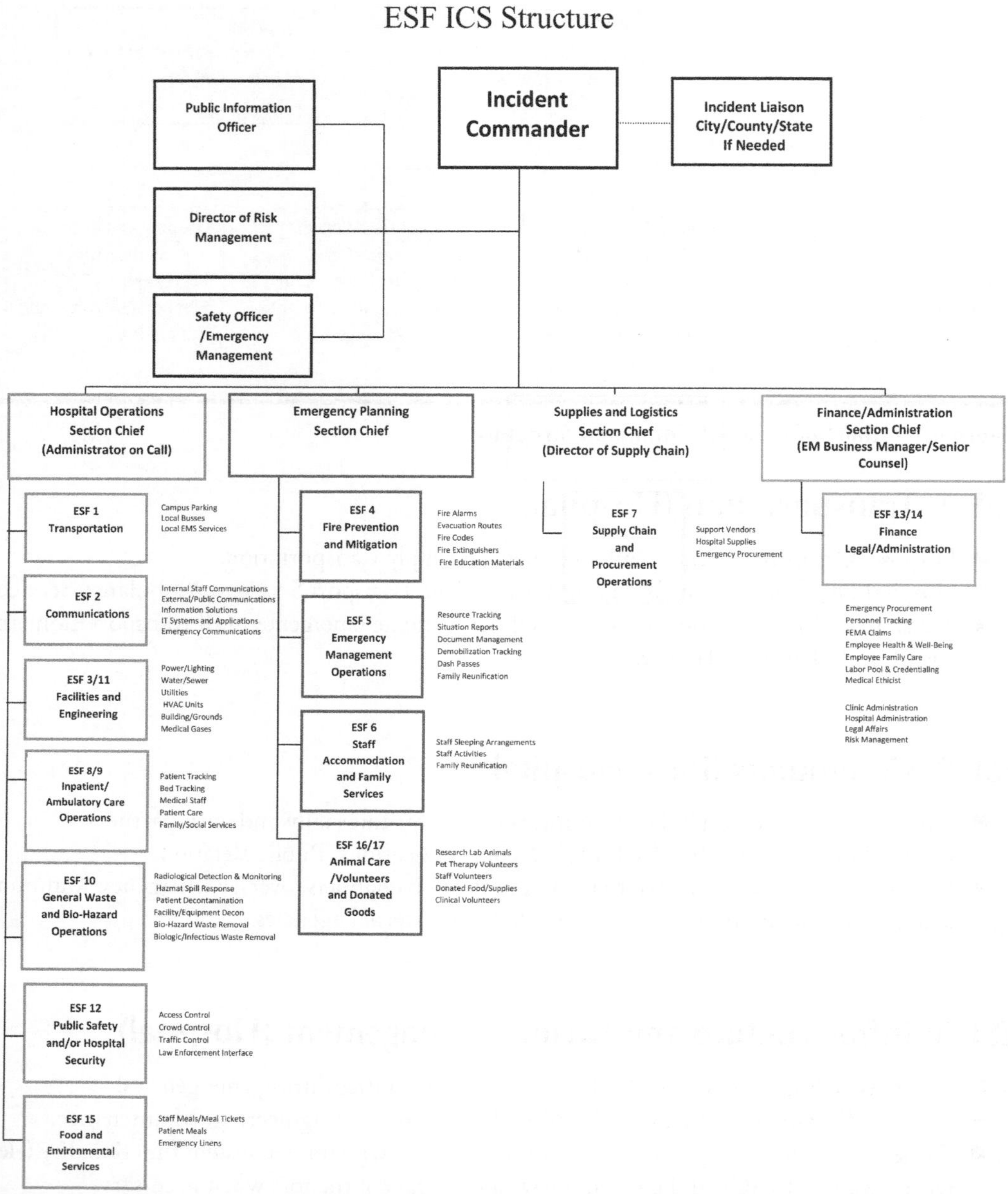

Figure 6.2 Chart of ESF Structure.

ESF 5: Planning and Information Management (Hospital)

- Function: Providing planning assistance and overseeing information management during emergency situations.
- Hospital Departments Involved: Emergency Management, Administration, and Legal departments play roles.
- Responsibilities: Developing and maintaining emergency response strategies, collecting and analyzing incident data, and ensuring adherence to regulatory requirements.

ESF 6: Patient and Family Support Services (Hospital)

- Function: Delivering care and assistance to patients and their families in times of crisis.
- Hospital Departments Involved: Social Services, Chaplaincy Services, Volunteer Services, and Staff Accommodations are contributors.
- Responsibilities: Providing counseling support, managing family reunification procedures, collaborating with community groups for aid services, or organizing shelter arrangements for staff during prolonged emergencies at the hospital.

ESF 7: Resource Management (Hospital)

- Function: Oversight of hospital resources encompassing supplies, equipment maintenance, and workforce management.
- Hospital Units Involved: Supply Chain, Human Resources, Finance.
- Duties: Ensure medical supplies and equipment are accessible, handle staffing requirements, and supervise assets in times of crisis.

ESF 8: Healthcare Operations and Patient Care (Hospital)

- Role: Supervise medical patient care during emergencies.
- Hospital Units Involved: Medical Staff, Nursing, Pharmacy, Emergency Department.
- Duties: Organize care, manage surge capacity, allocate resources, and maintain essential healthcare services.

ESF 9: Search and Rescue (Hospital)

- Role: Coordinate search and rescue activities within the hospital premises.
- Hospital Units Involved: Security, Facilities Management, Local Emergency Services.
- Duties: Locate and rescue patients or staff facing danger or trapped within the hospital; collaborate with search and rescue teams if needed.

ESF 10: Hazardous Materials (Hospital)

- Role: Handle material incidents within the hospital premises.
- Hospital Units Involved: Environmental Health and Safety, Laboratory Services, Facilities Management.
- Duties: Respond to hazardous material spills, contain them safely, decontaminate areas, and liaise with external HAZMAT teams as required.

ESF 15: Information and External Affairs (Hospital)

- Role: Handling communication with the public and media in times of emergency.

- Hospital Departments Involved: Public Relations, Communications, Legal.
- Tasks: Providing timely updates to the public, addressing media queries, and maintaining messaging across various channels.

Like a Federal, state, county, or local Emergency Operations Center (EOC) operates, a Hospital Emergency Operations Center (HEOC) is responsible for managing and responding to emergencies. However, their functions and responsibilities may vary in certain aspects. One significant difference lies in their focus and primary goals. Government-managed EOCs are responsible for coordinating responses across agencies and areas within a city, county, or region. They focus on addressing community impacts and overseeing responses to disasters, major accidents, or public health crises affecting the region. On the other hand, hospital EOCs mainly concentrate on overseeing hospital operations during emergencies such as casualty incidents, disease outbreaks, or specific facility crises. Their main priority is maintaining patient care standards, ensuring staff safety, and efficiently managing hospital resources. Both government Emergency Operations Centers (EOCs) and hospital EOCs work towards safeguarding health and safety during emergencies.

However, they encounter obstacles in ensuring that teamwork and clear communication are maintained in response to emergencies. While both share the goal of emergency response, differences in priorities, communication methods, and resource allocation can create challenges. During crises when hospitals are overwhelmed, County Emergency Operations Centers (EOCs) may find it difficult to coordinate with hospitals. Similarly, Hospital EOCs may face challenges aligning their strategies with county or regional plans, potentially leading to conflicts in resource distribution or logistics. Differences in decision-making authority and operational procedures between county EOCs and hospital EOCs could hinder collaboration. Establishing communication channels and a shared understanding of roles is vital to overcoming these challenges and responding cohesively during emergencies that impact both the community and hospital needs. It is crucial for the emergency manager of your hospital to establish connections with emergency managers in cities and counties in your area before any crisis arises. Building partnerships with government agencies, emergency services, and other healthcare facilities is essential for a preparedness plan. Efficient coordination and communication between these roles are pivotal for responding to any emergency scenario. Hospital leaders and emergency managers should actively participate in community emergency planning efforts, engage in training exercises with emergency responders, and establish mutual aid agreements to offer assistance during crises. These collaborative endeavors enhance the healthcare system's resilience.

To improve the ability to handle large-scale incidents in their areas, hospital emergency managers can collaborate closely with city, county, or regional emergency managers. This partnership allows for alignment of hospital needs and capabilities with response strategies at the county level. By working together, resources can be allocated efficiently, information shared promptly, and coordinated decisions made swiftly during fast-paced and complex emergencies. Building relationships between these players enhances understanding of their respective roles, strengths, and limitations facilitating effective communication and mutual aid when crises occur. The bond developed between hospital and county emergency managers fosters trust and confidence in each other's abilities, which is essential for establishing partnerships and overcoming challenges that may arise during emergencies. It enables them to establish communication channels quickly, exchange information, and make informed decisions that prioritize public safety while maximizing emergency response efforts. The collaboration between hospital emergency managers and county counterparts is essential for enhancing emergency preparedness and response efforts to ensure the community's health and safety are protected during crises.

When selecting a location for an HEOC within a hospital setting, various factors must be considered to ensure its functionality, accessibility, and effectiveness in times of crisis. The HEOC can be set up to function either in person, online, or in a hybrid format depending on the needs and size of the hospital or healthcare system. An in-person HEOC usually involves having a space where key personnel gather to coordinate emergency responses, enabling face-to-face communication, swift decision-making, and direct access to resources and documentation. On the other hand, if the internet is working, a virtual HEOC uses platforms to facilitate remote collaboration among team members, allowing them to participate from different locations without being physically present. This setup is especially beneficial for healthcare systems with staff dispersed across facilities, regions, or even across multiple states.

A hybrid HEOC model combines features of both in-person and virtual configurations. This strategy includes a location where essential staff can collaborate and lead response efforts while integrating virtual tools to involve remote team members or additional facilities within the healthcare system. For instance, decision makers and operational leaders may operate from a HEOC facility while representatives from facilities or external partners join meetings through video conferencing or collaborative platforms. The hybrid model offers flexibility and ensures that all relevant stakeholders can contribute to the response effort regardless of their whereabouts.

It also helps to link services in a healthcare system, allowing for teamwork across various locations, and improving how resources are used and communication. By using both face-to-face interactions and virtual tools, the HEOC can adjust to situations and guarantee a thorough and efficient emergency response. Hospital leaders and emergency managers must assess spaces to determine the best one for supporting the functions of the HEOC. Ideally, the HEOC should be centrally located within the hospital to allow access for personnel such as senior leaders, emergency management staff, and incident management team members. This central positioning is crucial for the mobilization and coordination of responses without disrupting hospital operations. The allocated space for the HEOC should be spacious enough to accommodate personnel, equipment, and resources for managing emergencies. It should have designated areas for workstations, communication tools like phones, computers, radios, real-time information-monitoring screens, and storage for emergency response supplies. Additionally, the selected space should support the functions of a HEOC, including information management, decision-making processes, and communication channels.

A dependable power source, internet connection, and backup systems are vital to ensuring operations during power outages or other disruptions. The layout should be designed in a way that promotes efficiency and collaboration among team members. Given the nature of emergency response activities, security and privacy are paramount within the HEOC to protect information related to patient care discussions, incident management strategies, and resource allocation decisions. This may involve implementing controlled access measures, such as communication channels and protocols, for data handling. It is crucial to prioritize spaces that can be easily adapted or repurposed as necessary during emergencies.

The ability to adapt allows the HEOC to modify its operations based on the seriousness and intricacy of the situation by adjusting staff or equipment as needed. When selecting a site for a HEOC within a hospital, factors like accessibility, functionality, security, and integration with hospital operations must be considered. By assessing spaces using these criteria, hospitals can establish an HEOC that improves their capacity to respond effectively during emergencies while ensuring continuity of patient care and safety.

The HEOC functions as the command post for the hospital's emergency response activities. It plays a pivotal role in coordinating efforts among different agencies, organizations, and departments involved in the response. The HEOC plays a part in collecting, analyzing, and disseminating information to assist the IC and team. It typically includes representatives from hospital departments and disciplines as well as external partners or stakeholders. Through coordination efforts, the HEOC ensures that resources, personnel, and information are deployed to meet both hospital and community needs. Coordinating resources is a responsibility of the HEOC, involving tracking personnel, equipment, supplies, and facilities for response and recovery efforts. Resource allocation is prioritized based on identified needs during incidents to optimize response efficiency. Planning for emergencies in healthcare settings is a process that requires consideration.

While the HEOC plays a role in overseeing and organizing hospital responses during emergencies, its success relies on coordinated operations and consistent functioning. The HEOC's tasks include coordinating departments, improving communication channels, and ensuring resources are managed effectively to meet the evolving needs of an emergency. To enhance coordination and readiness, hospitals should establish a routine within their HEOC. A clear battle rhythm offers an approach to managing emergency responses by promoting updates, prompt decision-making, and smooth transitions between shifts. This organized routine ensures team members are on the same page and critical information is communicated efficiently, and the response remains adaptable to changing circumstances. Implementing a battle rhythm can boost the efficiency of hospital HEOCs, leading to emergency management and optimal care provision in scenarios. An example of a partial HEOC Operational Rhythm may look like this:

0800-ESF/HICS Planning Meeting – Only staff listed on the ESF or HICS organizational chart attend. The purpose is to gather information, identify any unmet needs in response operations, and remove barriers to ensure ongoing preparedness.

0900-Day Shift Situation Meeting – All hospital staff are invited to attend this meeting (usually virtually) to understand the current situation of the event. This could include information about weather updates, road closures, staffing plans, logistical information for staff accommodation, parking information, etc.

1000-Local/County/State Briefings – Generally speaking, your hospital's emergency manager should attend meetings held by governmental agencies or coalition partners. These meetings occur at different times throughout the day but should be considered a priority within the hospital's operational rhythm so that information can be gathered and brought back to the response team. Decisions made at these meetings could have an operational impact on the hospital and may influence your decision-making. You will want to know about things like office or school closings, road closures, local curfews, or any other restrictions on local or state operations.

1200-System Wide Situation Meeting – If you have a large organization, this meeting allows corporate leaders to gather information from all areas of interest to get a full operational picture of the organization. This is similar in nature to a state holding a call for all State Emergency Response Taskforce (SERT) members. During times of crisis, like disasters or large emergencies, a SERT call plays a role in coordinating state-level resources and expertise. This structured communication method brings together representatives from state agencies and emergency management officials to share real-time information, assess the situation, and coordinate the deployment of resources to areas in need. Participants in the SERT call discuss the incident's status, identify needs, and plan response actions collaboratively for a unified approach. This teamwork streamlines decision-making, prioritizes resources, and ensures communication among government levels and emergency services. The SERT call serves as a centralized platform for coordination, enhancing the state's crisis response capabilities while ensuring alignment among all parties, in supporting communities. Just like a State Emergency Response Team (SERT) call functions as a communication and coordination tool during emergencies, a similar process takes place within a hospital system to ensure an organized and unified response. Just as the SERT call brings together representatives from state agencies and emergency management teams to evaluate the situation and coordinate resource deployment, an emergency call in a hospital system involves key personnel from various departments and facilities to address the immediate needs of the hospital network. During this call, participants such as hospital executives, department heads, and emergency response coordinators discuss the incident's status, allocate resources, and plan response strategies. The call enables real-time information sharing, helps prioritize tasks, and ensures that all facilities and departments work together effectively to manage the emergency. This centralized communication approach reflects the SERT call's aim of simplifying decision-making processes and maintaining collaborative efforts, tailored for a hospital system setting. By promoting collaboration and ensuring that all relevant parties are well informed and actively involved, both the SERT call and the hospital emergency call play crucial roles in optimizing response efforts and improving effectiveness in critical scenarios.

Enhancing your ability to respond to emergencies and uphold high-quality patient care within healthcare systems can significantly boost preparedness by adopting a comprehensive approach. This includes setting up emergency response protocols that clearly define procedures and responsibilities for scenarios ensuring all staff members are well trained and capable of implementing these protocols effectively. Conducting training drills and simulations is essential for reinforcing these protocols and acquainting staff with their roles under pressure. Efficient management of hospital resources is crucial, encompassing the acquisition, storage, and deployment of supplies and equipment to guarantee availability during crises.

Effective communication strategies also play a role in preparedness by facilitating accurate information exchange within internal teams and with external partners. Implementing communication systems and protocols ensures alignment among all stakeholders, enabling coordinated responses. Collaborating with partners like emergency services, public health agencies, and community organizations further fortifies the response network by providing additional assistance and resources as needed. Drawing insights from emergency incidents is key to improvement. By analyzing events, healthcare systems can extract lessons learned to integrate into their preparedness plans. Ongoing research and advancements in emergency management practices help refine strategies and incorporate approaches, enabling hospitals to address emerging challenges and enhance overall readiness.

As we wrap up this chapter on being ready, it is clear that a rounded and adaptable strategy is required. Covering the creation of protocols, training for staff, managing resources, communication tactics, and working with partners is crucial for a successful emergency preparedness blueprint. By adopting these methods and striving for enhancements, healthcare leaders and emergency managers can not only handle emergencies effectively but also guarantee top-notch care for patients even in the toughest situations.

Despite our efforts to anticipate challenges and create response strategies, unexpected factors and unique situations will always arise. Emergencies are inherently unpredictable, influenced by behavior and environmental variables that cannot all be accounted for in a plan. This uncertainty highlights the need for flexibility and adaptability in emergency preparedness. While careful planning sets the groundwork, it is just as vital to foster a culture of resilience and readiness that empowers teams to react effectively to circumstances. Recognizing that some elements are beyond our control encourages a flexible approach to emergency management, ensuring organizations can navigate real-world crises with agility and ingenuity.

In early March 2020 my daughter was set to celebrate her 10th birthday – a milestone we had eagerly anticipated. We had planned a party with her friends and invited our family members to join in the festivities. The excitement was palpable that Friday night as we looked forward to marking her special day with joy and laughter. My phone rang early on Saturday morning. It was one of the doctors from the ED. He let me know that several of the ED staff had tested positive for COVID. Some of the first cases in the state were at our facility. It was very concerning for many reasons, but all I could think about at that very moment was my own family and friends. My husband is a Critical Care Paramedic for a Pediatric Transport Team. Both of us are in and out of the ERs all the time. The gravity of the situation at this time when COVID was just emerging hit us hard, and the uncertainty of our own exposure made the situation even more alarming. We were faced with a difficult decision: prioritize the health and safety of our friends and loved ones or go ahead with the planned celebration. Considering the emerging pandemic, we made the heart-wrenching choice to cancel the party. It was a precautionary measure to protect my daughter's friends and our elderly family members from any potential exposure. It was a tough decision to make and. I will never forget the look on her face when she came downstairs full of anticipation for that day, and we had to tell her it was all canceled. We spent the day at home trying to make the best of the situation, even though it was far from what we had envisioned. We organized a small, impromptu celebration just within our household, (with way more cake and food than we could ever eat) and a few simple gifts. While it wasn't the grand party we had planned, we tried to make it special for her in our own way. While the cancellation of my daughter's 10th birthday party due to COVID-19 exposure concerns was a deeply disappointing experience for our family, it is essential to acknowledge that this incident pales in comparison to the far-reaching challenges and tragedies faced by many other families during the pandemic. For countless families, COVID-19 brought profound loss and hardship. Many experienced the heart-wrenching grief of losing loved ones to the virus, often unable to be by their side during their final moments or hold traditional funerals to mourn and honor their lives. The inability to say goodbye in person or to gather for communal support during such times of loss was a devastating blow that many families endured. In addition to personal losses, countless families faced significant economic hardships. Job losses, business closures, and financial instability created immense stress and uncertainty. The struggle to provide for families, coupled with the anxiety of navigating an unpredictable job market, added another layer of difficulty to the pandemic experience. Healthcare workers and frontline responders bore an extraordinary burden, grappling with overwhelming patient loads, emotional exhaustion, and the constant risk of exposure. Their dedication and sacrifices were nothing short of heroic, but they also faced intense personal and professional challenges that affected their well-being and the well-being of their families. Educational disruptions also had a considerable impact, with students and parents alike navigating the challenges of remote learning. For many families, the transition to online education highlighted existing inequalities and placed additional strain on parents who had to balance work, childcare, and educational responsibilities. The pandemic exacerbated social isolation for many, particularly for those living alone or in vulnerable populations. The inability to connect with friends and family, the lack of support networks, and the general sense of isolation contributed to significant mental health struggles.

The cancellation of my daughter's birthday party, though a significant personal disappointment, highlights a crucial lesson about preparedness and planning: while these elements are essential, they cannot always shield us from the unpredictable nature of unforeseen events. Our meticulous planning and preparation for the party were thwarted by a situation beyond our control, demonstrating how even the most well-thought-out plans can be upended by larger, uncontrollable forces. The sobering reality of that pandemic event illustrates that, despite our best efforts to prepare and plan, unforeseen events can profoundly affect our lives and test our resilience. It reinforces the value of being adaptable and compassionate in the face of adversity. While preparedness remains a critical component of managing emergencies, it is equally important to acknowledge and respect the diverse experiences of individuals and families who navigate challenges that far exceed our own. Ultimately, this reflection reminds us that while planning and preparation are crucial for mitigating risks and managing crises, they cannot eliminate the uncertainty of life's unpredictability. The ability to adapt, show empathy, and support one another during such times becomes just as essential as the plans we put in place.

~Kim Bailey

The Bibliography section reflects the source information for the concepts and frameworks described in this chapter.

Bibliography

Definitions and Distinctions between Emergency Management and Emergency Preparedness:

1. FEMA. (n.d.). *Emergency management.* https://www.fema.gov
2. Emergency Management Institute. (n.d.). *What is emergency management?* https://training.fema.gov/

Preparedness Cycle and Its Phases:

3. National Preparedness Goal. (2015). *The national preparedness goal.* https://www.fema.gov

Hospital Preparedness Planning and Framework:

4. Joint Commission. (2021). *Emergency management in healthcare.* https://www.jointcommission.org
5. APIC. (2021). *Emergency preparedness for healthcare facilities.* https://www.apic.org

Examples of Real-World Emergencies:

6. Christchurch City Council. (2011). *Christchurch earthquake: Report on the impacts and response.* https://www.ccc.govt.nz
7. U.S. Department of Health and Human Services. (2006). *The role of hospitals during Hurricane Katrina.* https://aspr.hhs.gov
8. World Health Organization. (2020). *COVID-19 pandemic: Lessons learned.* https://www.who.int

After-Action Reviews (AARs) and Feedback Mechanisms:

9. FEMA. (2020). *Conducting after-action reviews.* https://www.fema.gov
10. U.S. Department of Homeland Security. (n.d.). *Best practices for after-action reviews.* https://www.dhs.gov

Resource Management During Emergencies:

11. U.S. Department of Health and Human Services. (2020). *Resource management and logistics during emergencies.* https://aspr.hhs.gov
12. Centers for Disease Control and Prevention. (2018). *Managing medical supplies during an emergency.* https://www.cdc.gov

Hospital Incident Command System (HICS) Overview:

HICS is a standardized, role-based system designed for hospitals. It emphasizes a clear command structure with predefined roles such as Incident Commander, Operations, and Logistics.

13. U.S. Department of Health and Human Services. (n.d.). *Hospital Incident Command System (HICS) – Overview.* https://cdp.dhs.gov/training/course/AWR-934-V7

Hospital Emergency Operations Center (HEOC) Location and Functionality:
Considerations for selecting and designing HEOC spaces within hospitals.

14. American Hospital Association. (2020). *Hospital Emergency Operations Center (HEOC) – Design and functionality.* https://www.aha.org/emergency-management

Operational Rhythm for HEOCs:
Example of an operational rhythm for a hospital's HEOC to enhance coordination and efficiency.

15. Centers for Disease Control and Prevention. (2021). *Emergency Operations Center (EOC) Operational rhythm – Best practices.* https://www.cdc.gov

Chapter 7

Crisis Communication Strategies for Healthcare Leaders

Kimberly Bailey/Thomas Crawford

In times of crisis, effective communication is essential for healthcare leaders. It's not just about sharing information; it's about managing expectations, preventing misinformation, and building trust with the staff, patients, and the public. Transparent communication shows that leaders are in control and making informed decisions to safeguard everyone's well-being. It shapes the reputation of healthcare institutions – clear communication can enhance their image, while poor communication can have lasting negative effects. When people understand the reasons behind your actions, they are more likely to cooperate, ensuring a cohesive and efficient response.

This truth was starkly highlighted in June 2023, when a small coastal town in South Carolina was rocked by a shooting incident. The event required a coordinated response from over 15 local, state, and federal organizations. Just days before, I had shared a calm lunch with many of these same individuals – EMS leaders, county emergency management personnel, state FBI agents, and local fire department officials – completely unaware of the urgent collaboration that would soon be necessary. As chaos unfolded both at the scene and at the local Trauma Center where the patients were being brought in, my phone rang, and messages poured in with genuine expressions of support and offers of assistance. The calls came from those I had recently dined with – people who had become more than just professional contacts. They are also my friends. Our meetings are always casual, yet they forge connections that proved invaluable in times of crisis. What struck me most was the familiarity and ease with which these conversations occurred. We weren't slowed down by formalities or bureaucratic obstacles. Because we had already established trust and communication, our interactions were seamless and focused on swiftly mobilizing resources and expertise to save lives and support our community. The importance of these pre-existing relationships in times of crisis communication became glaringly clear as the situation unfolded. Reflecting

DOI: 10.4324/9781003529194-7

on that moment, I realized that the effort we put into fostering relationships before emergencies is not just professional networking – it's a strategic imperative for effective emergency management. It's about cultivating a network of trust and collaboration that transcends organizational boundaries and jurisdictional lines. These relationships enable us to communicate more swiftly, more effectively, and with greater resilience in the face of adversity. This experience reinforced my belief in the power of proactive relationship-building in emergency management. I urge you as healthcare leaders and hospital emergency managers to invest time in getting to know your partners, understanding their capabilities, and ensuring that when crisis strikes, you are not starting from scratch but standing shoulder-to-shoulder with a network of allies ready to support one another. Effective communication is the thread that binds these relationships together, allowing us to evaluate and adjust strategies in real-time, offer comfort and resources to both the public and staff, and uphold our ethical responsibilities. Building these relationships isn't just about preparing for the next crisis; it's about laying a foundation of resilience that strengthens our ability to protect and serve our community when they need us most. Through transparent and effective communication, we fulfill our roles as healthcare leaders, navigating emergencies with integrity and ensuring the well-being of those we serve.

-Kim Bailey

By the conclusion of this chapter, healthcare leaders will gain an understanding of how crucial communication is in managing emergencies. They will learn strategies and best practices to ensure that communication during crises is both impactful and compassionate while also aligning with the organization's objectives and values. Good communication can serve as a source of comfort and steadiness amidst turmoil.

As a healthcare leader, you are well aware that breakdowns in communication can have consequences on outcomes, safety, and the overall delivery of healthcare services. A study published in the BMJ in 2016 revealed that medical errors rank as the leading cause of death in the United States, with communication breakdowns being a contributing factor. The Joint Commission, responsible for accrediting healthcare organizations in the United States, has highlighted that communication lapses are a root cause of events – unforeseen incidents resulting in death or severe physical or psychological harm. From 2010 to 2013, over 70% of events reported to The Joint Commission attributed communication breakdowns as a contributing element.

In a research article published in the *Journal of the American Medical Association* (*JAMA*) in 2014 it was discovered that inadequate handoff communication between healthcare providers or facilities was responsible for 80% of medical errors.[1] When there is a lack of communication between healthcare professionals and patients, it can result in confusion regarding discharge instructions, medication plans, and aftercare. This breakdown in communication can heighten the likelihood of hospital readmissions. For instance, a study highlighted in the *Annals of Internal Medicine* revealed that close to one-fifth of Medicare patients end up being readmitted to hospitals within a month post discharge due to issues stemming from communication. These facts stress the essential role effective communication plays in healthcare operations. Nonetheless, why does crisis communication become more crucial during emergencies or disasters at facilities? During hospital emergencies, time is of the essence. Clear instructions on what actions to take can save lives. That

[1] The Joint Commission. (2014). *Inadequate handoff communication between healthcare providers or facilities was responsible for 80% of medical errors.* Journal of the American Medical Association.

is why effective communication during a crisis or emergency is the linchpin of successful healthcare emergency management.

On September 15, 2017, a significant incident occurred in Hawaii involving the accidental activation of the tsunami warning siren system. During a routine test of the system, which was intended to ensure functionality and readiness, an employee mistakenly selected the live alert option instead of the test option, causing the actual tsunami warning sirens to sound across the state. The blaring alarms, typically reserved for imminent and serious threats, caused immediate panic and confusion among the residents and tourists who were unaware that the alert was an exercise. People rushed to seek higher ground and safety, fearing a real tsunami was about to strike. The unintentional activation of the sirens triggered a wave of anxiety and disrupted daily activities as individuals scrambled to respond to what they believed was an urgent and life-threatening emergency. Local hospitals were immediately thrust into emergency mode, stretching their capacity as the false alarm created a sudden surge in demand for emergency services. Emergency departments had to manage an influx of people seeking information, reassurance, and medical assistance for stress-related symptoms. Elective procedures and appointments were delayed or canceled as staff prioritized emergency response protocols. Hospital staff had to manage not only the physical needs of their patients but also provide emotional support to alleviate fear and confusion. This event served as a real-time drill, testing emergency plans and the ability of hospital staff to handle sudden crises. Luckily, there were no reported fatalities directly resulting from the incident. State authorities quickly realized the error and worked to clarify the situation. Hospitals tried to disseminate accurate information to staff, patients, and the public to clarify that the alarm was false. This involved coordinating with state emergency management and public health officials to ensure unified and coordinated messaging. Emergency management officials issued statements and used other communication channels to inform the public that there was no actual threat and that the sirens had been activated by mistake during a test. Despite these efforts, the incident highlighted vulnerabilities in the alert system and underscored the importance of clear communication and proper procedural checks during drills. The event significantly impacted local area hospitals by straining resources, disrupting operations, and testing emergency response capabilities. It emphasized the critical importance of clear communication, efficient resource management, and robust emergency preparedness plans. The false alarm and subsequent handling by hospitals played a crucial role in maintaining community trust. Effective management and communication during the incident helped preserve the public's confidence in the healthcare system's ability to handle real emergencies. Conversely, any perceived mishandling could have led to a loss of trust and increased skepticism about emergency response systems. The accidental activation of the tsunami warning system served as a critical learning experience for Hawaii's emergency management agencies and emergency managers nationwide, including hospitals. We were prompted to re-evaluate our own alert systems, ensuring that safeguards were in place to avoid human error and improve verification processes. We looked at refining communication strategies, updating training programs, and improving coordination mechanisms to prevent similar incidents in the future and ensure a swift, effective response. The event also reinforced the necessity of clear and effective communication strategies, both for disseminating accurate information and for managing public response during crises. Additionally, it spurred a broader discussion on the integration of technology and human oversight in emergency management practices. Ultimately, the incident in Hawaii led to a renewed focus on enhancing the resilience and reliability of emergency alert systems, fostering a more prepared and responsive emergency management community across the country.

A hospital's emergency manager plays a pivotal role in crisis communications for healthcare leaders, acting as the linchpin that coordinates and implements the communication strategies essential for effective crisis management. The hospital emergency manager is responsible for developing comprehensive crisis communication plans as part of the broader emergency preparedness strategy. These plans outline the procedures for timely and accurate information dissemination during a crisis, ensuring that all communication efforts are coordinated and consistent. During a crisis, the emergency manager coordinates with the hospital's communications team to ensure the flow of information between various stakeholders, including healthcare leaders, medical staff, emergency services, government agencies, and the public. Together they ensure that messages are clear, accurate, and disseminated through appropriate channels, such as press releases, social media, internal memos, and public announcements. Emergency managers spend a lot of time networking and communicating on an almost daily basis with many external stakeholders. During times of crisis, the emergency manager should act as a liaison between healthcare leaders and external agencies, such as public health departments and emergency response teams. They should facilitate ongoing communication and collaboration, ensuring that the hospital's actions are aligned with broader public health strategies and regulations.

When a crisis occurs, your healthcare leadership team and the emergency manager will activate the crisis communication plan and oversee its implementation. This involves rapidly gathering information, assessing the situation, and ensuring that accurate and timely updates are provided to all relevant parties. Throughout the crisis, an emergency manager continuously monitors the situation and the effectiveness of communication efforts. They gather feedback from various sources, including staff, patients, and the community, and adjust the communication strategies as needed to address any gaps or issues that are identified. In many cases, your hospital emergency manager may serve as, or work closely, with your Public Information Officer (PIO). The PIO is the designated spokesperson during a crisis, responsible for communicating with the media and the public. Your emergency manager should ensure that the PIO has the most current and accurate information to share with your stakeholders.

Healthcare leaders should be able to rely on the expertise of the emergency manager to navigate the complexities of crisis communication. The emergency manager may provide guidance on the timing, content, and delivery of messages, helping leaders communicate effectively with internal and external audiences. Your hospital emergency manager is integral to the crisis communication process, ensuring that you as healthcare leaders have the tools, plans, and support necessary to communicate effectively during a crisis. Their responsibilities include planning, organizing, training, carrying out tasks, and assessing outcomes, all of which are crucial for building trust, ensuring safety, and effectively managing crises. Communication in times of emergencies involves aspects such as sharing information with external stakeholders. It serves various purposes. One key aspect is maintaining trust. Building and maintaining trust is fundamental to responding to crises. For healthcare leaders, clear and timely communication plays a critical role in establishing and upholding this trust. When facing a crisis like a disaster or major accident, patients, families, staff members, and the community at large rely on healthcare leaders for guidance and reassurance. How leaders communicate during these moments can significantly influence the public's confidence in their ability to handle the situation.

Above all else, transparent communication requires honesty about the nature and severity of the crisis. This honesty helps set expectations and prepares everyone involved for the challenges ahead. By sharing what is known, what remains uncertain, and efforts to gather information, healthcare leaders build credibility and demonstrate accountability. This transparency helps alleviate fear and uncertainty that could otherwise lead to panic or misinformation. Timeliness in communication is equally crucial.

During a changing emergency situation, any delays in sharing information can spark speculation, rumors, and a sense of distrust. Regular updates, even if the full picture is not crystal clear yet, indicate that healthcare leaders are actively involved and responsive. This shows a dedication to keeping everyone informed and engaged in the response efforts. Patients and their families feel trust when they believe their health and well-being are priorities. Clear communication about treatment guidelines, changes in healthcare services, and safety precautions reassures them that they're receiving care given the circumstances. Trust is also vital for healthcare staff to uphold morale and ensure adherence to emergency protocols. When staff members are kept informed and their concerns are addressed promptly, they are more likely to feel appreciated and supported – crucial for their performance and well-being.The larger community looks to healthcare leaders for guidance during crises. Public trust is key in promoting compliance with health advisories like distancing, vaccination, and quarantine measures. When the community trusts healthcare leaders, they tend to follow recommended actions, greatly impacting the crisis response's effectiveness. Upholding trust through communication plays a role in safeguarding the reputation of healthcare institutions. After a crisis, how an organization communicates and manages the situation will be closely examined. Being proactive and truthful in communication can improve the organization's reputation and establish trust in the community. Conversely, poor communication can result in lasting harm to the reputation and a loss of credibility. Trustworthy communication creates an atmosphere where patients, families, staff, and the community feel informed, supported, and involved – all crucial for achieving positive outcomes during emergencies. In crisis communication, ensuring safety and providing guidance are priorities. The hospital's emergency manager plays a role in facilitating this aspect. Communication is vital for delivering safety instructions like evacuation procedures, shelter-in-place guidelines, and details about resources. During crises such as disasters, mass casualty incidents, or public health emergencies like pandemics, effective communication is crucial for disseminating safety instructions to patients, staff members, and the wider community. Collaborating with healthcare leaders enables the emergency manager to effectively develop and deliver these instructions. For instance, a key duty of an emergency manager is to create safety protocols and evacuation plans ahead of any crisis. This strategy should detail the roles and duties, communication guidelines, message formats, and contact details. These guidelines ought to provide step-by-step guidance on how to deal with emergency situations, including evacuation routes, assigned gathering spots, and protocols for staying in place. Through planning and practicing these guidelines via drills and training sessions, the emergency coordinator guarantees that hospital personnel are well-equipped to implement them efficiently when necessary.

Communication plays a crucial role in notifying individuals about dangers and offering real-time updates on developing circumstances during an emergency. Using communication methods like announcements, digital displays, mobile notifications, and social media platforms, an emergency coordinator can aid in distributing vital information about safety measures, evacuation directives, and shelter, in place instructions. Clear directions help prevent chaos and uncertainty by giving people steps they can take to safeguard themselves. When individuals are aware of what actions to take, they are less likely to panic and more likely to react effectively. Emergency communications containing actionable guidance help ensure that individuals follow the required steps to protect themselves and others. For instance, directions to evacuate a location, seek refuge, or steer clear of areas can significantly decrease the likelihood of injury or harm during a crisis.

Effective crisis communication goes beyond giving safety instructions. It also involves informing people about the resources and support services available to them during a crisis. This could include details about facilities, emergency shelters, transportation options, and necessary supplies. A skilled hospital emergency manager will gather this information from sources as the situation unfolds to share with their team and those in the Emergency Department. By sharing information about resources and how to access them, the emergency manager can help reduce anxiety and uncertainty among those affected by the crisis. Communication channels can also be used to seek feedback and address concerns, making the crisis response more responsive and supportive. Safety instructions are crucial in crisis communication, with the hospital emergency manager playing a role in ensuring they are effectively communicated. By establishing protocols, using communication methods, and providing timely updates, an emergency manager helps protect individuals and communities during emergencies. Through planning, coordination, and open communication with the emergency manager, confidence can be instilled, and preparedness can be enhanced. The impact of emergencies lessened for both staff and patients. Effective communication plays a crucial role in ensuring that resources, personnel, and response efforts are well coordinated. It is vital for everyone involved to be on the same page and working together towards shared objectives. Coordination involves aligning resources, personnel, and response efforts to effectively tackle the challenges presented by emergencies. Central to this coordination is the accurate exchange of information, which is facilitated by the emergency manager through communication channels and established protocols. One of the responsibilities of an emergency manager during a crisis is to establish lines of communication among all parties engaged in the response process. This includes collaborating with healthcare leaders, medical staff, emergency services, government agencies, and community organizations. The frequency of meetings attended by a hospital's emergency manager with both internal and external stakeholders can vary based on the nature and severity of the crisis, as well as the unique needs and circumstances of the hospital. Nevertheless, it is common for emergency managers to partake in meetings throughout the crisis duration to ensure coordination and communication. Emergency managers frequently engage in meetings with hospital leadership, department heads, and essential personnel to evaluate the situation, make decisions collectively, and coordinate response actions.

During times of crisis, hospitals may hold meetings to make decisions and address important issues, such as resource allocation, patient care protocols, staffing requirements, and logistical plans. They often use a system like the Incident Command System (ICS) to organize their emergency response. These meetings help them stay updated on operations, set priorities, and deal with any challenges that arise. It is crucial for the emergency manager to play a role in these meetings by providing updates on communication efforts, coordinating support functions, and ensuring that everyone is working toward the goals. The structure of these crisis meetings closely resembles the framework of Emergency Support Functions (ESFs) commonly used in emergency management to coordinate resources and expertise across sectors during emergencies. Hospital emergency managers also gather representatives from departments such as nursing, facilities management, security, and public relations to coordinate various aspects of the response.

During crises, these gatherings aim to make sure that all departments are on the page exchanging details and tackling any obstacles or resource requirements that crop up. In emergencies or calamities affecting the broader community, hospital emergency coordinators should engage in discussions with outside parties such as local government agencies, public health authorities, emergency management groups, and community-based organizations. These discussions might happen multiple times a day during emergencies to share information, pool resources, and guarantee a coordinated response involving various sectors, including the hospital. Emergency coordinators may also need to provide updates and briefings to hospital staff, leaders, and external collaborators throughout the crisis period. These updates could be in the form of phone calls, video meetings, written reports, or face-to-face gatherings, based on the communication preferences and requirements of those involved. Essentially, your hospitals emergency coordinator may have to attend meetings with both internal and external parties during a crisis – from daily updates with internal teams to coordination sessions with external partners and community groups. These interactions play a crucial role in ensuring communication, coordination efforts, and collaboration throughout the crisis response phase; hence it's important for your emergency coordinator to actively participate in all these meetings. By encouraging communication, an emergency manager ensures that everyone stays well informed and understands their roles and duties. Holding updates and gatherings involving all parties helps to maintain a mutual understanding of the changing situation and aids in making unified decisions.

Good communication is crucial not only for sharing information and coordinating responses during a crisis but also for effectively managing the distribution and use of resources. In this aspect, the hospital's emergency manager collaborates closely with healthcare leaders to evaluate resource requirements, prioritize distributions, and mobilize assistance when needed. This cooperative approach allows for a comprehensive view of the hospital's resource landscape, enabling informed decision-making to tackle emerging challenges efficiently. Through communication and collaboration, an emergency manager facilitates the collection of real-time data on resource availability and demand. This involves evaluating the status of supplies, equipment, staff, and other essential resources for providing patient care and supporting response activities. By keeping lines of communication open with department heads, supply chain managers, and other key stakeholders, the emergency manager ensures that accurate information guides resource allocation decisions. Effective communication empowers an emergency manager to prioritize resource distributions based on changing priorities and critical requirements. In times of crisis, the need for resources can change quickly, requiring timely decision-making to distribute resources where they are urgently required. A skilled emergency manager can use real-time information and data-driven insights to pinpoint areas for resource allocation and ensure that scarce resources are distributed strategically to have the greatest impact on patient care and response efforts. The role of a hospital emergency manager is crucial in mobilizing help and resources when needed to strengthen the hospital's ability to respond effectively. This might involve collaborating with partners like government agencies, relief organizations, community groups, or healthcare alliances to access resources, staff, or expertise. For instance, healthcare alliances facilitate the coordination of resources among their member organizations. In times of crisis, when resources are limited or running low, being part of an alliance enables emergency managers to tap into supplies, equipment, staff members, and know-how from alliance members. By working in this way, resources can be directed where they are most required while boosting the collective response capabilities of the alliance. Through communication and teamwork, the emergency manager can utilize assistance to complement internal resources and strengthen the hospital's resilience in challenging situations.

Effective communication plays a role in helping the emergency manager enhance the hospital's response capabilities during a crisis. By collaborating with healthcare leaders, identifying resource requirements, prioritizing allocations, and mobilizing support when needed, the emergency manager strengthens the hospital's ability to handle emergencies efficiently, reduce risks, and ensure the safety of patients and staff. Through communication and strategic resource management, the hospital can effectively navigate crisis challenges with resilience and flexibility, ensuring care delivery while upholding high standards of patient safety and support. Apart from resource coordination, effective communication also ensures the integration of personnel into crisis response activities. The emergency manager works closely with department heads, team leaders, and frontline staff to communicate instructions clearly, offer guidance, and address any concerns that may arise. Clear communication regarding roles, expectations, and protocols empowers personnel to carry out their tasks effectively and contributes to the collective response effort.

On a Saturday evening at 7:37 pm, I received an alert on my phone notifying me that the incident assessment team would convene for a conference call at 7:45 pm to discuss an event. Joining the call immediately revealed chaos as members of the care team talked over each other, making it difficult for me to grasp the nature of the issue at hand. "Alright team, that's enough," I declared firmly. "I'm looking to hear from the Administrator on Call (AOC). I need to know the issue at hand, its consequences, and our course of action." However, a team member who was not the AOC piped up about not being able to access a third-party app we use for tracking hours. "Let me reiterate – I want input, from the AOC tonight. My main concerns are the well-being of our patients and our team members; everything else can wait until morning. So, what's the problem, its impact and what's our plan moving forward?" We addressed the issue at hand, assessed its effects, and devised a strategy to ensure operations without jeopardizing safety or staff well-being. The simple Problem, Impact, Plan (PIP) communication construct keeps the team focused and is now our standard methodology for looking at issues when they occur. On far too many occasions, communication fails because we provide too much information or not enough to the appropriate stakeholders, and we get distracted by addressable issues that do not matter in the moment. Case in point, during the unprecedented – the pandemic – I witnessed numerous health systems struggle to define how they would respond. Using our simple methodology, we worked through how we would communicate internally and to various stakeholders throughout the state and beyond. Problem – influx of COVID patients that could overwhelm our resources, and we needed to keep our care team members and the other patients safe. Impact – this was evolving; however, we needed to prepare for an influx of patients that could potentially overwhelm our health system and the limited resources we have throughout the state. Plan – remember this is where the focus on patient and care team member safety comes into play. We decided to divert and funnel – meaning we needed to keep non-acute/critical COVID patients out of our ambulatory spaces and emergency departments. Thus, we diverted by offering free tele-screenings for all non-acute/critical patients with COVID symptoms, and those that needed to be tested were funneled through one of our drive-through locations. We had a plan to handle those not requiring hospitalization and now we focused on what we needed to be able to safely care for the acute/critical COVID patients. Based on this and our need to communicate across four divisions, we focused on the minimum essentials required to provide care: staff (MDs, nurses, etc.), capacity (number of beds, vents, negative pressure rooms, etc.), and supplies (personal protective equipment, etc.). This became our common language and how we used the PIP format to ensure communication was organized and timely. If we had an issue impacting our ability to care for patients, we knew how to focus and how to help each other. Furthermore, we became a statewide resource and were able to help supply other hospitals with the equipment or supplies required to care for infectious patients. By fostering a sense of cohesion and shared purpose through a PIP model or a similar construct, your AOC and emergency manager can strengthen teamwork and enhance the overall effectiveness of the crisis response.

Dealing with the media during a crisis is crucial for healthcare leaders. They need to strike a balance between providing information, protecting privacy, and upholding the organization's reputation. In times of crisis, the media serves as a channel for sharing information with the public. How healthcare organizations interact with journalists and news outlets can greatly influence how people perceive and trust them. If a hospital lacks a communication team or an assigned Public Information Officer (PIO), the emergency manager often steps up to fulfill this role. In such situations, the emergency manager becomes the contact person for the media, ensuring that accurate updates about the crisis and the hospital's response are shared promptly and responsibly. This includes drafting press releases, coordinating press briefings, and conducting interviews, all while safeguarding confidentiality in accordance with privacy laws like HIPAA. A hospital emergency manager must also effectively communicate messages that underscore the organization's dedication to patient well-being and safety, which is crucial for upholding its reputation throughout and beyond crises.

A skilled emergency manager can foresee media inquiries, preparing suitable responses often in collaboration with healthcare leaders to ensure that the information shared is accurate and aligns with the hospital's crisis response plan. Effective media handling also involves rectifying misinformation and controlling the information flow to avoid causing alarm or confusion. Crisis communication frequently involves navigating dilemmas, such as patient confidentiality, consent, and upholding dignity and respect. Healthcare leaders and hospital emergency managers should be well informed about these challenges and ensure that communication practices adhere to the highest ethical standards. By stepping into the role of a Public Information Officer (PIO), the emergency manager can maintain the hospital's credibility as a source of information, thereby building public trust and confidence in the healthcare system during critical situations.

Clear communication is crucial for coordinating resources, personnel, and response efforts in times of crises. The hospital's emergency manager plays a role in facilitating this coordination by establishing communication channels, optimizing resource distribution, integrating staff into response activities, and fostering cooperation with external partners. Through communication approaches and proactive coordination initiatives, an emergency manager enhances the hospital's ability to respond effectively to emergencies while safeguarding the welfare of patients, staff, and the community.

Citations and influential documents for this chapter are present below.

Bibliography

1. Makary, M. A., & Daniel, M. (2016). Medical error—the third leading cause of death in the US. *BMJ.*, 353, i2139. https://doi.org/10.1136/bmj.i2139
2. The Joint Commission. (2016). *Improving patient safety: The role of communication.* https://www.jointcommission.org/resources/patient-safety-topics/communication
3. The Joint Commission. (2014). The role of communication in reducing medical errors. *JAMA.*, 312(6), 579–580. https://doi.org/10.1001/jama.2014.9184
4. Hernandez, A. F., Greiner, M. A., & Fonarow, G. C. (2010). Relationship between early physician follow-up and 30-day readmission among Medicare beneficiaries hospitalized for heart failure. *Ann Intern Med.*, 153(4), 237–245. https://doi.org/10.7326/0003-4819-153-4-201008170-00007
5. Peltier, E. (2017). Hawaii mistakenly triggers tsunami alert during routine test. *NBC News.* https://www.nbcnews.com/news/us-news/hawaii-mistakenly-triggers-tsunami-alert-during-routine-test-n804566
6. Ranney, M. L., Griffeth, V., & Jha, A. K. (2020). Critical supply shortages—the need for ventilators and personal protective equipment during the COVID-19 pandemic. *N Engl J Med.*, 382(18), 1664–1665. https://doi.org/10.1056/NEJMp2006863

Chapter 8

Resource Allocation and Management for Healthcare Facilities

Kimberly Bailey/Rocky Tucker/Jamie Blair

The extraordinary response to COVID-19 brought to light a critical reality often overlooked in healthcare and logistics planning: the pivotal role of the supply chain in ensuring community resilience. The impacts of regional and global shutdowns exposed the vulnerabilities of a "just-in-time" supply system, leaving medical professionals and emergency managers unprepared for the magnitude of disruption in medical services. As resources became scarce overnight, healthcare providers and their partners faced moral and ethical dilemmas regarding the allocation of dwindling supplies. The competition for essential items such as personal protective equipment (PPE), COVID testing materials, and vaccines became fierce, with both public and private entities vying for limited resources on a global scale. This intense rivalry led to compromises in quality control and a surge in counterfeit products, further straining healthcare systems already grappling with unprecedented patient volumes and acuity levels.

On a local level, the COVID-19 response demonstrated the importance of a whole-community approach to crisis management. The pandemic posed a prolonged medical crisis that affected communities of all sizes. Healthcare facilities faced not only diminishing clinical supplies but also a shortage of PPE for staff to safely administer care. Federal, state, and local partners played an instrumental role in locating PPE and ensuring its availability to healthcare providers. This often involved forging new relationships between government agencies and private sector vendors, which lasted throughout the initial response and established a framework for collaboration as COVID testing and vaccinations rolled out.

The acquisition and distribution of these resources presented significant challenges. Healthcare leaders and emergency managers had to work together to meet sourcing needs and provide distribution support, regardless of community size. Their collective efforts ensured that healthcare providers could continue to serve their communities effectively

DOI: 10.4324/9781003529194-8

during the pandemic. This experience highlighted the importance of robust supply chain management and the value of strong partnerships in maintaining community resilience during times of crisis.

~ Jamie Blair

Chapter 8 delves into how resources are managed in healthcare settings. By the conclusion of this chapter, healthcare leaders will have a grasp of how resources are allocated and managed during healthcare crises. They will be well equipped to make decisions about resource distribution while upholding patient-centered care principles and ethical norms. Effective resource management is crucial for ensuring the ability to deliver top-notch care in the face of limited resources. For example, as Hurricane Matthew neared South Carolina, the state prepared for its arrival. Evacuation orders led to individuals seeking shelter in arranged locations like schools and community centers. Many of these evacuees were elderly and had health issues requiring supplemental oxygen for breathing support. Community shelters quickly became overcrowded beyond expectations. The supply of oxygen tanks started running out as the number of people seeking refuge continued to rise. Emergency management offices received calls from shelter staff expressing worries about the depleting oxygen reserves. The situation was dire, with shelters facing the risk of running out of oxygen. Meanwhile, hospitals located inland were also feeling the strain from the influx of evacuees and patients in need of oxygen therapy. Already stretched thin while preparing for the storm's impact, these hospitals struggled to manage the surge in demand for oxygen tanks amid flooded roads and transportation challenges.

Despite facing obstacles, emergency managers, healthcare providers, and local suppliers joined forces to tackle the crisis head on. They worked tirelessly to coordinate the redistribution of oxygen resources from areas with surplus to those in critical need. In response to the emergency situation, local suppliers successfully delivered oxygen tanks to various locations, easing the strain on shelters and hospitals. Yet, this challenging situation exposed a weakness in our disaster preparedness plans that needed attention. The scarcity of oxygen tanks during Hurricane Matthew emphasized the need for disaster readiness, particularly in ensuring the availability of essential medical supplies and improving communication channels among shelters, hospitals, and emergency responders. In the aftermath of the hurricane, the lessons learned from this oxygen shortage prompted changes in how emergencies are handled statewide. Local authorities took measures by updating their strategies, implementing inventory control systems for medical supplies, and increasing resource stockpiling in vulnerable regions. Collaboration with healthcare facilities was also strengthened to ensure a coordinated response during future crises. These actions aimed not only at averting another disruption in the supply chain but at securing uninterrupted access to critical healthcare services for all individuals, especially those most at risk. This experience highlighted the importance of planning and cooperation in managing emergencies while reinforcing a commitment to enhanced preparedness for future challenges.

As healthcare leaders and hospital emergency managers devise strategies for addressing emerging crises, their goal is to achieve objectives. In this context, the focus is on directing resources towards solving problems. Properly identifying issues helps establish goals, which then aids in determining the resources needed to achieve those goals. Resource allocation and management play crucial roles in responding to and recovering from healthcare emergencies. The aim is to provide support effectively to ensure that appropriate capabilities are in place to meet objectives while minimizing adverse effects on patient care and enhancing overall organizational resilience.

Emergency managers work toward providing healthcare leaders with a shared understanding of events. The shared understanding creates a view that guides decisions on the resources and capabilities needed to achieve the specified goals for resolving, lessening, or recovering from a crisis. Additionally, emergency managers will organize the obtaining, delivery, and monitoring of resources once they are identified and utilized. This process may entail working with collaborating partners.

Earlier sections have covered the Hospital Emergency Operations Center (HEOC) and its role in crisis management. The HEOC serves as the hub for gathering information and managing resources. The individuals staffing the HEOC will offer expertise to advise leaders on resource requirements and locate resources from various sources to ensure timely and efficient resource delivery. It is the responsibility of the emergency manager to provide leadership and ensure objectives are set and met.

It is essential to recognize that in a healthcare setting, requested resources could include supplies for care or tangible items to fortify facilities and maintain operations. When it comes to supplies, HEOC Staff will approach those specialized sources with insight into transporting and handling unique equipment and materials. Sometimes existing supply chains may suffice. However, during crises, clinical staff may need to look beyond their organization for procurement solutions.

During emergencies, healthcare leaders work with staff to identify the resources needed to meet objectives. This collaborative effort is crucial for a response. Following FEMA guidelines, the first step is to assess requirements by determining resources like supplies, personnel, transportation, and communication tools. Accurate identification of needs is essential to prevent expenses. Once requirements are known, the next step is to procure the resources. Timely acquisition is vital to ensure resources are available when needed and to avoid delays, in response efforts. Finally, resources are deployed to where they are needed.

Effective mobilization plays a role in ensuring that resources are strategically positioned to offer support and aid, thereby minimizing the impact of emergencies on affected communities. It is vital to monitor and report on the status of these resources throughout the response period. This involves keeping track of resource usage, promoting utilization, and maintaining transparency through updates. Accurate monitoring and reporting not only facilitate resource management but also furnish essential data for decision-making processes.

Once immediate needs have been met and the situation stabilizes, the demobilization phase commences. This phase entails withdrawing resources that are no longer required and either returning them to their locations or reallocating them to areas in need. An executed demobilization process ensures that resources are conserved and kept ready for contingencies. The subsequent step involves restocking and replenishing supplies post emergency. It is crucial to replenish depleted resources, restock supplies, maintain equipment, and ensure all resources are primed for any emergencies. This systematic approach improves resource management efficiency and highlights the significance of preparedness and resilience in healthcare emergency management. While much of this process may be transparent for hospital leadership, aspects such as ordering, tracking, and restocking may necessitate certain leaders being regularly updated due to associated costs, procurement, and ongoing replenishment efforts.

Leaders should also consider consulting with HEOC personnel to ensure they have established tracking and reporting procedures in place right from the start of the event. These procedures will play a role in securing insurance or federal reimbursements if they become available after the event. Let us look at the process. An essential principle in the emergency management field is that all disasters originate and conclude locally. This means that no matter how big a disaster is, it starts and ends at the local level. When a disaster happens, the people who live in the affected area are the first to respond, and they are also the ones who deal with the aftermath once outside help leaves. Local communities are on the front lines from the beginning to the end of any disaster, and they play the most crucial role in both responding to and recovering from it. When it comes to resources, this principle emphasizes obtaining supplies to the end user as feasible. Prearranged agreements or contracts for services like transportation, ventilator rentals, staffing, or emergency fuel can guarantee that essential supplies or services are directly accessible to healthcare facilities.

If resources must be acquired from other sources, emergency managers will look to partner agencies within local municipalities, counties, or even the state to provide support. In some cases, the support may ultimately come from federal government sources but will always be managed through the lowest practical jurisdictional authority. Also, non-governmental organizations (NGOs) may support resource requests with volunteer staffing, services, and equipment. An example of NGO support could be Red Cross volunteers supporting hospital staff in areas where clinical experience may not be required.

Hospital Emergency Managers should be able to guide leadership and HEOC Staff through the resource ordering process. In most cases not involving predesignated agreements or contracts, EMs will coordinate with municipal or county Emergency Operations Centers for assistance in sourcing needed resources, so they should be very familiar with the process and the people they will be speaking to when they need to make these requests. Several outlets are available for ordering through partner agencies, but generally, an informal coordination will be followed by a request documented through an automated platform that the state or county has adopted for coordination. Counties and states use various platforms to request and track resources efficiently, which allows them to coordinate resources during emergencies. This kind of software provides real-time situational awareness, resource tracking, and incident management, allowing users to manage resource requests and coordinate responses across different agencies. Some have been specifically designed for healthcare resource management, enabling hospitals and emergency management agencies to monitor and request medical resources such as hospital beds, medical personnel, and supplies.

Various Crisis Information Management software platforms offer tools for resource management, incident reporting, and communication, supporting resource requests and coordination among agencies. These platforms enable counties and states to efficiently coordinate resources, ensuring timely and effective responses to emergencies and disasters. The documentation not only confirms an order but also initiates the process for tracking costs associated with orders. As mentioned several times earlier in this book, it is important that emergency managers establish relationships with local partners prior to catastrophic events to ensure mutual understanding of ordering and acquisition when time may be a critical factor. Ideally, Healthcare EMs exercise these processes with local partners to optimize resource utility.

While cost and usage factors may not be an immediate consideration in the face of a disaster, it is still the responsibility of the emergency manager and HEOC staff (ideally the Finance Chief) to maintain a running total of costs both financially and physically. Financial costs may continue to increase during an ongoing incident, while equipment operability and stockpiles of supplies decrease. A well-maintained tracking and reporting process allows emergency managers to keep leadership informed of costs while sustaining an effective program for reordering depleted supplies. Such a program will also ensure supporting staff members do not "burn out" by providing a mechanism for replacing staff members as long hours in tense environments contribute to fatigue.

Tracking costs associated with emergencies or disasters is crucial for hospitals to ensure financial accountability and sustainability. Accurate cost tracking helps hospitals manage their budgets effectively and provides a clear understanding of the financial impact of the event. Post event, this information can be used to apply for reimbursement from federal, state, or insurance programs, thereby recovering a significant portion of the expenses incurred. Additionally, detailed cost analysis enables hospitals to evaluate their emergency response strategies, identify areas for improvement, and allocate resources more efficiently in the future. It also supports compliance with regulatory requirements and facilitates transparent communication with stakeholders, including government agencies, insurers, and the community. Ultimately, thorough cost tracking and analysis help hospitals enhance their preparedness, resilience, and overall financial health. As a rule, any documentation generated by an incident should be kept for recordkeeping purposes. This is especially true for invoices, bills, timesheets, and other financially significant documents.

Further costs associated with disaster are those associated with restocking supplies and equipment used, or degraded, in direct response actions. Emergency managers and HEOC Staff should forecast these requirements as often as possible throughout the incident. This resource forecasting not only ensures depleted stocks are available as operations transition to recovery, but also allows the emergency manager and staff logisticians to keep leaders informed of resource status and any costs associated with restocking. As conditions begin to normalize and operations shift to recovery, these records of financial output will be critical for tracing costs and potentially supporting reimbursement of costs should it become available. Additionally, records of staff overtime, additional staffing requirements, and volunteer time serve to provide a picture of the overall incident response. Leadership will find these documents invaluable when assessing incident response and determining where capability gaps may lie.

As discussed earlier, the Incident Command System (ICS) is a structured framework used to manage emergencies. ICS Staff positions may be integrated into the HEOC in support of emergency managers. When utilizing the ICS General Staff, Operations and Plans Section Chiefs (or a modification thereof) will support the emergency manager by establishing objectives based on leadership guidance and determining resource requirements to meet those objectives. The Logistics Section Chief is responsible for acquiring and receiving resources. Tracking resources is traditionally a function of the Plans Section but remains a primary focus of all sections for accountability, cost efficiency, and, most importantly, safety. However, hospitals may choose to alter this process to fit the specific needs of their organization by decentralizing resource tracking responsibilities across various departments. For instance, the Logistics Section might take a more active role in tracking medical supplies and equipment, while the Finance Section could focus on documenting costs and financial resources. The Operations Section may monitor the deployment and utilization of personnel to ensure that staff are used effectively and safely. By involving multiple sections, hospitals can create a more comprehensive and integrated approach to resource management. This ensures that all aspects of resource utilization are monitored in real-time, enhancing overall accountability and efficiency. Additionally, hospitals can implement advanced resource tracking technologies, such as RFID tags, GPS tracking, and integrated software systems, to streamline the process and provide more accurate data. These modifications help hospitals adapt resource tracking practices to their unique operational structures, ultimately improving their ability to respond to emergencies and maintain safety standards.

It is important for healthcare leaders across the spectrum to forecast critical needs and requirements in the event of an emergency. While we cannot plan for all contingencies, there are certain resources that we know from training and experience should be readily available if disaster strikes. Additionally, existing supply chains should be reviewed routinely to ensure they will continue to be effective in the event of a disaster. Senior leaders and department heads should take time to work with emergency managers to ensure emergency stockpiles are readily available if needed.

Partnerships across the whole community are also necessary to ensure an efficient flow of resources when an incident occurs. The earlier discussion concerning resource ordering through local government and non-government sources underscores the need to establish these relationships early and exercise collaborative efforts often.

Seated in a room with around 120 people – fellow emergency managers and first responders – I couldn't help but notice that, amidst the crowd, there were likely just as many handguns as there were people. Yet, I felt an overwhelming sense of security. This wasn't an emergency; it was a routine meeting, one of many that I attend throughout the year in my role as an emergency manager. In our field, we quickly learn that our effectiveness hinges on the strength of our relationships. It's a truth we live by – you're only as good as your rolodex. No one can be an expert in every possible emergency scenario, but what sets apart strong emergency managers is their ability to quickly tap into a network of contacts who have the expertise, resources, and solutions needed in a crisis.

Meetings like this aren't just about exchanging updates or reviewing protocols; they're opportunities to strengthen these crucial relationships. Every face in the room represents a connection – a fire battalion chief who can deploy hazmat teams to your hospital, a deputy county administrator or county emergency manager with access to critical supplies, an official from the department of transportation who can help you coordinate evacuation routes for patients if there is need for evacuation, a federal law enforcement agent who understands your radiological capabilities and supports your hospitals radiological exercise every year, an EMS Operations Chief who understands your need to develop a robust mass casualty plan and works with you daily to ensure preparedness (you all know who you are). These relationships go beyond professionalism; they're built on mutual trust and a shared commitment to safeguarding our communities and they should be well developed in every community.

~Kim Bailey

For healthcare leaders, understanding and managing resource requirements specific to patient care is crucial for effective emergency response and overall hospital operations. Key resource categories include personnel, medical supplies and equipment, infrastructure, information technology, financial resources, and community resources. Each category presents unique considerations that must be addressed to ensure comprehensive preparedness and efficient management. Personnel encompasses healthcare professionals, support staff, and volunteers who are essential for providing patient care. Ensuring an adequate and well-trained workforce is fundamental to maintaining high-quality care during emergencies. This includes not only medical staff but also administrative and logistical support personnel who facilitate the overall functioning of healthcare facilities. Medical supplies and equipment are critical for treating patients and protecting healthcare workers. This category includes medications, medical devices, and personal protective equipment (PPE), among other essential items. Effective management of these resources involves maintaining an up-to-date inventory, understanding usage rates, and ensuring timely replenishment to prevent shortages during crises. Infrastructure refers to the physical resources required for patient care, such as hospital beds, facilities, and transportation systems. Adequate infrastructure ensures that hospitals can accommodate a surge in patients and provide necessary care without compromising safety or quality. This also involves contingency planning for alternative care sites and transportation logistics for patients and supplies. Information Technology (IT) resources are vital for maintaining data systems, communication infrastructure, and cybersecurity. Effective IT management supports patient tracking, medical supply and equipment inventory management, and the monitoring of usage burn rates. Robust IT systems enhance coordination and decision-making, ensuring that accurate information is available when needed. Financial resources are necessary for budgeting, insurance, and accessing emergency or contingency funding. Sound financial management enables hospitals to sustain operations during emergencies and invest in necessary resources and infrastructure. This includes planning for unexpected costs and ensuring that funding mechanisms are in place to support emergency response efforts. Community resources involve partnerships with other organizations, mutual aid agreements, and community support at local, state, and regional levels. Collaborating with external entities enhances resource availability and operational capacity, allowing for a more integrated and effective response to emergencies. Understanding the availability, accessibility, and operational requirements of these resources is fundamental to leveraging the full capabilities they present. A comprehensive understanding of all these resource categories and their specific considerations is essential for healthcare leaders to effectively manage patient care during emergencies. By ensuring that all resources are adequately available, accessible, and managed, healthcare facilities can enhance their preparedness, response, and overall resilience

Logistics concerns in the face of disaster are earmarked by a need to understand the situation, establish objectives, and focus resources toward meeting those objectives. Within a healthcare environment, resources may be of a clinical (medical) nature, or those material capabilities needed to sustain continuity of operations. Furthermore, depending on the impacts of the incident, time may be a critical factor in identifying a need and locating a source to meet the need. During disaster response and recovery, healthcare leaders are supported by the emergency manager's ability to establish a resource management function within the Hospital Emergency Operations Center. Logistics activities may involve enacting pre-existing contractual agreements, ordering through conventional supply chains, or linking into sourcing networks established by both government and non-government partners at all jurisdictional levels. Establishing local partnerships before a catastrophic event will optimize resourcing through external means. Healthcare leaders should familiarize themselves with those mechanisms put in place by Emergency Preparedness teams to better understand how they will be supported logistically in times of need.

Reference that influenced this chapter are in the below section.

Bibliography

1. Federal Emergency Management Agency. (n.d.). *Resource management in emergency operations.* https://www.fema.gov/emergency-managers/national-preparedness

Chapter 9

Recovery and Resilience in Healthcare Emergency Management

Kimberly Bailey/Thomas Crawford/Sam Hodge

Working for a coastal health system in a geographic region known as the Lowcountry makes us susceptible to hurricanes, tropical storms, and constant flooding. Predictably, we will go into emergency operations at least once a year, calling in our Team A to ensure we can continue to care for a reduced number of inpatients while we ride the storm out and let flood waters subside. We have mitigated the impact of flood waters on our buildings with storm barriers and we've elevated our generators to ensure we can maintain emergency power. Occurring at least once a year, we know how to prepare and respond/operate; however, historically, we were always slow to recover from the financial burden that comes with closing the clinics, cancelling operative cases and reducing our census for up to three days.

It was during a post event hotwash discussion that we walked through the cost of the storm – not based on the increased expense of staff being in the house for seventy-two hours – but the lost revenue. As a five billion-dollar a year health system, we would lose a healthy percentage of the nearly fourteen million dollars we generate a daily and it always created a budget burden that we would have to work our way out of for the remainder of the fiscal year.

"Why wait to recover?" a colleague asked. It was a profound question and it led us to a discussion on how we could recover while we prepared and responded to the event versus waiting until the end. Recovery by design meant that as soon as we began to cancel clinics and elective operative cases that we would immediately begin rescheduling them using evenings and weekends to create the additional capacity required to absorb the volumes lost during the storm. We made it an expectation and it has become a part of our culture – with recovery beginning before the first raindrop falls; thus, mitigating the financial burden and the burden placed on our patients that thought they would have to wait weeks to be rescheduled and months for the service to be provided. Do not wait until the end of an event to begin planning your recovery; on the contrary, run your recovery plans in parallel to the

DOI: 10.4324/9781003529194-9

planning and responding and you will mitigate the impact that emergency event will have on your finances and, more importantly, the patients that we serve.

~Tom Crawford

Healing and rebuilding are aspects of managing healthcare emergencies, with resilience being a journey. In Chapter 9, our attention shifts to the recovery phase, delving into the tactics that healthcare leaders can utilize to steer their organizations through emergency challenges, enabling them to emerge stronger and better equipped for future adversities.

Following a mass casualty event, the recovery process starts when the emergency happens, seamlessly blending with the response actions. Recovery following a mass casualty event is often the most prolonged phase, requiring meticulous attention and preparation. Navigating the recovery phase of healthcare emergencies is often challenging due to frequent changes. Healthcare leaders and emergency managers must exhibit flexibility and adaptability to effectively address these uncertainties. It requires being prepared to modify recovery plans and strategies in response to new information and evolving circumstances. Leaders should remain agile, making decisions based on insights to overcome any obstacles encountered. This may involve reallocating resources, adjusting timelines, or implementing solutions for continued care provision and progress in recovery endeavors. Flexibility also entails listening to input from staff and stakeholders being open to modifying approaches based on their feedback and experiences. In the aftermath of a healthcare crisis, it is crucial for leaders to stay adaptable, enabling them to tackle hurdles, reduce disruptions, and steer the recovery process smoothly. This flexibility is vital for fostering resilience within the organization.

Healthcare leaders should understand that while opportunities for reimbursement through FEMA exist, the process from submission to reimbursement can be lengthy, potentially spanning several years. Although reimbursement programs are available, it is crucial to be prepared for the possibility of having to cover expenses out-of-pocket initially. Hidden costs may arise, and it is essential to track all expenses comprehensively in a centralized location or account to facilitate accurate reporting and reimbursement claims. Engaging your organization's financial leaders or hospital foundation personnel could be highly beneficial in managing this task, as they are experienced in tracking and reporting costs associated with significant events. It is also advisable to anticipate and address the challenges of any required paperwork or expected documentation processes that any entity may require by providing prior training for staff responsible for documentation and expense tracking. This preparation can mitigate errors and ensure smoother processing of reimbursement claims. Most county (or parishes, or boroughs for our Louisiana and Alaska friends) emergency management offices can provide information on various courses offered through the Emergency Management Institute (EMI) that can help with understanding how to file for FEMA reimbursement after a disaster, particularly for a hospital system. These courses often provide information on eligibility requirements, documentation requirements, eligible expenses, and the process of applying for assistance. The FEMA Public Assistance Program and Policy Guide (PAPPG) is an essential resource for understanding the specifics of FEMA's Public Assistance Program, including eligibility, documentation requirements, and the reimbursement process.[1] Specialized consultants can be enlisted to assist with expense tracking and recovery

---

[1] Federal Emergency Management Agency. (2020). *Public Assistance Program and Policy Guide (Version 4)*. U.S. Department of Homeland Security. https://www.fema.gov/sites/default/files/2020-06/fema_public-assistance-program-and-policy-guide_v4_0.pdf

processes, but they can be expensive and a cost you may not be willing or able to incur after you have had to pay for an unexpected disaster.

Emergency procurement procedures are equally crucial during an event, as they ensure that necessary resources are acquired in a timely manner. It is imperative for hospitals to establish emergency purchasing procedures in advance of any incident. This is necessary to guarantee access to supplies that keep operations running smoothly, control expenses, and adhere to regulations. It will also strengthen resilience and allow hospitals to allocate resources efficiently and uphold quality and safety standards. These protocols play a role in the hospital's strategy for emergency readiness and response, allowing them to efficiently handle and bounce back from crises. Understanding which expenses are eligible for reimbursement from organizations like FEMA is essential for collecting and documenting the right information in the appropriate format. Proper knowledge and preparation in these areas are vital for maximizing recovery efforts and ensuring that all eligible expenses are accounted for and reimbursed efficiently.

During the recovery phase of healthcare emergency management, efforts are focused on returning healthcare services to their near-normal state. This stage marks the beginning of the healing and reconstruction process. A pivotal initial step in the recovery phase is assessment. This entails a review of how the emergency has impacted the healthcare institution, its patients, and the wider community. Assessment involves determining the extent of damage to healthcare facilities, evaluating health conditions, and understanding community well-being. Gathering and analyzing data from multiple sources is often essential in gaining an understanding of the situation. It is crucial to evaluate both operational consequences such as infrastructure damage, equipment losses, and disruptions in healthcare provision. Assessing social impacts on patients and healthcare personnel is indispensable.

The comprehensive assessment sets the groundwork for the recovery process, guiding decisions on how to allocate resources, prioritize repairs, and establish support systems for those impacted. After completing the evaluation phase, the focus shifts to recovering resources. This includes replenishing resources that were depleted or damaged during the emergency.

Human resources like healthcare professionals and support staff play a role in ensuring recovery. Prioritizing the well-being of staff members and ensuring they are rested and prepared to resume work is crucial. Material resources such as supplies, equipment, and medications need to be replenished to meet patient needs and sustain healthcare operations. This phase may also involve engaging with partners, suppliers, and government agencies to acquire resources.

Assessing infrastructure both prior to and following a mass casualty event is crucial for evaluating damage and supporting reimbursement opportunities. Conducting thorough pre-event infrastructure assessments establishes a baseline, allowing for an accurate comparison with post-event conditions. This comparative analysis can provide valuable insights into the extent of damage and the effectiveness of response and recovery efforts. In the aftermath of an event, leveraging resources such as the Army Corps of Engineers, which may be accessible through county or state programs, can significantly enhance the assessment process. These experts can offer specialized support in evaluating structural integrity and infrastructure damage, providing detailed reports that are essential for documenting and substantiating reimbursement claims. Engaging with these resources ensures a comprehensive assessment, which not only aids in recovery efforts but also strengthens the case for securing necessary financial support and reimbursement from relevant agencies.

Hospital or healthcare-related facility emergency managers should be equipped to handle requests for equipment and personnel that exceed the capabilities of standard vendors. Effective coordination and logistics are essential in making resources available to support healthcare services restoration. When traditional vendors are unable to supply critical resources, alternative solutions must be sought to ensure continuity of operations during an emergency event. Essential items that may be needed after an event, such as large water pumps, industrial fans, portable power sources, fuel trucks, refrigerated trailers, and mobile morgues, may be necessary to effectively manage hospital operations. In such cases, it is advisable to coordinate with your hospital's emergency management team, who can facilitate access to these specialized resources. They can leverage established networks, relationships, and protocols to procure and deploy these critical assets promptly. By utilizing these resources, healthcare leaders and response teams can maintain operational efficiency and address the diverse needs that arise during a major incident, ultimately supporting a more effective and organized response.

An often underestimated but crucial aspect of the recovery process is providing support to staff. The demanding nature of emergency situations can have an impact on healthcare professionals both physically and emotionally. It is essential for leaders to provide support through services like counseling, wellness programs, and sufficient rest periods to prevent burnout and maintain staff morale. A workforce that is resilient is better able to uphold quality patient care and operational stability during prolonged emergencies. Emergencies can have psychological impacts on patients, their families, and healthcare personnel. Offering support is vital in addressing the trauma and emotional requirements arising from the crisis. Support services may encompass counseling, mental health assistance, and group therapy for those impacted. It is crucial to provide a nurturing space that promotes self-care and mental well-being for healthcare professionals dealing with stress levels and burnout in emergency situations. Introducing initiatives like aid, stress management training, and peer support networks can greatly improve the overall welfare of the healthcare workforce. For patients and their loved ones, access to health resources and fostering an atmosphere are essential in aiding their recovery. Equally important is the well-being of healthcare staff, which is fundamental to maintaining a robust and effective workforce. Ensuring that employees are supported and cared for is essential to sustaining their performance and commitment. If organizations neglect the health and welfare of their staff, they risk diminished morale, reduced productivity, and ultimately, compromised patient care. By prioritizing the well-being of employees, healthcare institutions foster a positive work environment where staff are motivated and equipped to deliver high-quality care, thus reinforcing the overall resilience and efficacy of the organization during emergencies and beyond.

Rebuilding infrastructure sometimes plays a role in the recovery process by focusing on the restoration of healthcare facilities to their pre-emergency conditions or better. This can involve repairing buildings, replacing damaged equipment, and ensuring the functionality of systems such as power, water supply, and communication networks. In addition to addressing immediate downtime, long-term outage plans should be developed to manage extended disruptions effectively. The aim is to establish an environment where healthcare services can resume operations smoothly. Collaborating with engineers' construction teams and specialists is key during this phase to ensure that repairs are done effectively while meeting safety standards. Additionally, this phase offers an opportunity to integrate resilience measures like reinforcing structures against emergencies and upgrading systems for preparedness. Ensuring that healthcare facilities are operating effectively is vital for the community's recovery and the continued provision of health services. This includes identifying and preparing secondary locations for patient care, which can serve as temporary facilities if the primary site becomes untenable.

Continuity planning is essential for this reason. It ensures that an organization can maintain operations and deliver critical services during and after a mass casualty event or significant disruption. Comprehensive continuity planning involves developing robust downtime procedures and long-term outage plans to address various scenarios that may impact normal operations. Expanding these procedures involves detailing specific actions to be taken during periods of operational downtime or major disaster events, such as succession planning, alternative workflows, backup systems, and emergency protocols to minimize service interruptions. Planning for these secondary locations involves assessing their suitability, ensuring they are adequately equipped, and coordinating with relevant stakeholders to ensure seamless integration into the overall response strategy. By incorporating these elements into continuity planning, organizations can enhance their resilience, ensure continuity of care, and effectively manage the challenges posed by significant emergencies or operational disruptions. Continuity planning requires developing strategies to address risks, establish backup systems, and ensure that staff are ready to handle future crises. It also entails collaborating with stakeholders such as government agencies, community groups, and other healthcare providers to build a united and resilient response network. Continuity planning is crucial for organizations to ensure resilience and operational stability during and after significant disruptions or emergencies. Developing and expanding downtime procedures is a vital component of this planning, as it involves establishing detailed protocols for maintaining essential functions and minimizing service interruptions when primary systems or facilities are temporarily unavailable. These procedures should outline clear steps for managing the immediate impacts of downtime, including alternative workflows, backup systems, and communication strategies to ensure continuity of services.

It is important to address long-term outage plans to manage extended disruptions effectively. This entails creating strategies for sustaining operations over prolonged periods when primary resources or facilities are compromised. Key elements of these plans include identifying and preparing secondary locations for patient care, which can serve as temporary or supplementary sites to provide medical services if the main facility is rendered inoperable. These secondary locations should be evaluated for their capacity to meet patient needs, equipped with necessary medical supplies and infrastructure, and integrated into the overall continuity strategy. By incorporating these considerations into continuity planning, organizations can enhance their preparedness, maintain service delivery, and effectively navigate the challenges presented by significant operational disruptions.

Healthcare leaders and hospital emergency managers have a role in evaluating and prioritizing their organizations' needs during the recovery phase. Effective continuity planning necessitates comprehensive assessments of both immediate and long-term requirements essential for resuming normal operations after a significant disruption. This involves prioritizing critical aspects of care to ensure that all individuals receive the necessary medical attention and support. For example, during a mass casualty event or operational emergency, the Emergency Department (ED) often takes precedence over other hospital operations due to its central role in managing acute patient needs. Therefore, priority may be given to the ED, ensuring that it is adequately staffed and resourced to handle the surge in patients. This may involve reallocating resources and personnel from less critical areas, closing or scaling down non-essential departments, and redirecting ambulatory staff to support acute care areas. By concentrating efforts on maintaining robust front-line operations and optimizing the ED's functionality, organizations can effectively manage immediate patient needs and facilitate a more efficient response to the crisis.

Long-term planning must also address the gradual restoration of full operational capacity. This includes evaluating the ongoing needs for staffing, equipment, and facility repairs, and developing strategies for a phased return to normal operations. Such planning ensures that critical services remain uninterrupted while supporting a structured recovery process that allows for the stabilization and eventual normalization of all hospital functions.

Healthcare leaders and hospital emergency managers will need to pinpoint the areas that urgently need attention and allocate resources accordingly. It is crucial to prioritize the restoration of facilities since damaged infrastructure can significantly hinder healthcare service delivery. Leaders must assess which repairs and renovations are most pressing to ensure the safety and functionality of the healthcare setting. Additionally, replenishing supplies, equipment and medications is vital after an emergency may have depleted them. Evaluating inventory levels and collaborating with suppliers and partners are steps in restocking these resources. By identifying and prioritizing these needs, healthcare leaders and hospital emergency managers can effectively steer their organizations through the recovery phase, ensuring healthcare delivery.

Addressing supply chain challenges is critical for ensuring the seamless operation of healthcare facilities during and after significant events. Engaging in targeted exercises with the supply chain team can be instrumental in identifying potential issues and developing strategies to mitigate them before a crisis occurs. These exercises allow for the evaluation of existing supply chain processes, the identification of vulnerabilities, and the implementation of contingency plans to address potential disruptions.

Establishing redundancy in vendor options is a key strategy for enhancing resilience, much like the age-old wisdom of not putting all your eggs in one basket. Relying on a single vendor for critical supplies is akin to placing all your eggs in one basket – if that basket falls, all the eggs break. Similarly, if a sole vendor is affected by an event or disruption, the entire supply chain can be compromised. By diversifying vendor sources and building relationships with multiple suppliers, organizations effectively distribute their eggs across several baskets. This reduces the risk of supply shortages and ensures a more reliable flow of essential materials and resources, safeguarding the hospital's ability to respond effectively during emergencies. This strategy not only enhances preparedness but also ensures that the hospital can maintain operations and provide continuous care, even when faced with unforeseen challenges. This approach not only helps to alleviate supply chain issues but also strengthens overall preparedness, enabling organizations to maintain operational continuity even when faced with unexpected challenges. A well-structured supply chain strategy that includes redundancy and proactive exercises is vital for effectively managing the complexities of emergency response and recovery.

Leadership in healthcare often prioritizes bottom-line considerations, focusing on efficiency and cost-effectiveness. However, in the context of emergency events, traditional policies and procedures may not always align with the unpredictable nature of such incidents. Emergencies frequently present scenarios that deviate from established plans, requiring a flexible and adaptive approach. In these situations, it is crucial to rely on the expertise of a seasoned emergency manager. A strong emergency manager plays a pivotal role in navigating the complexities of crisis response, offering guidance and support tailored to the specific demands of the situation. Their experience and training equip an emergency manager to interpret and adapt existing protocols to fit the evolving circumstances, ensuring that the response remains effective and organized. By leveraging the knowledge and leadership of the emergency manager, healthcare organizations can better manage the inherent uncertainties of emergency events and maintain operational continuity amidst disruption, ensuring a bounce back.

A key duty of healthcare leaders during the recovery period is to extract insights from the crisis and integrate them into readiness strategies. This entails conducting event evaluations and discussions to pinpoint effective practices and areas needing enhancement. Leaders should seek input from employees, patients, and other stakeholders to gain a view of strengths and weaknesses in emergency responses and recovery efforts. These insights should be recorded, assessed, and translated into recommendations for bolstering readiness plans. By incorporating these learnings into strategies, healthcare leaders can fortify the organization's resilience and enhance its preparedness for upcoming crises. Embracing learning and improvement is fundamental in instilling a culture of preparedness within the healthcare entity. Adopting a proactive approach not only enhances an organization's capacity to recover from emergencies but also plays a critical role in safeguarding the well-being of patients, staff members, and the broader community. By anticipating potential challenges and implementing preventive measures, healthcare facilities can significantly improve their resilience and effectiveness in managing crises. This proactive stance ensures that the organization is well prepared to address and mitigate the impacts of emergencies, thereby protecting those it serves and supports.

To maximize the benefits of this approach, it is essential to establish a robust plan for tracking and implementing identified improvements. This involves developing a systematic follow-up process to monitor the progress of enhancements and ensure that they are effectively integrated into operational procedures. This is also the responsibility of the hospital's emergency management team. Regular evaluations and updates to the improvement plan will help to address any emerging issues and maintain the organization's readiness for future incidents. By committing to continuous improvement and diligent oversight, organizations can reinforce their emergency preparedness and response capabilities, ultimately fostering a safer and more resilient environment for all stakeholders. Establishing connections with the community plays a role in navigating through the post-crisis phase of healthcare emergency management.

Emergency managers understand that a successful recovery requires teamwork that goes beyond the hospital setting. By forming and nurturing partnerships with community groups, public health agencies, and local authorities, leaders can ensure a thorough approach to rebuilding healthcare services. These collaborations promote the exchange of resources, information, and expertise which are crucial for addressing the needs that arise during the recovery phase. Engaging with the community significantly enhances the effectiveness of recovery initiatives and fosters a stronger bond between healthcare institutions and the populations they serve. By actively involving community members in decision-making processes and recovery planning, healthcare leaders not only improve the alignment of their strategies with local needs but also cultivate trust and solidarity. This collaborative approach ensures that recovery efforts are informed by diverse perspectives and tailored to address the specific challenges faced by the community.

Building relationships characterized by mutual information exchange is particularly beneficial. When healthcare organizations proactively share information and seek input from community stakeholders, they demonstrate transparency and a commitment to inclusivity. This openness not only strengthens community support but also helps identify and address potential issues more effectively. Engaging with the community in this way underscores the organization's dedication to addressing the needs of its constituents and reinforces a sense of shared responsibility and partnership. By prioritizing such collaborative relationships, healthcare institutions can enhance the resilience of their recovery efforts and build a more cohesive and supportive community network. This engagement helps align recovery priorities with residents' needs and expectations, ensuring that recovery efforts are responsive to and resonate with community concerns. By integrating insights gained from emergencies, healthcare organizations can enhance their readiness and response capabilities. The process of recovery not only strengthens the healthcare system as a whole but also equips it to withstand and react efficiently to upcoming challenges. The establishment of collaborations with the community enables healthcare executives to tap into expertise and assets that may not be easily available within the healthcare institution itself. For example, community organizations could offer volunteer help, arrange donation drives for supplies, or grant access to spaces that can serve as facilities during facility upgrades. Health organizations and government bodies provide information on community health trends and emergency preparedness while also considering the regulatory aspects that impact recovery efforts in a locality. By engaging with the community, healthcare leaders help build resilience throughout the community's fabric and improve the community's crisis management capabilities. This promotes a culture of preparedness through their involvement in recovery projects. This cooperative strategy strengthens the healthcare organization's capacity to recover from emergencies and supports the community's wellbeing by guaranteeing that essential healthcare services are restored and preserved during critical times. Community involvement is not an obligation but a vital element in achieving a prosperous and enduring recovery in managing healthcare emergencies.

Creating resilience within healthcare organizations is an effort that extends beyond merely recovering from crises or emergencies. Leaders in the healthcare sector have a responsibility to enhance long-term resilience by putting in place strategies that strengthen readiness and response capacities. Regularly revisiting and refining emergency protocols and procedures is essential for maintaining preparedness. This includes evaluating responses to emergencies to identify areas needing improvement and integrating insights gained from each occurrence. By staying aware of evolving risks and industry standards, healthcare institutions can adapt their plans to effectively manage unexpected situations. Taking a proactive stance enables the organization to remain flexible and prepared to mitigate the effects of unexpected events or emergencies.

Maintaining readiness among healthcare workers is vital to conduct training sessions and exercises. These training sessions simulate emergency situations, allowing staff members to rehearse response procedures and improve their communication and teamwork skills when working with organizations. Training serves not only to enhance individual competencies but also to promote a sense of unity and enable staff to become familiar with their roles in stressful scenarios. Continuous training plays a role in reinforcing the expertise of employees and fostering a culture of preparedness within the organization. By updating and broadening the knowledge and abilities of staff members, training programs ensure that they are well equipped to handle both everyday tasks and unforeseen emergencies efficiently. This ongoing progress not only boosts personal skills but also helps strengthen the resilience of the organization, enabling it to face changing challenges and uphold top-notch performance levels consistently. Training sessions are regularly mandated by accreditation bodies that expect healthcare establishments to demonstrate their dedication to enhancing and sustaining staff skills. Adhering to these training mandates guarantees compliance with industry norms and elevates the credibility and efficiency of the organization. Hospital leaders and emergency managers should invest in training and make it a top priority to cultivate a culture that encourages quick and effective responses during emergencies. This approach empowers employees to handle crises confidently and competently, resulting in improved outcomes and strengthening the institution's overall readiness and ability to bounce back from challenges.

Integrating technologies into readiness plans is a key part of strengthening resilience in emergencies. Cutting-edge tools such as telemedicine and digital communication platforms can significantly boost the effectiveness of disaster response strategies. Progress in healthcare tech like data sharing and remote patient monitoring is crucial for improving response capabilities and optimizing resource allocation during crises. Immediate data sharing enables healthcare teams to exchange information smoothly and work together more efficiently in times of need. Continuous monitoring of patients from a distance enables the assessment of their health status while offering crucial information for making timely and precise interventions when necessary. Sophisticated decision-making aids facilitate well-informed choices to ensure the efficient allocation of resources and effective management of patient care under intense circumstances.

Using data and analytics is essential for strengthening resilience in healthcare settings. Healthcare leaders can analyze data and performance metrics to spot trends and patterns that can guide improvements in emergency response efforts. Insights from data-driven decisions help optimize resource allocation and shape risk management strategies. For healthcare organizations to enhance their emergency preparedness plans and adapt to changing challenges, it is vital to leverage data for continuous improvement. Through the collection and analysis of data, organizations can gain valuable insights into different facets of their emergency response capabilities and operational efficiency. For instance, the number of patients treated or types of injuries sustained in contrast to response times and resource use can guide the creation of better response procedures and supply use. Likewise, insights from evaluations conducted after emergencies and practice exercises outline performance indicators, and input from personnel aids in recognizing both strengths and areas needing enhancement in emergency preparedness.

In emergencies and crisis situations, having up to date information about equipment status and staffing levels is crucial for improving response tactics and distributing resources effectively. Analyzing incident frequency and resource utilization patterns can assist in prioritizing training sessions and drills to address urgent needs and improve preparedness gaps. Correlating risk factors like location and population demographics can aid in targeting mitigation strategies and making decisions about infrastructure development. By combining and examining data sources like these, the healthcare sector enables organizations to boost their readiness for emergencies and improve training methods, and enhance risk management practices, thereby strengthening their ability to tackle upcoming obstacles effectively.

Creating resilience within healthcare organizations involves a strategy that includes planning ahead effectively, integrating technology, providing support to staff, and utilizing data efficiently. Emphasizing these elements not only improves an organization's ability to respond to emergencies promptly but also cultivates a resilient culture that promotes continuous readiness and operational excellence in the face of uncertainties. Proactively investing in resilience guarantees that healthcare systems can maintain their standards of care and support for their communities, even during challenging times.

I began my journey in public safety shortly after graduating high school in 1984, driven by the inspiration of the TV show EMERGENCY! My aspiration was to emulate heroes like Johnny Gage and Roy DeSoto. My first significant encounter with emergency management came in 1989 during Hurricane Hugo. This Category 4 storm, with winds reaching 135-140 mph, left a trail of devastation just north of Charleston, South Carolina. The storm surge, estimated at 13 feet above sea level, caused severe flooding and destruction. My own home experienced about 4 feet of storm surge damage, and the impact of Hugo was a vivid reminder of nature's power and the critical need for effective planning and response. While our makeshift donation center at the fire station helped, it was clear that improved planning and coordination were essential.

In 2007, I transitioned into emergency management with Georgetown County, working under Director Louis Dougan, whose mentorship was invaluable. As Director, I led responses to multiple presidential-declared disasters, including major floods and hurricanes. These experiences highlighted the importance of not only immediate response but also long-term recovery and resilience. Effective recovery strategies and building community resilience are crucial for ensuring that affected areas can return to normalcy and that healthcare facilities can continue to serve their communities effectively.

In September 2019, I took on a new challenge at Conway Medical Center as Director of Emergency Management and Safety. The COVID-19 pandemic was a pivotal moment, revealing the vulnerabilities and demands faced by healthcare systems. The pandemic underscored the need for hospitals to remain operational and resilient, not only for the public but also for first responders. It also emphasized the necessity for comprehensive recovery plans to address long-term impacts and to enhance the resilience of healthcare facilities.

Healthcare facilities play a vital role in community resilience and recovery. It is imperative that hospitals have a thorough understanding of emergency management principles and the incident command structure. Facilities that are part of larger healthcare systems have an advantage in patient evacuation and resource management, but every facility must be equipped to handle emergencies and support recovery efforts.

Building and nurturing relationships is foundational to effective emergency management. Hospitals must engage in regular training, exercises, and regional collaborations to strengthen these connections. Participation in regional healthcare coalitions and Local Emergency Planning Committees (LEPCs) fosters trust, enhances communication, and improves overall preparedness. These relationships are crucial not only for immediate response but also for effective recovery and long-term resilience.

My journey from a volunteer firefighter inspired by a TV show to a seasoned emergency management professional reflects a deep commitment to protecting communities and advancing the field. The lessons learned from Hurricane Hugo, numerous hurricanes, and the COVID-19 pandemic underscore the importance of continuous improvement, collaboration, and preparedness. They highlight that recovery and resilience are integral to ensuring our healthcare systems and communities can withstand and recover from any disaster.

–Sam Hodge, Horry County Director of Emergency Management

Recovery, within healthcare emergency management, is a stage that requires both effort and transformation. It signifies a moment where healthcare leaders must apply the lessons learned from the emergency response to aid in healing, rebuilding, and establishing long-term resilience within their organizations. While navigating through this phase is undeniably tough, it also brings forth opportunities for progress, development, and fortification across various aspects.

In the process of recovery, healthcare leaders are responsible not only for fixing structures and replenishing essential resources but also for addressing the emotional impacts on patients, families, and staff. This comprehensive approach involves evaluating the extent of the emergency's effects on healthcare operations, patient care services, and community well-being. Through assessments, leaders can effectively prioritize recovery efforts by pinpointing areas that require attention and setting clear goals to restore normalcy.

The recovery stage provides healthcare organizations with a chance for reflection and enhancement. It encourages leaders to examine and improve emergency response protocols, operational practices, and communication methods based on real-life experiences and feedback obtained during the crisis. This continuous process ensures that the organization enhances its capabilities and strengthens its preparedness to handle emergencies efficiently. At the core of recovery lies the development of resilience within healthcare institutions. Resilience is more than bouncing back from tough times; it is about being able to adjust, learn, and come up with new ideas when faced with ongoing obstacles. Leaders in the healthcare sector have a role in nurturing resilience by fostering a culture of improvement, encouraging staff involvement in recovery efforts, and incorporating strategies to build resilience into everyday practices. Armed with this knowledge, leaders can ensure that their organizations not only recover from crises but also emerge more resilient and better equipped to protect the health and well-being of their communities in the face of future challenges. The recovery phase following a significant crisis, such as the COVID-19 pandemic, represents not merely a period of restoration but rather a transformative journey toward building a more resilient healthcare system. This journey emphasizes the need for organizations to evolve their capacity to adapt, respond effectively, and remain robust amidst uncertainty. The unprecedented impact of COVID-19, despite its inclusion in risk assessment tools, far exceeded initial expectations, revealing critical vulnerabilities and prompting substantial modifications across the healthcare landscape.

In response to the pandemic, extensive modifications were made to support operational continuity and enhance preparedness. These changes included the rapid adaptation of infrastructure and design standards to better accommodate emergent needs. For instance, the implementation of negative pressure rooms became a priority to effectively manage airborne contaminants and prevent the spread of infectious diseases. Hospitals and healthcare facilities also invested in advanced ventilation systems, increased capacity for intensive care units (ICUs), and redesigned patient care areas to ensure safe and efficient treatment environments.

New industry standards emerged, focusing on enhanced infection control measures, flexibility in facility design, and improved patient flow management. This included incorporating modular design elements that allow for the rapid reconfiguration of spaces to meet varying patient volumes and clinical requirements. The integration of advanced technology for real-time monitoring and telemedicine capabilities also became more prevalent, supporting both patient care and staff safety. These adaptations not only address the immediate impacts of the pandemic but also lay the foundation for a healthcare system that is better equipped to handle future challenges, demonstrating a commitment to continuous improvement and resilience in the face of evolving threats. These sources provide comprehensive insights into the evolving standards and practices in healthcare design and infection control, offering evidence to support the implementation of new industry standards in response to emerging challenges.

I always leave my door open when I am in the building. My office is kind of like the kitchen at my house, where people naturally come together. It's a place usually filled with chatter, spontaneous meetings and occasional laughter amidst the chaos. It serves as a comforting space for sharing updates seeking advice and fostering teamwork in times of crisis. But today my door was shut. I sat quietly at my desk. I needed some time to reflect. As someone who has dealt with many emergencies as an emergency manager and a former first responder, the challenges posed by the COVID 19 pandemic had truly tested my strength and resilience like never before. The pandemic had been a journey for all of us, pushing our nation's healthcare system to its limits, revealing both its strengths and weaknesses.

Alone in my office that day, memories of the months of responding to the pandemic came rushing back. The nation was engulfed in uncertainty and fear during those first weeks. I found myself adapting to become more prepared than I ever had before even though I live in a coastal community prone to hurricanes. During the rush to secure supplies for our own home before the panic set in across the globe, I had the foresight to think about the importance of essentials we might need. My husband Brad (a Critical Care Paramedic) and I changed from a couple used to being reasonable about assessing risk to something resembling survivalist preppers due to the uncertainty and the sense of gravity we felt was at hand. Our children ages 20, 16 and 9 were alarmed at the unusual items that were arriving from our regular delivery service every day. Cases of hand sanitizer, gloves, disinfectant, face masks and thermometers were on the short list. I did not forget the toilet paper. We had plenty for the duration of the COVID event. But one evening one of our leaders came into the HEOC looking a little worried. His wife couldn't find toilet paper anywhere. With two daughters at home, they were running out fast. I felt relieved and a little proud knowing I had enough at home that I could share. I promised to bring some for him the next day, and I did. It may have been just a gesture, and we laughed about it a little in the moment, but it highlighted the sense of community and support that was crucial for all of us to feel safe during those challenging times. It served as a reminder to me that preparedness went beyond supplies and protocols; it involved anticipating and meeting the needs that arose in a crisis, even if that just meant the comfort of toilet paper.

Each day of the COVID pandemic presented new obstacles for all of us in healthcare. There were moments when our standard protocols seemed insufficient in the face of such an unprecedented crisis. Like hospitals nationwide we faced a surge in patients, dwindling supplies and the overwhelming uncertainty that hung over us all. I remembered the nights, the calls for help and the urgent quest to secure an adequate supply of personal protective gear for our clinical teams. The urgency was palpable. The stakes were undeniably high. However, amidst the turmoil I also witnessed displays of resilience. Doctors and nurses at every hospital in the area worked tirelessly. Often putting their own wellbeing at risk to provide care for patients.

I witnessed the community coming together to donate supplies and show support for healthcare workers in every way. During a day filled with activity, a small but very impactful gesture lifted the spirits of our tired staff. A local lawn sign company acknowledging the dedication of our healthcare heroes gifted a "Heroes Work Here" sign. It was placed prominently at the hospital entrance and quickly became a symbol of pride and motivation. Whenever staff members passed by, they were reminded that their efforts and sacrifices were acknowledged and valued by the community. Though simple the sign carried meaning lifting morale and reinforcing our determination to overcome challenges together. I also observed innovation flourishing through advancements in telemedicine and new patient management protocols developed swiftly to address the influx of cases. These experiences filled me with pride and so much gratitude to be part of this amazing care team.

As the pandemic progressed our hospital's role expanded beyond its boundaries. Local emergency managers often sought my advice and insights recognizing our hospital as a symbol of readiness and strength, not to mention where most of the action was happening. It was humbling to be viewed as a source of support for my emergency management family, and a glaring reflection of the trust we had established well before this event began within our emergency management network throughout this state. We aligned our strategies, gave progress updates and shared the valuable lessons learned. Our discussions ranged from the best way to distribute protective equipment or sharing resources needed for providing mental health support for frontline workers to our disappointment about major community events and annual conferences we all looked forward to that would sadly not be taking place that year. The collaboration between the emergency management community proved invaluable time and time again as it established a network of shared knowledge and resources that bolstered our hospital's and our state's response. These interactions reaffirmed my belief that unity's key in any crisis. Through efforts sharing insights and offering support we were able to tackle challenges more efficiently and ensure our communities remained resilient and well prepared for whatever came our way.

In that moment I found myself contemplating the lessons we had learned. I realized that the resilience displayed during COVID 19 could be applied beyond pandemics to all types of emergencies. The key lay in recognizing our strengths and leveraging them further. I pondered on the importance of readiness and flexibility. As I reflected on these teachings a fresh sense of purpose filled me. I believed that the strength we demonstrated during the challenges of COVID 19 could be utilized to enhance our readiness, for any crises. It involved fostering a culture of preparedness, where everyone comprehended their responsibilities and had the tools to take action. It meant establishing communication channels and guaranteeing that support mechanisms were in place for those at the forefront.

Standing up from my seat a wave of determination swept through me. The journey had been demanding yet enlightening. Our healthcare system, and numerous others nationwide, had exhibited resilience. It was now our collective responsibility to carry forward those insights. With that mindset and an unwavering dedication to progress I believed we could confront any obstacle that awaited us. I opened the door again. Stepping out of my office into the hallway I was prepared to guide my team towards a future where resilience wasn't merely a measure but an integral aspect of our operations. I was resolute in ensuring that the lessons gleaned from COVID 19 would guide us through times and leave us stronger, on the other side, and it was time for a coffee.

~ Kim Bailey

Bibliography

Flexibility in Facility Design

1. American Society for Health Care Engineering (ASHE). (2020). *Designing for flexibility: Health care facility design trends*. ASHE Journal.
2. Healthcare Design Magazine. (2021). *Adapting healthcare spaces: Flexibility and resilience in design*. Healthcare Design.
3. Architectural Record. (2021). *The future of healthcare facility design: Flexibility and adaptation*. Architectural Record.

Improved Patient Flow Management:

4. Journal of Healthcare Management. (2021). *Optimizing patient flow in healthcare settings: Best practices and innovations*. Journal of Healthcare Management.
5. Institute for Healthcare Improvement (IHI). (2020). *Improving patient flow and reducing delays in healthcare delivery*. IHI Report.
6. The New England Journal of Medicine. (2021). *Strategies for managing patient flow in emergency situations*. NEJM.

Chapter 10

Leveraging Emergency Management to Influence Other Hospital Programs

Kimberly Bailey/Thomas Crawford

From a Chief Operating Officer's perspective, the synergies between emergency management principles and other hospital programs should not be organic, it needs to be purposeful. The first tenet of emergency management is mitigation and to mitigate you must continuously review your environment of care (hazard vulnerability analysis), document any material weaknesses, and operationalize a plan that mitigates the impact on your care environment. We, at times, may use different terminology; however, the premise between a hazard vulnerability and a failure mode and effects analysis (FMEA) are very similar in their approach to mitigating risk. Emergency management in healthcare focuses on preparing for, responding to, and recovering from emergencies, disasters, and other disruptions that could impact care delivery and hospital operations to the point that patients and care team members are put at risk. A Failure Mode and Effects Analysis is a systematic approach to identifying potential failures in a process or system before they occur and, once again, implementing corrective actions to prevent or mitigate their occurrence. Although emergency management is broader in scope, again the premise is the same, how do we ensure a perpetual state of readiness for our health system? By leveraging an emergency management mentality and its guiding principles to influence all processes, systems and programs that make up the construct of your care delivery model.

-Tom Crawford

A hospital's emergency management program plays a role in safeguarding the well-being of patients and staff. The various safety initiatives and programs developed by the organization contribute to a resilient preparedness stance, creating a secure healthcare environment. It is essential to integrate the emergency management program with hospital programs for these reasons. The systematic approach of emergency management significantly boosts the hospital's readiness and resilience. Incorporating emergency management principles into hospital projects ensures a

DOI: 10.4324/9781003529194-10

coordinated response to incidents, whether they are minor disruptions or major disasters. This integration fosters a culture of safety and preparedness across the organization, aligning all departments and staff for improved patient care and safety. Leveraging the expertise and resources of the emergency management program helps in refining protocols for hospital programs, enhancing efficiency, reducing vulnerabilities, and strengthening the healthcare delivery system through consistent standards and practices.

This teamwork across departments readies the hospital for unexpected situations and also enhances day-to-day functions, making the institution more adaptable and resilient to changes. Integrating emergency management with hospital programs that adhere to accreditation standards in emergency management holds advantages. Accreditation bodies often outline requirements for emergency readiness within their standards. By aligning your hospital's emergency management program with these accreditation criteria, you can ensure compliance and enhance your performance during accreditation assessments. This alignment establishes a framework for enhancement, guaranteeing that the hospital upholds top-notch care and preparedness standards.

Consider a Workplace Violence Program as an example. A hospital's emergency management program can greatly bolster a workplace violence program by including preventive measures, response tactics, and support mechanisms. The fusion of a hospital's emergency management program with a Workplace Violence Program can substantially fortify the safety and security protocols within a healthcare facility. By collaborating on risk evaluations, these programs can collectively assess the hospital's susceptibility to workplace violence, integrating actions and response tactics into emergency planning strategies. Exchanging information on incidents and trends related to workplace violence informs emergency management approaches.

Staff training and education programs can be tailored to prepare individuals for workplace violence incidents and emergencies, encouraging a response strategy. Consistent communication protocols help in alerting and coordinating responses during instances of violence and broader emergency events. By incorporating workplace violence response protocols into emergency plans and conducting simulation exercises, readiness and response capabilities are strengthened. Implementing security measures collectively, such as forming threat assessment teams, addresses both the prevention of workplace violence and preparedness for emergencies. Coordinating support services and offering health assistance to affected employees ensure care. Regular reporting mechanisms and data analysis from these programs aid in identifying trends and areas that need improvement. Adhering to standards in both workplace violence prevention and emergency management programs ensures compliance while enhancing safety within the hospital environment. Integrating workplace violence prevention strategies into emergency management practices helps hospitals establish a unified approach to safeguarding the well-being of their staff, patients, and visitors. This holistic strategy fosters a culture of safety and resilience in healthcare settings. Emergency management initiatives can significantly impact the effectiveness of infection prevention programs within hospital systems by providing support.

Hospitals can ensure an effective response to disease outbreaks by setting up clear protocols. Regular training sessions are crucial for assessing the staff's readiness in handling emergencies and improving preparedness. Communication coordination during outbreaks is essential for sharing information, facilitating quick decision-making and response coordination. During disease crises, hospitals can manage increased demand by implementing strategies such as setting up isolation units or expanding treatment areas, ensuring sufficient resources are available. Working with infection prevention teams helps develop strategies for disinfection, waste management, and patient isolation to prevent infections from spreading within healthcare settings. Including infection prevention measures in emergency response plans is crucial for reducing disease transmission during disasters or mass casualty incidents, enhancing resilience. Using technology for real-time monitoring of infection rates assists in the detection of outbreaks, enabling prompt proactive measures to be taken. It is imperative for hospital emergency management to collaborate closely with facility leaders to ensure an approach to protecting infrastructure.

It is crucial to prioritize the protection of hospital facilities and utilities, as any disruptions could have an impact on hospital operations and patient care. By working strategically with other programs, emergency management teams can create plans to reduce risks, enhance the resilience of infrastructure, and guarantee that essential services continue to function during emergencies. Equally important is maintaining a supply chain for resources to enable hospitals to operate effectively in times of crisis. Joint efforts between emergency management and facilities teams can help identify weaknesses, establish supply channels, and develop contingency measures to handle interruptions. Another critical aspect of collaboration involves ensuring that hospital buildings are structurally resilient. Through collaboration, emergency management and facilities teams can evaluate weaknesses, make upgrades or reinforcements, and create protocols for building evacuation or sheltering in emergencies. Planning for utility failures and implementing backup systems are elements of this partnership since reliable utilities are vital for hospital operations. By coordinating their actions, emergency management and facilities teams can set up backup systems like generators or alternate power sources to ensure services in case of utility failures.

Collaboration between hospital emergency management and facilities is vital for safeguarding infrastructure. By working to address issues concerning the protection of facilities, maintaining supply chains, ensuring structural resilience, and preparing for utility failures, hospitals can improve their readiness and response capabilities. This ultimately helps in safeguarding care and staff safety during emergencies. Collaboration between hospital emergency managers and the risk department is vital for managing safety and risk aspects within healthcare settings. Joint efforts are crucial for planning the storage and handling of materials to prevent accidents and reduce risks. Through coordinated efforts, emergency managers and the risk department can establish decontamination procedures to respond swiftly in cases of material exposure incidents, ensuring the safety of patients, staff and visitors. Cooperation between these departments also facilitates the development of protocols for handling chemical spills safely. Proper training on managing substances is essential for staff preparedness in responding to chemical spills. Working together enables emergency managers and the risk department to ensure that employees are well equipped to handle incidents, minimizing impacts on patient care and hospital safety overall. Fire safety is a priority in healthcare facilities, underscoring the importance of collaboration between emergency managers and the risk department in this area.

They work together to create fire evacuation strategies customized to fit the hospital's design and patient demographics, guaranteeing organized evacuations in case of emergencies. Some hospitals incorporate the fire and life safety program into their emergency management efforts, bringing together safety measures within a framework. This unified method enables coordination and synchronization of fire safety procedures with emergency response tactics.

By including the fire and life safety program within the emergency management framework, hospitals can establish a unified approach to safety and emergency readiness. This helps in maximizing resources and improving communication channels during situations. The integration typically leads to efficiency, consistency, and effectiveness in handling both safety procedures and emergency responses. Conversely, some hospitals opt to maintain a separation between the fire and life safety program and the emergency management program due to needs and regulatory factors. Keeping these programs distinct can offer attention on fire safety compliance, regulatory requirements, and particular life safety protocols. Hospitals following this approach may prioritize meeting industry regulations related to fire safety, building codes, and life protection measures that demand expertise. By segregating these programs, hospitals can adopt a targeted approach toward enhancing compliance with regulations governing fire safety standards in their sector. Ultimately, whether hospitals decide on integration or separation of fire and life safety programs from emergency management depends on factors like setup, regulatory obligations, resource distribution, and the desired level of expertise in addressing fire safety measures and life protection protocols.

Both approaches have their advantages, and the decision to combine or separate these programs should be tailored to the needs, priorities, and operational factors of the hospital in order to effectively ensure the safety of patients, staff and visitors during emergencies and non-emergencies. Offering fire prevention training for both staff and patients also boosts safety awareness and readiness, decreasing the chances of fire incidents and fostering a safety-oriented culture within the hospital setting. Collaboration between hospital emergency managers and the risk department can improve safety measures, mitigate risks, and cultivate a sense of preparedness within the healthcare facility.

In hospitals with radiation capabilities, collaborative efforts between emergency managers and the radiology department are crucial for developing emergency protocols to address radiation incidents. Training staff on handling emergencies equips them with the expertise to respond appropriately in such scenarios, minimizing potential risks and ensuring everyone's safety. Planning for handling or transferring materials on site necessitates coordinated actions involving external partners at local, state, and Federal levels to uphold stringent safety standards and prevent any oversights that could jeopardize the wellbeing of patients, staff, and the nearby community. Building connections between the emergency manager at your hospital and the IT department is vital to ensure operations and efficient responses to emergencies in healthcare settings. A key reason for this partnership is the creation of procedures for handling system downtime, which are crucial for managing IT failures that could affect important hospital functions. By collaborating with the IT team, emergency managers can help establish downtime protocols that detail steps for maintaining essential services during system outages, reducing disruptions to patient care and operational continuity. The growing threat of cybersecurity breaches in healthcare highlights the significance of teamwork between emergency management and IT professionals. Safeguarding electronic health records and sensitive data is essential to protect confidentiality and uphold data integrity. Through collaborative efforts, emergency managers and IT experts can enforce comprehensive cybersecurity measures to prevent unauthorized access, data breaches, and cyber threats that may jeopardize patient information or disrupt hospital activities. It is also crucial to have strategies in place for dealing with cyber threats and attacks. Collaborative initiatives allow for the development of approaches, incident response procedures, and recovery plans to swiftly address and mitigate the impact of cyber incidents, enhancing the hospital's resilience against evolving cybersecurity challenges.

The connection between hospital emergency managers and the IT department is crucial for dealing with downtime procedures, cybersecurity issues, and the overall resilience of IT systems in healthcare environments. By collaborating, these departments can improve readiness, response capabilities, and strategies to reduce risks. This collaboration helps protect information, ensure continuity, and strengthen the hospital's ability to handle IT emergencies and cyber threats.

Emergency management plays a role in supporting hospital programs that involve partners like state or local corrections departments. Building partnerships with these entities is key to developing emergency plans tailored to the unique needs of incarcerated individuals in healthcare facilities. Specific evacuation plans must be put in place for hospitals housing incarcerated individuals to guarantee their safety during emergencies. These plans should consider factors such as supervision, security procedures, and coordination with staff for an evacuation process during crises. Emergency management can collaborate with authorities to integrate these evacuation protocols into the hospital's overall emergency response framework for seamless coordination and effective implementation, during drills or real emergency scenarios.

By setting up ways to communicate, organizing training drills, and creating detailed procedures designed for inmates, emergency preparedness can improve the hospital's ability to handle crises while focusing on the safety and welfare of everyone, including those in custody.

Incorporating emergency preparedness into the training and education curriculum for hospital staff is crucial to guaranteeing an efficient response to crises. By integrating emergency preparedness into staff training, hospitals can offer guidance on emergency procedures, protocols, and best practices, empowering employees to react confidently in emergency situations. This ongoing training serves to reinforce staff readiness, improve their understanding of emergency protocols, and ensure a coordinated response across all departments. Providing staff with skills through cross-training is essential for maximizing resource utilization during emergencies. By equipping employees with capabilities through training initiatives, hospitals can enhance their flexibility in adapting to dynamic emergency scenarios, filling key roles as required, and collaborating effectively in multidisciplinary response teams. Including emergency preparedness in staff training programs cultivates a culture of readiness and resilience among employees. It also enables the hospital to efficiently mobilize its workforce to mitigate risks, safeguard patient well-being, and sustain operational continuity during crises.

Certain departments or functions within a hospital could significantly benefit from participating in emergency management due to their roles in patient care and the necessity for specialized response procedures during emergencies.

In any Emergency Department across the country, there is a possibility for it to become the point of contact during an emergency in the community it serves, even if only temporarily. Collaboration with emergency management is crucial to manage increases in numbers, ensure effective triage, and have all required resources and protocols ready. Similarly, trauma centers must always be prepared for events like mass casualty incidents, natural disasters, and other emergencies that could result in a surge of injured patients. Working closely with emergency management helps ensure that trauma teams are well trained and well equipped to handle situations efficiently. In the event of a hospital evacuation affecting a transplant program, maintaining continuity of patient care is vital. Transplant patients require attention both before and after their procedures to prevent organ rejection and manage infections effectively. Managing medication becomes a challenge as well; transplant patients rely on specific immunosuppressants that are often sensitive to temperature changes, so any disruptions in their supply or administration can pose life-threatening risks. Coordinating with Organ Procurement Organizations (OPOs) and ensuring the transport of organs during an evacuation becomes more complex due to the critical nature of maintaining organ viability.

In addition, it is important to have access to health records (EHRs) and ensure that all patient information is transferred smoothly for care. However, disruptions in IT systems can complicate this process. Moving equipment and ensuring that the new facility can cater to transplant patients with the necessary sterile conditions present additional challenges. Evacuating staff members who play a role in offering top-notch transplant care adds another layer of complexity, especially considering their own evacuation needs. Communication difficulties during an evacuation can impede coordination among the transplant team, patients, families, and external entities, making the situation more challenging. The emotional toll on patients, vulnerable due to their health condition, is substantial as the stress and anxiety of evacuation can impact their well-being and recovery journey. Dealing with ethical and financial obstacles, such as adhering to standards and bearing the significant costs of evacuation, highlights the diverse range of challenges faced by a transplant program in critical times like these. Nonetheless, close collaboration with the hospital's emergency manager can help alleviate many of these hurdles by enabling planning and efficient allocation of resources to prioritize supplies and equipment for transport.

They can also set up communication channels to stay in touch with OPOs and other important stakeholders, simplify tracking and access to EHR, and make sure that all regulatory and compliance requirements are followed during the evacuation process. This collaboration can greatly reduce the strain on patients and staff by providing a structured, clear plan of action in times of emergency. ICUs need to be ready for power outages, equipment malfunctions, and other disruptions that may arise during emergencies. Emergency management plans help ensure that critical care services continue without interruption. Operating rooms and surgical teams should have strategies in place for evacuation, handling surgical cases during disasters, and ensuring the availability of necessary supplies and equipment. Pediatric Units and Neonatal Intensive Care Units pose unique challenges. These units must have specialized emergency protocols to safeguard infants and children. This involves evacuation strategies, maintaining controlled environments, and ensuring care for high-risk patients.

The collaboration between emergency management and accredited programs promotes an approach to risk management. Accreditation standards often mandate training sessions, drills, and assessments which're fundamental elements of efficient emergency management. By meeting these criteria, hospitals can boost their preparedness level and their capacity to respond effectively in emergency situations.

This does not just help the hospital follow regulations better; it boosts trust among patients, staff, and the community in the hospital's emergency response capabilities. In the end, integrating emergency preparedness into hospital initiatives and aligning with accreditation requirements enhance the hospital's ability to deliver efficient and dependable healthcare services.

References that influenced this chapter are in the below section.

Bibliography

1. American College of Emergency Physicians. (2019). *Emergency medical services: Clinical practice and systems oversight.* Dallas, TX: American College of Emergency Physicians.
2. American Hospital Association. (2017). *Hospital emergency preparedness and response: Assessing hospital emergency management programs.* Chicago, IL: American Hospital Association.
3. Association of Healthcare Emergency Preparedness Professionals. (2020). *Integrating emergency management into hospital operations.* https://www.ahepp.org
4. Centers for Disease Control and Prevention (CDC). (2019). *Infection control in healthcare personnel: Infrastructure and routine practices for occupational infection prevention and control services.* Atlanta, GA: CDC.
5. Federal Emergency Management Agency (FEMA). (2010). *Developing and maintaining emergency operations plans: Comprehensive preparedness guide (CPG) 101.* Washington, DC: U.S. Department of Homeland Security.
6. Federal Emergency Management Agency (FEMA). (2013). *Continuity of operations (COOP) planner's workbook.* Washington, DC: U.S. Department of Homeland Security.

7. Institute of Medicine. (2011). *National standards for culturally and linguistically appropriate services in health and health care: A blueprint for advancing and sustaining CLAS policy and practice.* Washington, DC: National Academies Press.
8. Institute of Medicine. (2012). *Crisis standards of care: A systems framework for catastrophic disaster response.* Washington, DC: National Academies Press.
9. Joint Commission. (2019). *Emergency management in health care: An all-hazards approach* (2nd ed.). Oakbrook Terrace, IL: Joint Commission Resources.
10. National Fire Protection Association (NFPA). (2016). *Healthcare facilities code handbook (NFPA 99).* Quincy, MA: NFPA.
11. Occupational Safety and Health Administration (OSHA). (2008). *Best practices for hospital-based first receivers of victims from mass casualty incidents involving the release of hazardous substances.* Washington, DC: U.S. Department of Labor.
12. U.S. Department of Health and Human Services. (2017). *Hospital emergency preparedness and response during a mass casualty event.* Washington, DC: U.S. Government Printing Office.
13. U.S. Department of Homeland Security. (2017). *Healthcare and public health sector-specific plan.* Washington, DC: U.S. Department of Homeland Security.
14. World Health Organization. (2011). *Hospital emergency response checklist: An all-hazards tool for hospital administrators and emergency managers.* Geneva: World Health Organization.

Chapter 11

Case Studies for Healthcare Emergency Management

Kimberly Bailey/Thomas Crawford

In Chapter 11, we shift our focus to real-life examples that showcase the principles, difficulties, and achievements of managing healthcare emergencies. By the conclusion of this chapter, healthcare leaders and emergency managers will gain an understanding of how these principles can be applied in real-life situations. They will recognize the value of drawing lessons from real-life cases and be better equipped to make informed decisions within their organizations by leveraging the experiences of others who have successfully dealt with the challenges of healthcare emergency management. You will acquire a grasp of response tactics and the intricacies involved in overseeing healthcare during emergencies or disasters, enabling you to utilize the insights from these case studies to enhance readiness, response, and recovery efforts. These case studies provide perspectives on how healthcare leaders have handled emergencies, offering practical guidance and motivation for future readiness and response endeavors.

Utilizing case studies as tools in healthcare emergency management is fundamental for gleaning insights from events. These instances present engaging narratives that allow healthcare leaders to delve into the complexities of emergency scenarios. By examining both accomplishments and setbacks, leaders can identify decisions and resource allocations that shape responses.

Healthcare leaders develop an understanding of the difficulties presented by emergencies, like disasters, mass casualty incidents, and public health crises. Each situation requires strategies for managing and recovering from them. Real-life examples also shed light on the leadership styles and communication methods used in high-pressure situations. These examples highlight how effective coordination and clear communication can help prevent chaos and improve outcomes. Additionally, they showcase organizations that have shown resilience in times by emphasizing the importance of planning, adaptable strategies, and strong partnerships in ensuring operational continuity and patient safety during emergencies. By learning from these case studies, healthcare leaders can promote a culture of improvement within their organizations, making them more resilient to challenges while upholding a commitment to excellence in emergency preparedness. The case studies will explore a variety of healthcare emergency scenarios:

DOI: 10.4324/9781003529194-11

- **Case Study 1: Mass Casualty Incident**: Insight into the response to a large-scale mass casualty response impacting the hospital operations. (Kim Bailey-Vegas Shooting)
- **Case Study 2: Natural Disaster:** Insight into the response to a hurricane and flooding impacting the operations of a hospital. (Kim Bailey-Hurricane Maria)
- **Case Study 3: Public Health Emergency**: Insight into the response to a pandemic impacting a healthcare system. (Tom Crawford-COVID 19 Pandemic)
- **Case Study 4: Cybersecurity Incident:** Insight into a response to a data breach and cyberattack targeting a healthcare system. (Kim Bailey-Wanna Cry Cyber Attack)

Case Study 1: Mass Casualty Incident: Insight into the Response to a Large-Scale Mass Casualty Response Impacting Hospital Operations – Kim Bailey

Introduction

The tragic mass shooting that took place in Las Vegas on October 1, 2017, stands out as one of the most extreme instances of gun violence in U.S. history, deeply affecting the many individuals who were present at the Route 91 Harvest music festival. With a gunman firing from a Mandalay Bay Resort and Casino hotel room, over 60 people lost their lives. More than 800 others sustained injuries in the horrifying incident. This event occurred amidst the nightlife atmosphere of Las Vegas, highlighting how quickly and profoundly mass casualty situations can unfold.

In response to the tragedy, local law enforcement, fire departments, and medical teams acted swiftly to provide aid and evacuate those in need amid the scene. The coordinated efforts of these emergency responders were instrumental in bringing stability to the situation and eliminating the threat posed by the shooter. The hospitals throughout Las Vegas faced challenges as they worked tirelessly to care for a number of critically injured patients, putting their emergency response capabilities to the test.

The repercussions of the Las Vegas shooting went beyond loss of life and physical injuries; they also had an economic impact on the city's tourism and hospitality sectors.

The shooting had a lasting impact on the survivors, witnesses, and the community leading to a focus on health support and trauma counseling. Lessons learned from the incident emphasized the importance of being prepared, receiving training, and working together across agencies during emergencies. Effective communication channels played a role in sharing information with the public and coordinating response efforts, with social media being used for updates and safety guidelines. Following the shooting, discussions around changes such as gun control laws and public safety policies gained urgency at levels of government. Healthcare facilities revisited their emergency plans to enhance their ability to handle surges in patients and respond to events. Efforts to build community resilience were also heightened, stressing the importance of educating people on emergency procedures and personal safety measures. The tragic event in Las Vegas served as a reminder of vulnerabilities in public gatherings and underscored the need to improve emergency response capabilities. It sparked a reassessment of policies and practices aimed at creating communities that are better equipped to handle future crises effectively.

Background

The tragic mass shooting in Las Vegas on October 1, 2017, took place during the Route 91 Harvest music festival near the Mandalay Bay Resort and Casino on the Las Vegas Strip. While festivalgoers were enjoying the concert, a shooter positioned himself in a hotel room on the floor of Mandalay Bay and unleashed gunfire upon the crowd using a collection of powerful firearms. This horrifying act of violence claimed the lives of more than 60 individuals. Left over 800 people were injured, marking it as one of the deadliest mass shootings in recent American history. The immediate emergency response involved an effort by various organizations and agencies. Local emergency services such as the Las Vegas Metropolitan Police Department (LVMPD) and Las Vegas Fire & Rescue, along with responders, quickly arrived at the scene to secure the area, evacuate survivors, and provide medical aid to those wounded. Their swift actions were crucial in managing the situation, capturing the gunman, and preventing harm to concert attendees and residents nearby. Government agencies at all levels, ranging from local to national authorities, also played significant roles in responding to this tragedy and carrying out subsequent investigations. The LVMPD spearheaded law enforcement efforts by conducting a probe into the motives and methods of the shooter. Government agencies, like the FBI, offered assistance in analyzing evidence, collecting intelligence, and working together with national security bodies to uphold safety and capture any potential associates. Key players in the crisis response included hospitals and medical facilities throughout Las Vegas tasked with the job of caring for critically wounded individuals. Emergency medical teams diligently triaged patients, conducted lifesaving surgeries, and handled the surge in demand for healthcare services. The American Red Cross and local community groups also sprang into action to aid survivors and their loved ones by providing shelter, counseling, and other essential support during this period. The Las Vegas tragedy showcased the resilience and collaborative efforts of emergency responders, healthcare providers, and community organizations in dealing with a crisis. It emphasized the significance of readiness, swift response capabilities, and efficient coordination among stakeholders to minimize the impacts of tragic incidents and assist impacted individuals and communities in their recovery endeavors.

Timeline of Events

This timeline delineates the series of events, actions taken and decisions made by stakeholders during and following the Las Vegas tragedy, shedding light on the coordinated response initiatives and continuous effects on the community's well-being as well as emergency response protocols.

Before the Shooting (Leading Up):

- September 2017: Stephen Paddock checks into a suite on the 32nd floor of the Mandalay Bay Resort and Casino.
- September 28–30, 2017: Paddock transports numerous firearms and ammunition into his hotel room unnoticed.

During the Shooting:

- October 1, 2017:
- 9:59 PM: The shooting begins as Paddock opens fire on the Route 91 Harvest music festival crowd from his hotel room.

- 10:05 PM: First emergency calls reporting gunfire and casualties are received by 911 dispatchers.
- 10:08 PM: Police officers arrive on the scene and start securing the area and evacuating concertgoers.
- 10:15 PM: Las Vegas Metropolitan Police Department (LVMPD) establishes a command post near the venue and initiates a full-scale response.
- 10:30 PM: Multiple hospitals in the Las Vegas area receive the first wave of injured patients by ambulance and private vehicles.
- 10:45 PM: LVMPD identifies the location of the shooter and begins efforts to breach the hotel room.
- 11:20 PM: SWAT teams breach Paddock's hotel room and find him dead from a self-inflicted gunshot wound.
- 11:30 PM: Las Vegas hospitals activate mass casualty protocols, calling in additional medical staff and resources to handle the influx of patients.

Following the Shooting:

- October 2, 2017:
- Early Morning: LVMPD identifies the gunman as Stephen Paddock, a 64-year-old retired accountant.
- Throughout the Day: Authorities secure the crime scene, gather evidence, and interview witnesses to reconstruct the events leading up to the shooting.
- Emergency Response: Hospitals continue to treat patients, some in critical condition, and begin identifying victims through a makeshift Family Assistance Center.
- October 3, 2017:
- Investigation Intensifies: The FBI and other federal agencies join the LVMPD in investigating the motive behind the shooting and any potential accomplices.
- Community Support: Vigils and memorials are held across Las Vegas to honor the victims and support their families.
- October 6, 2017:
- Victim Identification: Authorities released the names of all 58 victims who died in the shooting.
- October 7–10, 2017:
- Continued Investigation: Law enforcement continues to interview witnesses, review surveillance footage, and analyze the shooter's background.
- October 11, 2017:
- Funerals and Memorials: Funerals and memorial services for victims begin, attended by thousands from across the country.
- October 12–15, 2017:
- Community Healing: Counseling services and support groups are established for survivors, families, and first responders dealing with trauma.
- October 16, 2017:
- Final Victim Identified: The last victim, who succumbed to injuries days after the shooting, has been identified.
- October 17–20, 2017:
- Law Enforcement Briefings: LVMPD and FBI provide updates to the public on the progress of the investigation.

- October 21, 2017:
- Shooter's Motive: Authorities conclude that Stephen Paddock acted alone and that no clear motive for the shooting could be determined.
- October 22–31, 2017:
- Recovery and Reflection: Las Vegas begins to heal as residents and the nation mourn the loss of life and discuss ways to prevent similar tragedies in the future.
- In October 2017, ceremonies and services were held to honor the victims of an event drawing crowds from all over the country. Following this, support networks and counseling sessions were set up for those affected by the incident. As days passed, the final victim was identified. Law enforcement agencies provided updates on their investigation to the public. It was eventually determined that the perpetrator acted alone with no motive. In the latter part of October efforts focused on healing. Reflecting on the tragedy in Las Vegas as communities came together to mourn and seek ways to prevent such incidents in the future.

Impact Assessment

The aftermath of the Las Vegas shooting on October 1, 2017, had a far-reaching impact across aspects underscoring how interconnected human, environmental, economic, and social spheres are in the aftermath of such tragic incidents.

- Human Impact: The tragic event led to the loss of 58 lives. Less than 850 individuals were injured, marking it as one of the deadliest mass shootings in recent U.S. history. Families and friends of the victims grappled with sorrow and trauma, while survivors faced injuries along with enduring psychological effects like post-traumatic stress disorder (PTSD) and anxiety. The psychological ramifications extended beyond the victims to encompass first responders and the wider Las Vegas community.
- Environmental Impact: Although there was no damage to ecosystems or pollution caused by the shooting, from a standpoint its indirect impact on community well-being can be viewed as an environmental consequence affecting emotional health and social unity in the area.
- Economic Impact: The economic repercussions were multifaceted. Immediate expenses involved costs for treating victims and implementing security measures. The aftermath of the event in Las Vegas had far-reaching economic consequences, such as a decline in tourism and visitors, impacting the local economy heavily reliant on hospitality and entertainment. Businesses near the incident site faced disruptions. The city grappled with challenges to its reputation as a tourist destination.
- Social Impact: On a level, the shooting put the strength and unity of the Las Vegas community to the test. Following the incident, there was a display of support for victims and their families through community-driven initiatives and fundraising efforts. The tragedy sparked discussions on gun control laws and public safety measures, leading to debates across the country. Despite this, it brought people together in sorrow and solidarity, with candlelight vigils and memorials becoming symbols of healing and remembrance.
- Assessment Methodology: In terms of assessment methods, official reports and hospital records were used to gather data on casualties, injuries, and financial impacts. Through means like interviews with survivors, victim families, first responders, and community leaders, as well as stakeholders' perspectives, provided insights into psychological and social repercussions. These interviews also shed light on response actions taken by agencies during recovery phases following the incident.

Response Effectiveness

In the aftermath of the mass shooting in Las Vegas on October 1, 2017, hospitals demonstrated their ability to respond effectively by mobilizing resources, coordinating care, and delivering crucial medical treatments. Their proactive measures included activating casualty protocols, ensuring surgeries, and managing patient flow to save lives and aid in community recovery. Following the incident, hospitals in Las Vegas played a role in addressing the medical needs of the victims. Emergency departments activated mass casualty protocols to efficiently receive and prioritize patients. Trauma centers like University Medical Center (UMC) and Sunrise Hospital and Medical Center promptly organized trauma teams, surgical staff, and support personnel to handle the influx of injured individuals. Their quick response and effective triage processes ensured attention, surgeries, and critical care interventions that were essential in stabilizing patients and preventing further loss of life.

The hospital response efforts were characterized by coordination, communication, and resource allocation. Collaborating closely with EMS services, law enforcement agencies, and local emergency management authorities facilitated transport and resource distribution. Communication channels were set up to offer real-time updates on statuses, bed availability, and medical supply requirements. Hospitals brought in staff, including nurses, doctors, and support personnel to handle the increase in numbers efficiently. The allocation of resources like equipment, blood products, medications, and surgical supplies was carefully handled to address the changing needs of care. The promptness and suitability of hospital response actions played a role in lessening the impact of the emergency situation. Hospitals swiftly activated their incident command systems to ensure coordination of resources and staff. Swift patient evaluation and triage enabled treatments such as surgeries and critical care interventions. The appropriateness of response actions was evident in hospitals' capacity to mobilize teams, like trauma surgeons, orthopedic experts, and intensive care unit (ICU) personnel to deliver tailored care based on the severity of injuries sustained by individuals.

The effectiveness of hospital responses was demonstrated by University Medical Center (UMC) serving as Las Vegas' Level I Trauma Center during the crisis. UMC received a number of injured patients and utilized its trauma expertise and specialized capabilities to manage intricate cases. Sunrise Hospital and Medical Center, a trauma center, also played a role by executing its mass casualty plans efficiently and collaborating closely with local authorities. Both medical facilities offered assistance to patients and their families, including counseling services and organizing follow-up care.

In general, the joint efforts of hospitals, law enforcement, EMS, and other stakeholders significantly mitigated the impact of the emergency. Patients received appropriate attention, leading to lower mortality rates and better outcomes. The collaborative actions of Las Vegas hospitals emphasized the importance of readiness, effective communication, and coordinated responses in handling mass casualty incidents.

Lessons Learned

The response to the Las Vegas mass shooting uncovered lessons for responders and healthcare facilities. Successes included initiating emergency protocols and efficient coordination among law enforcement, EMS, and hospitals. Challenges identified involved the necessity for communication systems to manage information influxes and integrating health support into emergency plans to address psychological impacts on victims and responders alike. The incident underscored the significance of community resilience and preparedness in addressing large-scale emergencies.

Several effective strategies and best practices emerged during the response that proved successful in handling the crisis. First responders quickly set up a command structure enabling decision-making and resource allocation. Hospitals implemented triage protocols to prioritize care based on injury severity, ensuring attention for critical patients. Innovative approaches included utilizing units to expand treatment capabilities and incorporating technology for real-time patient tracking and resource management. These methods facilitated the response and improved patient outcomes.

Recommendations to enhance emergency preparedness, response and recovery efforts focus on various areas. For responders, investing in training programs simulating mass casualty incidents can enhance coordination and decision-making under pressure. Strengthening communication systems, such as radio networks and digital platforms, is essential for improving awareness and information sharing during emergencies. Hospitals should continue refining their mass casualty plans to be adaptable to various scenarios, including provisions for surge capacity and mental health support. Collaborative exercises involving all stakeholders can further improve readiness and coordination. Community engagement initiatives should also be emphasized to raise awareness and resilience in the event of incidents. By following these suggestions, communities can enhance their readiness and response to crises, ensuring an efficient and collaborative approach that saves lives and aids in community recovery.

Implications for Policies and Practices

Following the mass shooting in Las Vegas on October 1, 2017, significant implications for policies and practices emerged, influencing emergency management procedures and laws. The incident highlighted the necessity for policies addressing mass casualty incidents (MCIs) involving active shooters and large public gatherings. It prompted a reassessment of emergency response protocols, especially concerning law enforcement strategies, medical responses, and inter-agency coordination. The event exposed gaps in existing laws related to gun control and public safety, leading to discussions on firearm regulations and security measures enforcement at events. It also sparked conversations about improving surveillance systems to reduce risks linked with such acts. The incident underscored the role of community resilience in coping with and recovering from events of this magnitude. To enhance frameworks, policymakers and emergency management authorities have called for training and resources for first responders, healthcare providers, and community leaders.

Establishing procedures for dealing with shooter situations and improving communication systems among law enforcement, emergency services, and hospitals are key priorities. Collaboration between agencies is central to reform efforts focusing on streamlining response actions and enhancing information sharing across state and federal levels. Recommendations include coordination and joint training exercises to ensure a cohesive and effective response in emergencies. Community resilience initiatives involve residents in readiness activities, promoting trauma-informed support, and expanding health services for survivors and affected families. The tragic Las Vegas mass shooting prompted a review of emergency management policies and procedures, leading to efforts to strengthen frameworks, improve inter-agency cooperation and enhance community resilience in anticipation of future crises. By addressing these challenges head-on, policymakers aim to reduce risks, enhance response capabilities, and build a society capable of effectively navigating crises of all kinds.

Conclusion

The Las Vegas mass shooting on October 1, 2017, provided lessons in emergency management that can guide preparedness strategies and responses.

The recent event brought to light the challenges involved in handling large-scale mass casualty incidents in dynamic and public settings. The response showcased both successes and areas needing improvement across aspects of emergency management. The impact of this emergency response event extends to influencing policies and practices in emergency management. It triggered a review of protocols and procedures, resulting in training for first responders, healthcare workers, and community leaders. The incident emphasized the importance of coordination and communication among response teams, advocating for systems and joint drills to enhance preparedness and response times. Themes like learning, adaptation, and innovation emerged as factors in creating resilient and responsive communities. The incident underscored the necessity for readiness efforts, including educating the public on emergency response protocols and trauma-informed care. Technological advancements, such as enhanced surveillance systems and communication tools, were recognized as facilitators in improving awareness and response capabilities. The Las Vegas mass shooting highlighted the importance of enhancing emergency management practices. By drawing lessons from events, adjusting strategies to evolving threats, and fostering an environment of innovation, communities can better equip themselves to handle emergencies effectively.

The occasion acted as a driving force to enhance resilience and preparedness at every level, highlighting the dedication to protecting public safety and welfare in challenging times.

References

1. Centers for Disease Control and Prevention. (2017). Mass shooting: An American public health crisis. Retrieved from https://www.cdc.gov/massviolence/
2. Federal Emergency Management Agency. (2018). A whole community approach to emergency management: Principles, themes, and pathways for action. Retrieved from https://www.fema.gov/whole-community-approach-emergency-management
3. Ghafil, C. (2019). Emergency preparedness: A literature review on policy, legislation, and practices. Journal of Emergency Management, 17(2), 45-63. doi:10.1177/1545592319839987
4. National Academies of Sciences, Engineering, and Medicine. (2018). A national trauma care system: Integrating military and civilian trauma systems to achieve zero preventable deaths after injury. Washington, DC: The National Academies Press. doi:10.17226/23511
5. National Association of Emergency Medical Technicians. (2018). Principles of mass casualty incident management. Retrieved from https://www.naemt.org/initiatives/education/mci-management

Case Study 2: Natural Disaster: Insight into the Response to a Hurricane and Flooding Impacting Operations of a Hospital – Kim Bailey

Introduction

Hurricane Maria, a Category 5 hurricane, made landfall in Puerto Rico on September 20, 2017. This study focuses on the impact of the hurricane on healthcare infrastructure and emergency response in Puerto Rico. It delves into the challenges faced by healthcare providers, coordination among response agencies, and lessons learned for disaster preparedness and response efforts.

Background

The powerful Hurricane Maria wreaked havoc across parts of the Caribbean and Puerto Rico in September 2017. As a Category 4 hurricane hitting Puerto Rico, it brought winds, heavy rainfall, and widespread flooding. The storm caused damage to infrastructure like homes, businesses, roads, utilities, and transportation systems, exacerbating vulnerabilities in the healthcare system. The island's electrical grid suffered extensive damage, leading to prolonged power outages that lasted for months. Following Hurricane Maria's aftermath, emergency responders, along with government agencies and relief organizations, came together to assist affected communities. International aid was also mobilized to support search and rescue operations, provide emergency medical care, and distribute essential supplies like food and water. The aftermath of Hurricane Maria had a lasting impact on Puerto Rico. The island's economy took a hit, leading to damage in infrastructure and a decrease in productivity. Additionally, the storm revealed weaknesses in Puerto Ricos healthcare system, governmental institutions, and emergency readiness and response capabilities. Communication systems also began to malfunction making it difficult for healthcare facilities and emergency responders to coordinate and share information effectively.

Event Timeline

This timeline provides an overview of the significant events that occurred during and after Hurricane Maria, highlighting the challenges faced by hospitals in Puerto Rico and the response efforts undertaken to address the impacts of the storm on healthcare infrastructure and patient care.

- September 20, 2017:
- 6:15 AM: Hurricane Maria makes landfall in Puerto Rico as a Category 4 storm, with sustained winds of 155 mph and heavy rainfall.
- Morning: Hospitals across Puerto Rico activate emergency protocols in preparation for the storm, including securing facilities, stocking up on supplies, and implementing contingency plans for patient care.
- Afternoon: Power outages begin as the hurricane's strong winds topple utility poles and damage electrical infrastructure, leading to widespread blackouts across the island.

- Evening: Hospitals start experiencing power failures, forcing them to rely on backup generators to maintain essential services. Communication systems also begin to fail, hindering coordination and information sharing among healthcare facilities and emergency responders.
- September 21, 2017:
- Morning: Hospitals report damage to infrastructure, including roof leaks, flooding, and structural damage from hurricane-force winds and storm surges. Medical equipment, such as MRI machines and X-ray equipment, suffer water damage, rendering them inoperable.
- Afternoon: Access roads to hospitals become impassable due to fallen trees, debris, and flooding, complicating efforts to transport patients and supplies. Emergency medical services (EMS) teams struggle to reach affected areas to aid and evacuate patients in need of critical care.
- September 22, 2017:
- Morning: Hospitals face shortages of medical supplies, including medications, IV fluids, and oxygen tanks, as supply chains are disrupted by the hurricane. Healthcare workers ration supplies and prioritize patient care to conserve resources.
- Afternoon: Morgues at hospitals reach capacity as the number of fatalities increases, overwhelming staff and storage facilities. Hospitals collaborate with government agencies and relief organizations to establish temporary morgues and facilitate the identification and processing of deceased individuals.
- September 23, 2017:
- Morning: Hospitals continue to operate on emergency power, with limited fuel supplies for backup generators. The lack of electricity hampers medical procedures, diagnostic tests, and patient monitoring, putting critically ill patients at risk.
- Afternoon: Healthcare workers face exhaustion and burnout as they work around the clock to care for patients and respond to emergencies. Mental health support services are mobilized to provide counseling and support to hospital staff experiencing stress and trauma.
- September 24, 2017:
- Morning: International aid organizations and military personnel arrive in Puerto Rico to assist with relief efforts, including the provision of medical supplies, personnel, and logistical support to hospitals and healthcare facilities.
- Afternoon: Hospitals begin to stabilize operations as fuel deliveries replenish generator supplies and communication networks are restored. Relief efforts focus on restoring power, water, and transportation infrastructure to facilitate the delivery of aid and support to affected communities.
- September 25, 2017:
- Morning: Hospitals resume elective surgeries and outpatient services as conditions improve and infrastructure repairs progress. Healthcare facilities prioritize patient discharges and transfers to free up bed space and accommodate new admissions.
- Afternoon: Recovery efforts shift towards long-term rebuilding and restoration of healthcare infrastructure, including repairs to damaged buildings, replacement of medical equipment, and strengthening of emergency preparedness plans to mitigate future disasters.

Assessment of Impacts

Hurricane Maria resulted in more than 3,000 deaths, with many attributed to delays in receiving medical care and essential services. Hospitals in Puerto Rico struggled significantly during and after the hurricane. Already strained by the storm's effects on infrastructure, staffing, and resources, hospitals faced challenges with an influx of fatalities. The facilities, morgues, and emergency departments prepared for handling a large number of deceased individuals experienced capacity issues. This led to overcrowding and logistical difficulties in managing the deceased. The hurricane's destruction disrupted supply chains, making it hard to access resources like body bags, refrigeration units, and medical supplies for handling fatalities. Shortages of these resources complicated efforts to manage the deceased effectively. Additionally, damage to hospital infrastructure, such as power outages and structural issues, added hurdles in dealing with fatalities. Hospitals faced challenges in maintaining storage conditions for bodies due to the lack of electricity or backup generators, which raised concerns about decomposition and hygiene. Issues with communication and logistics created obstacles in coordinating efforts between hospitals, emergency responders, and government agencies dealing with fatalities. This resulted in delays and inefficiencies in sharing information, allocating resources, and executing response plans. Infrastructure such as hospitals, clinics, and water treatment facilities suffered damage. The destruction extended to homes, businesses, and critical infrastructure causing lasting impacts.

The aftermath of the storm led to the displacement of residents, disrupted communities, and hindered access to healthcare services. Hurricane Maria inflicted harm on hospital structures with roof collapses, flooding incidents, and structural integrity issues. Hospital Damas in Ponce experienced roof damage that resulted in water seepage and flooding within parts of the facility. This compromised patient care spaces as medical equipment and supplies necessitated patient evacuation and service relocations. The hurricane's fierce winds and storm surge caused power outages and utility failures across the island. As a result, hospitals were left without services, like electricity and water supply systems, leading to challenges.

During the power outages at Hospital Pavia in Santurce, critical medical equipment such as ventilators and life support systems failed due to the lack of generators and sufficient fuel supplies. This led to challenges in maintaining services and providing care to patients.

The damaged roads, bridges, and transportation networks made it hard for patients in those in areas to reach healthcare facilities. Hospital Menonita in Caguas encountered difficulties receiving patients because of road closures and transportation issues caused by debris and flooding. As a result, access to healthcare services was limited, causing delays in treatment for patients with needs and increasing the risk of complications.

The disruption of supply chains and communication networks affected hospitals' ability to acquire supplies and mobilize healthcare staff. Hospital Auxilio Mutuo in San Juan faced shortages of medications, medical equipment, and personnel following Hurricane Maria. Without resources and staffing, hospitals struggled to address patient needs, worsening the impact of the disaster on public health.

Hurricane Maria's widespread destruction led to a surge in healthcare demand as hospitals were already grappling with resource limitations and infrastructure damage. UPR Hospital in Carolina, Puerto Rico, saw a rise in the number of patients seeking care, causing the emergency departments and critical care units to operate at capacity. The surge in patients overwhelmed the hospital's resources and staff, resulting in delays in treatment, overcrowding, and compromised patient outcomes.

The emotional strain of dealing with deaths after Hurricane Maria weighed heavily on hospital personnel, including healthcare workers, first responders, and support staff. Witnessing the devastation and loss of life, alongside the challenges of providing care under such circumstances, led to heightened levels of stress, burnout, and trauma among healthcare providers.

Response Effectiveness

Assessing the response effectiveness to Hurricane Maria highlighted both successes and difficulties encountered in meeting the needs of affected individuals and communities. This evaluation encompassed coordination issues among state and federal agencies that caused delays in delivering aid to impacted areas. Despite collaboration efforts by agencies on different levels (local, federal, international), logistical obstacles arose, leading to delays in distributing resources due to disruptions in communication and transportation infrastructure.

Enhancing responses through communication systems and streamlined coordination protocols is crucial for ensuring efficient resource allocation and alignment of efforts at all response levels. Issues with communication led to challenges in sharing information and coordinating response efforts, affecting the timeliness and effectiveness of the overall response. Challenges related to resources and logistical issues hindered the delivery of medical supplies, personnel, and equipment to areas requiring assistance.

Following Hurricane Maria, emergency response efforts rapidly mobilized aid and local resources to provide support to affected communities. Search and rescue operations, emergency medical care, and the distribution of vital supplies such as food, water, and medicines played a pivotal role in the initial phases. However, significant challenges arose due to devastation and infrastructure damage in reaching remote regions promptly. This emphasized the importance of positioning resources and establishing clear protocols for swift deployment during future emergencies.

Response actions varied in terms of timeliness; initial needs like search and rescue operations were prioritized effectively. Challenges persisted in restoring services, like power supply and healthcare access, because of prolonged logistical hurdles and extensive destruction. During the response to Hurricane Maria, there was a display of aid and support, yet there were areas that could be improved in terms of coordination, communication, and resource allocation. Strengthening preparedness, training, and infrastructure resilience can equip response teams to handle disasters efficiently and enhance overall response effectiveness.

Lessons Learned

In reflecting on the outcomes following Hurricane Maria, it became evident that island hospitals needed to focus on enhancing their disaster preparedness, resilience, and collaboration to respond to emergencies. The suggested recommendations were put forward to bolster the healthcare system's ability to withstand disasters and safeguard patient care and public health. These lessons are transferable across all healthcare organizations.

Key Findings and Recommendations:

- Hospitals were advised to invest in infrastructure upgrades to better withstand storms by fortifying buildings against winds and flooding, installing backup power systems, and safeguarding essential equipment.
- It was crucial for hospitals to ensure emergency power and maintain a supply of fuel for backup generators. Establishing protocols for fuel delivery and storage was highlighted as a necessary step.
- Maintenance protocols for equipment needed implementation alongside redundancy measures for devices to minimize disruptions in patient care during power outages or equipment malfunctions. Regular inspections, testing, and servicing were recommended practices.

- Enhancing communication systems and protocols was deemed vital for the coordination of response efforts and the dissemination of information during emergencies.
- Hospitals should set up communication methods, like satellite phones or radio systems, to stay connected in case regular networks go down. It is crucial for hospitals to create plans for moving and transporting patients during emergencies to ensure access to medical care and minimize risks. This involves mapping evacuation routes, collaborating with transport services, and establishing procedures for moving patients to care facilities.
- Regular training and education sessions for hospital staff on disaster readiness and response protocols are vital. These sessions should include drills, simulations, and exercises to train personnel on emergency procedures, roles, responsibilities, triage, crisis communication, and stress management.
- Building relationships with state and federal agencies, along with community groups, is essential for better coordination in emergency responses. Hospitals need agreements, mutual aid pacts, and communication guidelines in place to share information effectively and allocate resources during crises.
- Getting involved in public health campaigns and community outreach programs is critical for promoting disaster preparedness at the community level. Hospitals can contribute by educating the public on emergency readiness, sharing materials, and offering assistance to communities.
- To prepare for emergencies, healthcare facilities may need to store medications, medical equipment, and essential supplies. They should also establish guidelines for maintaining and repairing equipment.
- Continuous training and education for healthcare staff on how to handle disasters and manage crises are crucial. This includes conducting drills and simulations to familiarize employees with their roles during emergencies. Training should cover triage, trauma care, and providing aid.
- Improving communication systems is vital for sharing real-time information among hospitals, emergency responders, and government agencies. Investing in communication methods like satellite phones can ensure connectivity during power outages or network failures.
- Collaborating with communities is important for raising awareness about disaster risks and promoting preparedness. Hospitals can work with schools, businesses, and community groups to create outreach programs and support networks for populations.
- Building partnerships with government agencies, relief organizations, and other healthcare providers can enhance response capabilities during emergencies by sharing resources.
- This might include setting up agreements, collaborating on mutual aid arrangements, and engaging in training exercises to enhance coordination and collaboration during emergency situations.
- Implementing public health programs to address the broader health needs of the community, such as disease prevention, sanitation, and mental health support. Hospitals can take part in community health initiatives, vaccination campaigns, and outreach programs to promote well-being in the aftermath of a disaster.

Successes

Despite the difficulties and destruction caused by Hurricane Maria, there were accomplishments and positive outcomes in the response and recovery efforts. The achievements concerning hospitals and healthcare in Puerto Rico during and after Hurricane Maria highlighted the resilience, adaptability, and dedication of healthcare professionals in handling emergencies and ensuring the well-being of their communities. These successes offer insights for disaster preparedness, response, and recovery endeavors.

- Community resilience and unity in times of adversity, along with grassroots organizations' mobilization efforts aided by volunteers, provide support.
- Hospitals and healthcare providers exhibited resilience and ingenuity when responding to the crisis. Despite infrastructure damage and supply shortages, medical professionals tirelessly delivered care to patients through emergency treatments, surgeries, and critical care services. Hospitals successfully relocated patients to places, such as other healthcare facilities and shelters to ensure their well-being and ongoing care. Emergency medical teams organized transportation logistics and medical assistance to help transfer patients, including those with conditions or special requirements.
- To meet the demand for services, field hospitals, and mobile clinics were set up in heavily affected areas to provide extra healthcare capacity. These temporary facilities offered consultations, triage services, and basic treatments to residents who couldn't access hospital services due to damage or displacement.
- Healthcare providers worked closely with government agencies, relief organizations, and volunteer groups to coordinate response efforts and make the most of resources. Joint command centers were established to enhance communication, resource distribution, and decision making among stakeholders for an efficient response to the healthcare needs of impacted communities.
- Despite facing professional struggles, healthcare workers displayed resilience and commitment in looking after patients and assisting their communities during the crisis. Many healthcare professionals put in hours in challenging conditions while showing empathy, professionalism, and determination in overcoming difficulties. After Hurricane Maria, hospitals and medical facilities worked hard to recover and rebuild, aiming to restore services and fortify their resilience against disasters. They focused on repairing infrastructure, replacing equipment, and enhancing emergency preparedness plans to improve the healthcare system's capacity and readiness.
- Healthcare professionals got involved in public health initiatives to address the health needs of the community, including disease prevention, hygiene practices, and mental health support. They set up outreach programs, educational campaigns, and partnerships within the community to promote health and well-being in the disaster scenario.

Policy and Practice Implications

Regarding policy and practice implications, Hurricane Maria highlighted the importance of having disaster preparedness and response strategies in place. This includes investing in infrastructure, healthcare systems, and building community resilience. Policy changes may involve updating emergency management practices, enhancing disaster response policies, and allocating funds towards disaster preparedness activities. Furthermore, it is crucial to consider the impact of emergency response events on policy-making processes, legislation development, as well as emergency management practices. Discussions should revolve around reforms needed to strengthen frameworks, foster better collaboration among different agencies involved in emergencies, and boost community resilience for future crises.

Conclusion

The aftermath of the hurricane highlighted weaknesses in infrastructure readiness and logistical planning, stressing the importance of improving disaster preparedness and response strategies. Hurricane Maria emphasized the significance of learning, adjustment, and creativity in constructing communities. The hurricane exposed flaws in Puerto Ricos healthcare system and emergency response capabilities, leading to a reassessment and strengthening of disaster readiness frameworks. Utilizing advancements in technology, like communication systems and data analysis for risk evaluation, can boost the efficiency and effectiveness of responses. To sum up, the lessons from Hurricane Maria stress the need for emergency management practices that prioritize resilience and quick reactions. By incorporating these lessons into policymaking and community development, stakeholders can enhance readiness for disasters, reduce risks and protect affected populations' well-being. Continuous learning and adaptation play a role in nurturing a culture capable of enduring unexpected challenges, ensuring that communities are better prepared to confront future crises.

References

1. Puerto Rico Department of Health. (2018). Hurricane Maria: Impact on healthcare infrastructure and emergency response.
2. Federal Emergency Management Agency (FEMA). (2018). After-action report: Response to Hurricane Maria in Puerto Rico.
3. Centers for Disease Control and Prevention. (2018). Public health response to Hurricane Maria in Puerto Rico, US Virgin Islands, and Florida. Retrieved from https://www.cdc.gov/disasters/hurricanes/pdf/hurricane-maria-ph-response.pdf
5. Federal Emergency Management Agency. (2018). Hurricane Maria: Federal response timeline. Retrieved from https://www.fema.gov/disaster/4339
4. National Hurricane Center. (2017). Hurricane Maria advisory archive. Retrieved from https://www.nhc.noaa.gov/archive/2017/MARIA.shtml

Case Study 3: Public Health Emergency: Insight into Response to a Pandemic Impacting a Healthcare System – Tom Crawford

Introduction

Despite our continuous emergency management cycle of mitigation, preparation, operations, and recovery – with an ongoing hyperfocus on mitigation – there are times that you and your team may find yourselves completely unprepared for an unforeseen event that is destined to impact your hospitals, clinics, and the communities they serve. Case in point, the COVID-19 pandemic was an unprecedented event in our lifetimes – that challenged and strained an already fragile national healthcare system. From the first patient being diagnosed in Wuhan, China on November 17, 2019, to the first patient being diagnosed in the United States on January 21, 2020 – no health system had any experience on how to handle the inevitable influx of acutely ill and highly infectious patients that would overwhelm hospitals, emergency departments, and clinics around the country. On the contrary, we were all left trying to quickly forecast the impact on our ability to deliver care in a resource-constrained environment that kept our patients, care team members, non-COVID patients, and family members/visitors safe.

My mind was racing. After thirty years in healthcare, I never thought for an instant that I would be in a meeting reviewing a scoring system that would be used for the allocation of our scarce resources, such as ventilators. This was in preparation for the potential of the pandemic-induced demand stripping our capacity to care for patients; meaning, with limited resources, which patient would receive the life-sustaining device when there were not enough for all those in need – a sobering and, frankly, horrifying thought. With this stated, the purpose of this case study is as follows:

- To highlight how you can plan for the unplanned/unprecedented by leveraging the collective intellect of your team versus depending on a few individuals.
- To underscore how simplifying communications will increase efficiency and create a common operational language across a large system of care.
- To outline how to conduct fluid emergency planning during the event when the variables are changing rapidly.
- To highlight the framework required to recover from the financial burden and lost patient volumes during the event versus waiting for the operational impact to diminish.

Background

I vividly remember sitting in a conference room in late January/early February of 2020, discussing how we are going to prepare for the pandemic. At this time, there were horrifying reports coming in from Italy, and the impact on New York City hospitals was reported incessantly on the nightly news. With no one in the room having experience, the conversation was hypothetical with no real follow-up tactics to work through, with one exception. One of my colleagues knew the COO of a New York hospital that was at ground zero for the pandemic in the United States and suggested that I connect with him to better understand what we needed to prepare for. It was 6:30 pm when I was able to touch base with the New York COO, and what I heard was beyond troubling:

- Acute and critically ill COVID patients saturated their ICU and Med/Surg capacity, meaning no inpatient beds were available, with patients on stretchers in the Emergency Department and in the hallways.
- Staff members contracted COVID at a rate that jeopardized their ability to keep inpatient units and other hospital functions open.
- The rate of staff infections was complicated by their inability to keep enough personal protective equipment (PPE) in stock to protect their care team members, patients, and visitors.
- A need for additional equipment – ventilators, air scrubbers, etc. is required to safely provide care.
- The economic impact due to a loss of their elective business – patients were canceling their elective surgeries and ambulatory visits because they were simply too afraid to go to where the outbreak was.
- Staffing with temporary labor – at 2 to 3 times the cost of an employed nurse, tech, etc., to handle the surge and to supplement the units that had been devastated by the number of care team members infected with COVID.
- A growing amount of work-related and emotional stress due to being understaffed and overwhelmed by a growing number of deaths.
- An uncertainty about whether they would be able to sustain operations at the current pace was compounded by the demand for emergent services growing exponentially.

The picture he was painting sounded hopeless, and the stress in his voice was palpable. I thanked him for his feedback and reminded him that Charleston is one of the most visited locations in the world. His advice for me: "Get ready."

Event Timeline

As previously referenced, the first COVID-19 patient diagnosed in the United States occurred in January 2020, and frankly, we didn't know what to expect. However, after my phone-call with the New York City COO, we ramped up our planning meetings to twice a week to ensure we covered the academic tertiary/quaternary campus as well as our regional health network.

We – the emergency management team – decided to surround ourselves with physician leaders, clinical leaders, administrative leaders, and selected care team members. With zero pandemic experience, we were determined to place our trust in our collective intellect versus the direction set by a single individual. This immediately paid dividends. "What are we the most worried about?" was the first question asked. Reflecting on the feedback I received from my colleague in New York, I immediately replied, "Keeping our patients, care team members and visitors/family members safe." This was the catalyst for our "divert and funnel" strategy for those COVID patients that were symptomatic yet not acutely ill enough to require an emergency department visit and/or hospitalization. We simply did not want these patients coming to our clinics, EDs, etc., which would elevate the risk of infecting our staff, other patients, and visitors.

We had the ability to perform symptom screening via telehealth in an effort to divert symptomatic non-acute and potentially infectious patients; however, we didn't have a location to funnel them through for testing. During one of our planning meetings, one of our infectious disease physicians asked if he could show us something. "Of course," I responded. He proceeded to pull up a YouTube video from South Korea that showed how they were performing drive-through testing. At the end of the video, he asked, "Can we do this?"

The collective wisdom in the room came up with and implemented a "Divert and Funnel" strategy by offering anyone in the State of South Carolina who was experiencing COVID symptoms the opportunity to be screened via telehealth for free. Those needing testing were sent to a local mall – we took over a large section of their parking lot – where we would begin offering COVID testing 7 days a week beginning in early March 2020, beating the first drive-through for patient care that was established in New York by several days.

We learned many lessons and had numerous successes via our collaborative planning process – from how to create additional negative pressure rooms with a piece of plywood and an air scrubber to our decision, before the pandemic began to impact the Southeast, to significantly over-order PPE and to lease additional ventilators for our system. We were well ahead of the impact on the South Carolina system of care, so when we started feeling the care burden brought by the influx of COVID patients, we were able to help other hospitals by providing PPE and, when needed, additional ventilators. We also learned that we needed to simplify the way we communicated across 15 hospitals and 750+ care locations. Based on this premise, we decided to go back to basics and focus on the minimum requisites required to take care of an inpatient: capacity (inpatient beds), staffing (MDs, nurses, techs, etc. – this was fluid due to care team members being infected), and supplies/equipment (from PPE to ventilators). We started with the PIP format – Problem, Impact, Plan – and under the planning, we went through each division's capacity, staffing, and supplies/equipment. It was seamless, and we were able to communicate across thousands of stakeholders in four divisions in a matter of minutes a minimum of three times a day.

Lastly, we learned that to be successful amid the unprecedented times, we needed to be fluid and move quickly – even if the decision was difficult. Case in point, our health system is a state institution; meaning we do not have an investment portfolio or a large endowment that we could use, or turn into, liquid assets to cover our loss of business. On the contrary, we only have 60 days cash-on-hand. Therefore, when 50% of our elective/ambulatory business was lost due to patients not wanting to go to hospitals and clinics, we had to act quickly as our days of cash-on-hand began to rapidly decline. We started planning our cost reductions on Wednesday, and this culminated on Sunday night at 9:00 pm when I presented a plan to furlough 1,200+ care team members. Specifically, our plan was to furlough on the following Monday and mitigate the impact on our employees by enrolling each of them in unemployment and covering the cost of their benefits so there would be no break in service.

The furlough occurred the next day, and our System CEO assembled his senior leadership team the following Tuesday (less than 24 hours later) and asked a simple question of his team, "How do we get our people back?" Again, relying on the collective intellect in the room, we began to chart our recovery strategy – running emergency operations in parallel with normal operations – in the middle of the pandemic, and this fluid approach resulted in our ability to quickly recover financially, well before the pandemic ended.

Impacts Assessment

- Post After Action Report meetings – the following impacts were noted and presented as a part of our commitment to continually learning and refining our emergency response:
- Patient Impact – we were able to segregate our critically ill patients from those who could recover in isolation. This dramatically decreased the number of other patients, family members, or care team members that got infected while receiving or providing care.
- Care Team Member Impact – we were able to create an environment that was safe for our team to provide care, and our focus on running emergency operations and normal operations in parallel meant we had fully recovered financially during the pandemic. Our employees returning to work while other hospitals and health systems were just beginning to announce their reductions in force, highlighting the need for timely and fluid planning.
- Human Impacts – our approach to "diverting and funneling" symptomatic patients that did not require hospitalization provided a level of insulation to our clinics and emergency departments. Just as importantly, it kept the family members and loved ones safe as we ensured that those afflicted with COVID-19 isolated themselves until their symptoms had resolved.
- Economic Impact – by quickly recognizing the lost volume's impact on cash flow and through a quick reduction of our operating expenses, not only were we able to recover quickly by bringing our furloughed employees back, but we made budget even though health systems around the country were posting historic losses.
- Social Impact – our health system's proactive and fluid response led to the State of South Carolina providing funding for our health system to set up fixed and pop-up testing and vaccinating locations throughout the state (impacting every county). This resulted in hundreds of thousands of South Carolinians getting vaccinated and over 1,000,000 COVID tests being performed.

Response Effectiveness

- Effectiveness – although we had no experience, the leveraging of the collective intellect of the team led to proactive and fluid planning that resulted in outcomes-based objectives (example – keeping non-acute patients out of our EDs and ambulatory clinics). We were able to absorb the influx of patients without having to deploy the field hospital we established, and we became a statewide resource for testing, vaccinating, and for helping to provide the supplies and equipment needed for other non-affiliated hospitals to sustain operations.
- Coordination and Communication – Externally, our health system was in lockstep with other hospitals, local municipalities, and with numerous state regulatory agencies. Internally, additionally and again, we created our own response language (staffing, capacity, and supplies/equipment) – this is the way we looked at our care delivery operationally, and it helped us to relegate the "noise" that comes with emergency events and to remain hyperfocused on the items that would keep our patients, care team members and visitors safe.
- Timeliness and Appropriateness of the Response – we were proactive; meaning, we were actively planning before the first COVID patient was diagnosed in South Carolina. Not only were we able to absorb the additional infectious volume of patients in a safe and efficacious manner, but we became a statewide resource for testing and vaccinating and a resource for providing additional PPE or equipment to hospitals that were challenged by the increased demand for services. Additionally, our emergency operations team helped guide the operational responses of other health systems in and out of the state.

Lessons Learned

- We learned numerous lessons during our pandemic journey. Note – the following list is not exhaustive – but it does include the salient takeaways that we'll use moving forward:
- Proactive and Fluid Planning – we planned early, and it provided the outcomes we established through the enhanced safety of care delivery for our patients and care team members. We continued to plan – at times daily – as the prolonged event progressed. This allowed us to be perpetually ready and led to our rising to meet the needs of not only our patients but the needs South Carolinians and other healthcare providers throughout the state.
- Consistent, Timely, and Simplified Communication – by distilling our communication down to the Problem, Impact, and Plan with the "plan" looking at capacity, staffing, and supplies/equipment – every team member knew what to expect from each meeting and knew, down to the hospital and/or clinic level our level of preparedness for the day (updated in four-hour increments).
- Recovery, Recovery, Recovery – one of the greatest lessons imparted to me over the years is that the disruption to patient care and the financial impact of unplanned emergency management events can be mitigated during the event. For example, if we cancel elective surgeries and ambulatory visits due to inclement weather, we'll open up Saturdays and have 90%+ of all lost volume rescheduled before the storm begins to subside. We used this foundational knowledge to respond quickly to our cash flow issue, decreased expenses, and consequently, learned to run emergency operations contemporaneously with normal operations – which led to our quick recovery and the health system meeting budget when other systems across the country we are reporting unprecedented losses.

Policy and Practice Implications

- The one policy implication/reform opportunity that was evident to health system operators across the country was that the United States needs to focus on bringing more of our critical medical supply manufacturing back to the United States. What most individuals outside of healthcare do not realize is that our supply chain coming out of China was disrupted pre-pandemic, with bioburden being found on different supplies, including surgical gowns. The disruption was magnified with a lack of PPE, ships being unable to access ports, etc.

Conclusion

- The key takeaway from this case study is that you do not have to have experience or access to experience to prepare for an emergency management event. You simply need to be able to articulate the potential issues and facilitate the inter/multi-disciplinary team discussion until you come up with potential solutions.
- Additionally, simplified and continuous communications will keep everyone in lockstep as you continue to navigate unknown waters. Coupled with the expectation that planning is ongoing/fluid, this will allow you to adjust as needed with your team already connected to the "why."
- Lastly, I'm going to underscore a recurrent theme within this text – recovery. You do not have to wait until the event has concluded to recover. Had my health system waited, it would have put us in a perilous cash position, and we would have been challenged to recover all of our pre-pandemic services that we offered. I have never understood the premise behind waiting, so don't and mitigate the impact on your patients waiting to receive care, as well as the financial burden that is analogous to emergency events.

Case Study 4: Cybersecurity Incident: Insight into a Response to a Data Breach and Cyber Attack Targeting a Healthcare System –Kim Bailey

Introduction

In May of 2017, the global WannaCry ransomware attack highlighted weaknesses in healthcare cybersecurity. This harmful software quickly spread through computer networks, locking up data and making systems unusable until a ransom was paid. Healthcare facilities in the United Kingdom felt the brunt of the impact, with the National Health Service (NHS) experiencing chaos. Hospitals had to cancel appointments and procedures as staff were denied access to systems for patient records, diagnostics, and administrative tasks. The event not only emphasized the importance of cybersecurity measures to safeguard sensitive health information but also showcased how cyberattacks can severely disrupt patient care and safety. The WannaCry incident acted as a reminder for healthcare institutions to enhance their cybersecurity defenses to better protect against future threats.

Background

The WannaCry ransomware took advantage of a flaw in versions of the Windows operating system, specifically targeting systems that had not yet installed a crucial security update. It quickly spread through networks using the EternalBlue exploit, which was originally created by the National Security Agency (NSA) and later leaked by a hacker group. The initial infections often originated from phishing emails, where users unintentionally clicked on attachments or links resulting in the ransomware being downloaded. Within a network, WannaCry moved sideways, encrypting files on each affected system and effectively blocking users from their data. It demanded payment in Bitcoin for the decryption keys necessary to regain access.

In the United States, this attack had real-world consequences for healthcare systems. For example, a major nonprofit healthcare provider serving Maryland and Washington D.C. experienced significant impacts. The ransomware compelled the organization to close down its email and electronic health record systems to prevent the spread, leading to disruptions in patient care. Staff had to resort to paper records and manual procedures, causing treatment delays and administrative confusion. The impact of WannaCry on healthcare systems emphasized the risks of depending on software and highlighted the importance of strong cybersecurity measures to defend against such destructive attacks.

Event Timeline

- Attack Phase: Beginning on May 12, 2017, WannaCry infected over 200,000 computers across 150 countries within a few days.
- Impact on Healthcare: Hospitals and healthcare facilities, including NHS hospitals, experienced widespread disruption to patient care as critical systems, including electronic health records (EHRs) and appointment scheduling, were inaccessible.

Impacts Assessment

- Human Impacts: The impact of the WannaCry attack on care was deeply felt by humans as the disruption to hospital systems directly affected the quality and consistency of medical services. The downtime of IT infrastructure made it difficult for healthcare providers to access health records (EHRs) efficiently, causing significant delays in retrieving essential patient information. This situation made it challenging for doctors and nurses to make decisions about patient care, often having to work with outdated records. In some instances, the inability to access histories, lab results, or imaging studies led providers to delay treatments or procedures until the systems were back online, potentially worsening health conditions. Many appointments were canceled, disrupting planned care schedules for patients. For individuals with ailments or those in need of checkups, these delays could have severe consequences since gaps in treatment could result in their health deteriorating or their illnesses progressing. Patients requiring emergency care were at risk due to delays that could lead to life-threatening situations. The attack also had an impact on care continuity. When patients move between healthcare providers or departments at a hospital, not having current medical records can make it difficult to ensure that care is well coordinated. This fragmented process raises the chances of mistakes, like incorrect doses or overlooked diagnoses, which can put safety at risk. The worry and unease felt by patients dealing with uncertainty about their care add to the harm as their trust in the healthcare system dwindles due to the breakdown in its capability to provide dependable, seamless care.
- Operational Impacts: Hospitals faced disarray during the WannaCry attack, leading to disruptions in their daily operations. Many surgeries had to be rescheduled or postponed,

resulting in a backlog of procedures and potential negative effects on health due to delays. Ambulances were redirected to nearby centers, putting pressure on those hospitals and increasing response times for emergencies. The administrative workload skyrocketed as staff worked tirelessly to handle the crisis, dealing with tasks like processing patient data, coordinating care, handling a surge in inquiries, and addressing hurdles. This operational chaos strained hospital resources and worsened the impact on patient care and overall system efficiency.
- Financial Impacts: Remediation costs, including IT recovery efforts, cybersecurity upgrades, and potential fines for data breaches, imposed significant financial burdens on affected healthcare systems.

Response Effectiveness

- Coordination and Communication: Healthcare providers collaborated with cybersecurity experts, government agencies, and law enforcement to contain the spread and mitigate the impact of the attack.
- Resource Allocation: Hospitals redirected resources to IT security upgrades, enhanced staff training on cybersecurity awareness, and implemented incident response plans.
- Timeliness of Response: Prompt identification of the attack and rapid deployment of patches and security updates helped mitigate further spread and limit damage.

Lessons Learned

- Successes: Enhanced cybersecurity awareness, improved incident response capabilities, and strengthened collaboration among healthcare providers and cybersecurity experts.
- Challenges: Outdated IT infrastructure, lack of cybersecurity funding, and the global scale of the attack highlighted vulnerabilities and gaps in preparedness.
- Recommendations: Advocate for continuous IT infrastructure updates, robust cybersecurity measures, and comprehensive staff training to mitigate future cyber threats.

Policy and Practice Implications

- Policy Changes: The WannaCry attack prompted governments to review and update cybersecurity policies, emphasizing the importance of regular software updates and cybersecurity resilience in critical infrastructure sectors, such as healthcare.
- Practice Improvements: Healthcare systems globally reinforced cybersecurity measures, including improved patch management, data encryption, and incident response planning to safeguard patient data and operational continuity.

The WannaCry ransomware attack had significant impacts on hospital operations, particularly affecting patient care and administrative functions. Here are specific examples of how some hospitals were impacted.

Disruption of Patient Care:

1. Appointment Cancellations: Hospitals had to cancel outpatient appointments and non-emergency surgeries due to the inability to access patient records and scheduling systems.

2. Delayed Treatments: Patients experienced delays in receiving treatments and surgeries, impacting their health outcomes and the continuity of their care.
3. Emergency Room Diversion: Some hospitals had to divert ambulances to other facilities due to operational constraints and the need to manage critical resources effectively.

Administrative Chaos:

1. Electronic Health Records (EHRs) Unavailable: Healthcare providers were unable to access patient medical histories, test results, and medication information stored in EHR systems, hindering clinical decision-making.
2. Appointment Scheduling Disruptions: Systems for scheduling patient appointments and managing hospital resources were paralyzed, leading to administrative challenges in managing patient flow and staffing.

Financial and Operational Strain

- Remediation Costs: Hospitals had to deal with challenges while fixing their IT systems following the WannaCry ransomware attack. These expenses covered the costs of implementing crucial security updates and recovering data from backups but also included investments in enhancing cybersecurity infrastructure to prevent future cyber attacks. The process of system restoration was often intricate and time-consuming, requiring IT assistance, leading to increased expenses. The financial pressure was exacerbated by the need to address disruptions in hospital operations, making the recovery efforts both expensive and demanding in terms of resources.
- Productivity Loss: The outbreak of the WannaCry attack had a significant impact on the efficiency of staff at healthcare facilities that were affected. Healthcare professionals had to divert their attention from care to deal with cybersecurity issues. Following the attack, doctors, nurses, administrative personnel, and IT staff encountered difficulties due to the loss of access to digital systems. Physicians and nurses, who usually rely on electronic health records (EHRs) for information and treatment plans, had to resort to manual methods. This change not only slowed down their tasks but also increased the risk of errors since handwritten notes are more prone to mistakes or misplacement. The additional responsibility of recording data meant less time for direct patient care, resulting in treatment delays and a drop in care quality. Administrative staff responsible for hospital operations also faced challenges. Without tools, activities like appointment scheduling, billing processing, and communication, with patients and other healthcare providers became more complex and time consuming.

The manual processes introduced inefficiencies that contributed to a drop in productivity. IT staff, who played a role in responding to the incident, faced a workload as they worked on containing the ransomware spread, restoring affected systems, and implementing stronger security measures. While their efforts were vital in managing the crisis, diverting IT resources from maintenance and support tasks to emergency response created a backlog of technical issues further impacting hospital operations' efficiency. The attack significantly impacted staff productivity. Healthcare professionals, already under pressure due to their demanding roles, now had to handle a cyber crisis on top of their existing responsibilities. Managing the incident consumed time and energy that could have been devoted to patient care, resulting in increased stress levels, burnout, and decreased job satisfaction. The prolonged disruption caused by the attack meant that after systems were back online, staff had to catch up on delayed work and address any errors or issues stemming from the processes. In the long run, reduced productivity also had consequences for healthcare facilities. The extra time needed to handle the emergency situation, along with the likelihood of overtime expenses and the cost of bringing in workers to cover shifts, all contributed to an increase in operational expenses. The decrease in effectiveness in treatment and administrative tasks also meant that hospitals found it harder to effectively support their communities, possibly resulting in a drop in earnings as patients sought treatment elsewhere. In essence, the shift of time and resources towards dealing with the cybersecurity incident had an effect on efficiency, patient care quality, and the financial well-being of the impacted healthcare facilities.

- Reputation Damage: The impact of the WannaCry attack on hospitals went beyond operational disruptions. It significantly affected the reputation of healthcare institutions and eroded trust. When hospitals faced challenges in delivering care due to system issues, appointment cancellations, and postponed surgeries, it shook the confidence of patients and the community. People expect healthcare facilities to be safe, dependable, and effective during times of crisis. The sight of hospitals struggling with a cyberattack not only raised concerns about protecting health data but also questioned their readiness for emergencies.

This loss of trust could have long-term consequences. Patients might hesitate to seek treatment at compromised facilities, fearing for their privacy or the hospital's ability to provide services in the future. Media coverage post attack tarnished public perception of these institutions. News reports highlighting the disorder within hospitals during the attack reinforced perceptions of vulnerability and inefficiency. Reputational harm often leads to repercussions.

Hospitals might see fewer patients as people opt for alternative care options, leading to a drop in revenue. Additionally, dealing with system restoration, enhancing cybersecurity measures, and managing regulatory issues can strain finances. In some instances, hospitals may need to invest resources in public relations to regain trust and assure the community of their dedication to patient safety and data protection.

The lasting financial repercussions could involve insurance costs, potential legal settlements, and ongoing cybersecurity enhancements. These various elements contribute to a burden that persists after the initial crisis is resolved. The incident highlights the significance of cybersecurity measures, not for operational reasons but also for maintaining patient confidence and the financial stability of healthcare organizations.

Staffing and Communication Issues

- Communication Breakdown: The WannaCry ransomware incident highlighted vulnerabilities in the communication networks of hospitals and healthcare systems, adding complexity to an already challenging situation. Communication methods like email, messaging platforms, and internal phone systems were frequently unusable. This disruption made it extremely challenging for healthcare teams to organize aspects of patient care and operational responses. For instance, the inability to access health records (EHRs) and other digital platforms forced staff to resort to manual communication methods like handwritten notes or face-to-face meetings, which were time consuming and prone to mistakes. The breakdown in communication impeded the transmission of information, resulting in delays in patient care, confusion among staff members, and heightened levels of stress. With communication channels compromised, hospitals faced difficulties in managing patient transfers, sharing crisis updates, and coordinating actions across various departments and facilities.

- Staffing Challenges: The cyber incident also had an impact on hospital staff, worsening existing issues and introducing new challenges. Medical professionals, already dealing with high-pressure situations, had to shift their focus from tasks to aid in IT recovery efforts or adjust patient care methods due to the system disruptions. The IT team faced pressure as they worked tirelessly to contain the attack and restore critical systems functionality. During this time, healthcare workers had to adapt to the sudden loss of digital resources and records, often putting in extra hours to handle the increased workload and ensure patient well-being. Some hospitals experienced staff shortages in staff during the attack due to employees being reassigned for crisis management or difficulties in maintaining staffing levels amidst operational turmoil. This pressure complicated patient care delivery as fatigued and understaffed teams struggled to uphold service quality amid uncertainty and chaos.

These impacts underscored the vulnerability of healthcare systems to cyberattacks and emphasized the critical need for robust cybersecurity measures, contingency planning, and rapid response protocols to safeguard patient care and operational continuity during future cyber incidents.

Conclusion

The recent cyberattack using WannaCry ransomware on healthcare networks emphasizes the importance of taking steps in cybersecurity, having plans for responding to incidents, and fostering cooperation between different industries to lessen cyber vulnerabilities and safeguard patient well-being. By drawing lessons from this event and putting in place cybersecurity strategies, healthcare institutions can boost their ability to withstand and respond to changing cyber threats. This real-life example showcases the consequences of cyber assaults on healthcare systems and underscores the continuous endeavors to reinforce cybersecurity measures and uphold the confidentiality of patient information on a global scale amidst an atmosphere of unpredictability and disturbance.

Bibliogarphy

1. National Health Service (NHS) Digital. (2018, February). *Lessons learned review of the WannaCry ransomware cyber attack*. NHS England. https://www.england.nhs.uk/wp-content/uploads/2018/02/lessons-learned-review-wannacry-ransomware-cyber-attack-cio-review.pdf
2. Cybersecurity and Infrastructure Security Agency (CISA). (2017, May 12). *Alert TA17-132A: Indicators associated with WannaCry ransomware*. U.S. Department of Homeland Security. https://www.us-cert.cisa.gov/ncas/alerts/TA17-132A
3. U.S. Department of Health and Human Services (HHS). (n.d.). *HHS cybersecurity program resources*. https://hhscyber.hhs.gov/
4. Federal Bureau of Investigation (FBI). (2017, June). *Ransomware prevention and response for CISOs*. https://www.fbi.gov/file-repository/ransomware-prevention-and-response-for-cisos.pdf/view
5. Symantec. (2017). *The WannaCry ransomware attack: A retrospective analysis*. https://www.symantec.com/blogs/threat-intelligence/wannacry-ransomware-attack
6. Kaspersky Lab. (2017). *WannaCry and the vulnerabilities of the healthcare sector*. https://www.kaspersky.com/resource-center/threats/wannacry-ransomware

Chapter 12

The Road Ahead: Sustainable Healthcare Emergency Management and Emerging Trends

Kimberly Bailey

I have always taken pride in my planning and my composed demeanor when faced with challenges. Lately I am encountering a situation that pushes me beyond my expertise and comfort zone. Many people around me are now boldly moving towards incorporating data analytics, artificial intelligence (AI) and cloud-based communication systems into their emergency response strategies. The potential advantages are evident; better real-time decision making, allocation of resources and enhanced coordination among departments. At first, I was hesitant. For years emergency managers had been accustomed to manual methods. Writing emergency plans manually, using walkie talkies during drills, and relying on simple methods of communication. The thought of embracing AI algorithms and cloud technologies felt overwhelming and unfamiliar. Nevertheless, I realized that ignoring these emerging trends was not an option. The healthcare industry is changing rapidly. Keeping up requires adapting to technologies. Determined to overcome my doubts I made the decision to fully engage in this endeavor. I dedicated some evenings to researching examples of other emergency management departments that had adopted these technologies and sought advice from colleagues who were more knowledgeable about tech innovations.

The process of learning can be quite challenging, with moments of frustration. Delving into AI algorithms and navigating cloud-based systems is akin to mastering a language. However, with each understanding I am increasingly aware of the potential these technologies offer. A pivotal moment occurred during a mass casualty event when utilizing the cloud-based communication platform enabled seamless coordination with external agencies and first responders. The clarity and efficiency of communication were unparalleled highlighting that these innovations are not merely tools but transformative enhancements

 DOI: 10.4324/9781003529194-12

to our emergency response capabilities. Embracing change may be challenging but it is also undeniably thrilling. I felt revitalized by seeing how blending emergency management principles with cutting edge technology could enhance our healthcare environment's resilience and responsiveness. While my core mission remains unchanged – to safeguard lives and ensure our hospitals preparedness – the methods are evolving in many ways. I aspire for my journey of adaptation and growth to inspire my team and peers positively. I aim to encourage a culture of enhancement motivating individuals to maintain a sense of curiosity and receptiveness to concepts. As a team we have welcomed innovation guaranteeing that our healthcare system stays ahead in emergency preparedness. By pushing beyond my boundaries, I experienced career growth while also contributing to building a stronger and more resilient healthcare system.

-Kim Bailey

In Chapter 12, we shift our focus to the ever-evolving landscape of healthcare emergency management. By the end of this chapter, healthcare leaders will have a clear perspective on the latest advancements in the field, allowing them to anticipate future needs and opportunities for enhancing their healthcare emergency management strategies. This chapter explores the latest trends and innovations in the field, providing healthcare leaders with insights into cutting-edge strategies, technologies, and approaches that can enhance preparedness, response, and recovery efforts. We will address the need for healthcare leaders to stay abreast of emerging trends and innovations to ensure their organizations remain at the forefront of effective emergency management.

The history of emergency management is a tale of growth, adaptability, and creativity. To truly grasp the progress made, it is worth embarking on a journey to the 1970s and 1980s, a time when emergency management was still in its early stages, navigating its way through the modern era against the backdrop of those memorable decades. In the 1970s, the field of emergency management was as rough and authentic as the rock melodies blasting from transistor radios. The tunes of that era could have symbolized every fire chief's role, resonating with the urgency and intensity of that period. Emergency management resembled a patchwork quilt of initiatives rather than a unified approach, much like the diverse mix of music genres on a 70s playlist. During that era, fire stations stood at the core of response operations where firefighters were not just responders to fires but to incidents like car accidents and natural calamities. Radios, with only a few channels, served as the link connecting responders to one another and the central command post, much like the simple yet strong bond between a record needle and vinyl. Disaster plans, if they were in place, were usually handwritten and stored in a filing cabinet alongside a collection of beloved LPs. In towns across the country, local fire chiefs took on the role of emergency managers, making crucial decisions with just a map, a radio, and a phone. The nature of their work was unpredictable.

With the arrival of the 1980s came a wave of professionalism that swept through emergency management like the driven revolution that transformed the music industry. The establishment of FEMA in 1979 reshaped the landscape. Local emergency managers began to establish themselves as a profession similar to how new wave artists carved out their own space in a music world dominated by rock and disco. The introduction of the Incident Command System brought a standardized approach to disaster response, mirroring how MTV revolutionized the music scene by introducing a visual format with round-the-clock video plays. Technology started making its way into the field and pagers and early computers became tools of the emergence. Despite these advancements, the core principles remained unchanged – the commitment to readiness and response was as steadfast as the resilience and optimism.

Over time, emergency management has evolved into a coordinated and technologically advanced domain. The incorporation of technology is as significant as the impact of streaming services on the music business. Emergency operations centers now buzz with real-time data, GIS mapping, and social media updates. Roles have expanded, with official emergency managers assuming leadership roles by integrating systems similar to how contemporary music producers blend genres and technologies to craft something entirely unique. The COVID pandemic of 2020 caught us all off guard, bringing forth changes that propelled the field into new territories, much like how surprising collaborations have led to the birth of fresh musical genres.

As we gaze towards the future, the progression of emergency management is poised to persist, with innovations that will revolutionize the field just as music videos revolutionized pop culture in the 1980s. Advancing technologies such as artificial intelligence, drones, and sophisticated data analysis will assume roles akin to synthesizers in the hands of figures from the 80s, acting as cutting-edge tools that will redefine what can be achieved.

Although technology will undoubtedly shape what lies ahead, the essence of emergency management will endure – a dedication to safeguarding communities, a foundation built on planning and the capacity to remain composed and lead during crises. The insights gleaned from decades set against a backdrop of rock, disco, and synth-pop tunes from the 70s and 80s will continue to guide generations of emergency responders. The journey from yesteryear to today has been extraordinary. As we stand at the threshold of breakthroughs, we do so with wisdom gained from history illuminating our path. The narrative of handling emergencies is a journey, like the timeless melodies from those memorable eras; it will persist in motivating and transforming. The world of healthcare emergency management is in a constant state of flux, driven by advances in technology, changes in the healthcare industry, evolving risks and threats, and lessons learned from past emergencies. Integrating data analytics and artificial intelligence (AI) into a healthcare emergency management program can revolutionize the way hospitals prepare for and respond to crises. By harnessing the power of advanced data analytics, hospitals can analyze vast amounts of historical data to identify patterns and trends that may indicate potential emergencies. AI algorithms can then be utilized to predict and forecast potential risks, allowing hospitals to proactively allocate resources and plan responses accordingly. The real-time monitoring capabilities of AI can provide early detection of anomalies and alert healthcare providers to emerging threats, enabling swift and effective interventions. Moreover, AI-driven decision-making tools can assist in optimizing resource allocation during emergencies, ensuring that critical supplies, personnel, and equipment are deployed efficiently. AI technologies can enhance the decision-making process by providing evidence-based recommendations and predictive insights to healthcare leaders. By leveraging machine learning algorithms, hospitals can develop more effective emergency response strategies tailored to specific scenarios. AI systems can also support the automation of routine tasks, freeing up healthcare staff to focus on critical patient care activities during emergencies. AI technology can automate a wide range of routine tasks, such as data entry, documentation, scheduling, and communication, which are essential but time-consuming activities in a hospital setting. By offloading these tasks to AI systems, healthcare staff can devote more time and attention to critical patient care activities during emergencies, thereby improving overall patient outcomes and satisfaction. For example, AI-powered chatbots can assist in triaging patients by gathering initial symptoms and information, directing patients to appropriate care pathways, and providing basic medical advice. This can help alleviate the burden on emergency department staff and streamline the intake process, ensuring that patients receive timely and accurate care. Additionally, AI-driven predictive analytics can optimize patient flow within the hospital, predicting surges in patient admissions and adjusting staffing levels and resource allocation accordingly to prevent bottlenecks and minimize wait times.

AI-enabled monitoring systems can also track vital signs and patient data in real-time, alerting healthcare providers to any concerning changes or abnormalities. This continuous monitoring can aid in the early detection of deteriorating patient conditions, allowing for prompt intervention and potentially preventing adverse outcomes. AI algorithms can also analyze large volumes of medical data to identify patterns indicative of specific conditions or complications, aiding in accurate diagnosis and treatment decisions during emergencies. By automating routine tasks and augmenting healthcare staff with AI-powered tools, hospitals can improve efficiency, streamline processes, and enhance patient care delivery during emergencies. The integration of data analytics and AI into a healthcare emergency management program can greatly improve preparedness, response, and recovery efforts, ultimately enhancing the safety and well-being of patients and staff within the healthcare environment. Virtual platforms have emerged as indispensable tools in all areas of emergency management, including healthcare, offering versatile solutions for communication, coordination, and resource allocation during crises. These platforms facilitate remote collaboration among healthcare professionals, emergency responders, and decision-makers, enabling swift and effective responses to emergencies such as natural disasters, pandemics, or mass casualty incidents, among other scenarios.

In recent years, emergency management has taken on a more prominent role in special event planning and coordination, particularly during high-stakes situations like Election Day. In November 2020, one of South Carolina's county elections departments encountered a significant technology issue with mail-in ballots. The county's emergency management department was called in to assist. The situation required a manual count of ballots, demanding a well-coordinated response to ensure accuracy and timeliness. The emergency management team quickly developed a plan to count each ballot within a tight time frame, organizing separate teams for initial and secondary counts. This effort also involved coordinating with the media and managing logistics to set up the space, provide necessary resources, and support the employees involved. The use of advanced technology from a neighboring jurisdiction played a crucial role in maintaining a clear operational picture throughout the day. This technology provided real-time information, such as traffic conditions, vehicle locations, and active incidents, which was vital for ensuring a smooth and secure process. The success of this operation underscored the importance of staying current with emerging trends and technology in emergency management. This example highlights why it is essential for emergency management professionals to keep up with current trends and continually seek innovative solutions. In a world where unexpected challenges can arise at any moment, the ability to adapt quickly and leverage new tools and strategies can make a significant difference in the effectiveness of response efforts. By embracing innovation and staying informed about the latest developments, emergency management can better serve communities, ensuring that critical events are managed efficiently and with minimal disruption.

Picture a situation where a hospital is struck by a natural calamity like a hurricane that brings about widespread flooding and structural destruction. The physical HEOC situated inside the hospital premises becomes inoperable due to power failures and impassable roads, which hinder personnel from assembling in person. In such a circumstance, the hospital can promptly switch to a virtual emergency operations center for hospitals. Utilizing a digital platform enables hospital leaders, emergency management teams, and healthcare workers to organize their response from remote locations. By using video calls and shared data in real time along with teamwork tools, leaders can maintain smooth communication and decision-making processes, ensuring that patient care is not disrupted. This online system enables the distribution of resources, monitoring patient conditions, and working together with external emergency services and government bodies. In this situation, there are advantages: it offers a reliable option in case the physical infrastructure is at risk of disruption and guarantees seamless operations while boosting the hospital's capacity to react promptly and efficiently to changing emergencies. By utilizing technology effectively, the hospital can manage its operations efficiently, support its employees, and provide medical treatment to patients amidst unprecedented difficulties. Virtual emergency operations centers and stakeholders can come together through a combination of hybrid methods to exchange real-time information and plan response strategies collaboratively. This approach allows for resource deployment even in situations when gathering in a physical centralized location is not feasible.

Virtual platforms also aid in facilitating telemedicine and virtual healthcare services by enabling healthcare providers to evaluate and treat patients – an approach that helps alleviate strain on healthcare facilities facing high demand and significantly reduces the risk of disease spread. Additionally, the incorporation of intelligence and data analytics into virtual platforms improves overall situational awareness, enabling predictive modeling, early identification of outbreaks, and better decision-making processes. As the landscape of healthcare emergency preparedness and response plans are adapting to rely more heavily on virtual platforms to establish robust and flexible healthcare systems that can effectively address the intricate issues of today's world. Telemedicine and virtual healthcare services are transforming how emergencies are managed in the healthcare sector by guaranteeing continuity of care during crises and establishing a pattern that is anticipated to influence the direction of responses in the future. Telemedicine makes use of communication technologies to provide medical services from a distance, allowing healthcare professionals to diagnose patients and provide treatment and monitoring without being physically present with them. This advancement proves beneficial in emergencies like natural disasters or pandemics when access to traditional healthcare facilities is restricted or risky. Through the use of video calls, remote monitoring devices, and mobile health apps, telemedicine guarantees that patients receive medical care while also easing the strain on overwhelmed emergency departments and curbing the transmission of contagious illnesses.

The integration of healthcare in emergency preparedness is both groundbreaking and a direct response to the growing need for convenient and effective medical services. This shift is fueled by progressions in expanded internet availability and the growing usage of smartphones and other smart gadgets. During emergencies, telehealth platforms can promptly adjust to the spike in requirements, offering a flexible solution that conventional healthcare setups frequently find challenging to keep up with. Telemedicine offers patient care, follow-up appointments, and mental health assistance, which are vital aspects of holistic emergency services. Incorporating AI and data analysis into healthcare platforms boosts the capacity to forecast and address health crises. AI programs can evaluate information to detect trends and anticipate possible outbreaks, enabling preemptive actions instead of reactive measures. This proactive strategy can greatly reduce the effects of emergencies, enhance results, and optimize resource distribution. The growing use of platforms and telemedicine in emergency preparedness demonstrates a wider shift towards digital advancement in healthcare and emergency response efforts. It shows how technology can help fill gaps in care during emergencies and emphasizes the significance of innovative approaches in building strong healthcare systems.

Community-driven disaster preparedness is an advancement in healthcare emergency management that indicates a move towards inclusive and cooperative strategies for disaster readiness. Instead of the conventional hierarchical methods of emergency response, community-based disaster preparedness focuses on engaging local communities in recognizing risks, creating response strategies, and enhancing their ability to lessen the effects of disasters. This approach recognizes that communities are usually the initial responders during emergencies and hold important local insights and assets that can support formal healthcare systems. When community members come together with healthcare providers and government agencies to plan and train for disasters collaboratively, community-based disaster preparedness efforts work to create a sense of ownership and empowerment among individuals involved. This ultimately results in more effective and long-lasting disaster resilience strategies being put in place.Technology plays a significant role in driving innovation within community-based disaster preparedness. Using digital platforms and technology tools helps to facilitate communication and engagement within communities. Virtual hubs online social networks, and mobile apps all serve as avenues for sharing information, coordinating volunteer efforts, and managing responses promptly during emergencies. These online tools help communities quickly gather resources and communicate information while reaching out to external aid organizations in times of crisis to better adjust and react to changing challenges. Community-led disaster readiness takes an approach to managing emergencies that extends beyond conventional healthcare systems to consider social factors like economics and the environment's impact on health. By incorporating fairness and sustainability principles into disaster preparation and response efforts, this movement aims to lessen gaps in healthcare access and bolster resilience within marginalized groups. Community-driven efforts to prepare for disasters may include educating healthcare volunteers and forming emergency response squads within neighborhoods while also enhancing infrastructure to endure natural calamities, all aimed at enhancing the ability of communities to handle crises effectively. The approach of community-based disaster preparedness signifies a change in how healthcare emergencies are managed by emphasizing the value of grassroots involvement and collaborative efforts across disciplines to foster innovation and resilience in local communities. The ongoing adoption of cutting-edge technologies and new methods is set to have an impact in shaping the future of healthcare emergency management. These advancements aren't merely passing fads; they represent agents of change that aim to boost community resilience and readiness while lessening the effects of disasters in public health. Key strategies such as Resilient Infrastructure and Sustainability programs are gaining importance as hospitals prioritize constructing infrastructure capable of enduring different risks and embracing eco-friendly practices for reducing their environmental impact in crises. This combined strategy improves the running of operations and lessens the environmental effects in the long run to bolster the community's resilience as a whole. Public-private partnerships (PPP) are crucial in enhancing healthcare readiness and response capabilities as well. Collaborations between healthcare institutions and private businesses merge various skills and resources to enhance access to vital equipment, technology, and knowledge. These alliances facilitate stronger planning, cooperation, and response initiatives, leading to a more efficient and thorough emergency management structure. Advancements in Mental Health and Psychosocial Support are transforming how healthcare institutions handle the psychological effects of crises on individuals and their loved ones, as well as staff members. Elevated methods for offering tailored assistance can alleviate lasting trauma and enhance the general welfare of communities following a disaster. Mobile Health Applications (known as mHealth apps) have become instruments for instant data exchange, communication, and organization in times of crisis. These applications allow healthcare professionals to promptly access and share information and coordinate responses among organizations to provide prompt care to affected communities in times of crisis. Their flexibility and ease of use make them extremely valuable during emergencies by enabling quick and well-informed decision-making that can greatly influence the outcomes of emergency responses.Together, these progressions highlight a changing trend towards a more cohesive and technology-driven strategy for managing healthcare emergencies. By embracing these advancements and being open to future developments in healthcare technology and practices, organizations can enhance their capacity to effectively handle emergencies while also setting the foundation for a stronger and more flexible healthcare system ready to tackle upcoming obstacles confidently.

The pandemic illuminated the critical need for healthcare providers, especially those without emergency departments, to innovate and prepare for delivering services in the field or off-site. As testing became a priority, many providers faced challenges in planning and executing testing sites, often requiring logistical support from local jurisdictions. In several cases, there was an underestimation of the complexities involved in what is largely a logistics mission. From identifying adequate hardstand surfaces to leveraging technology, ensuring PPE supply, coordinating feeding and hydration, and managing public information, our emergency management department was instrumental in bringing structure and efficiency to the testing process. However, the pandemic also revealed that not all local emergency management departments or jurisdictions are equipped to support large-scale field operations. This gap highlights the importance of innovation and the need for more active participation in regional healthcare coalitions and preparedness initiatives. These coalitions are vital in bridging the gap between public safety and healthcare, fostering collaboration, and ensuring that all stakeholders are prepared to meet the demands of future crises. By embracing innovation and strengthening these partnerships, we can enhance our ability to respond effectively to emergent challenges.

-Mario Formisano, Deputy County Administrator, Dorchester County

Chapter 13

Conclusion and Call to Action

Kimberly Bailey

This section really speaks to me as it highlights the role of leadership in managing healthcare emergencies effectively. It goes beyond dealing with current crisis situations; it emphasizes the importance of building a sustainable legacy of readiness and strength. As leaders in this field, it's not our job to handle today's challenges but also to share essential wisdom and perspectives with the generations to come. This heritage is not about passing along methods and rules but, about fostering an environment where preparedness and flexibility are core values. In the paced realm of healthcare emergency response planning and coordination leadership goes beyond quick decision making to encompass encouraging creativity and forward thinking. It calls for an approach that involves consistently predicting and readying ng for the unexpected. Adjustingg, to the shifting environment of healthcare emergencies requires flexibility and a readiness to adopt new technologies and tactics. By fostering these attributes within ourselves and our team members we can guarantee that our institutions not endure but flourish in challenging circumstances. Furthermore the tradition of leading in healthcare emergency response goes beyond the limits of organizations and includes working with various partners to form alliances and encouraging a community wide dedication to readiness This comprehensive method guarantees that we are not only reacting efficiently to emergencies at present but also establishing a strong groundwork, for the days ahead As I ponder upon the insights acquired and experiences gathered over my professional journey I am reminded of the significant influence that capable leadership can wield in healthcare emergency response Lets inspire each other to grow and share our knowledge with the leaders who will uphold the important task of protecting public health and welfare during challenging times.

~Kim Bailey

At the conclusion of this chapter, healthcare leaders and emergency managers will feel compelled to apply the insights and expertise acquired from this book. They recognize the role of their leadership and dedication in safeguarding the security and welfare of their institutions and the communities they support in times of crisis.

This chapter takes us on an exploration of the key components that healthcare leaders encounter as they handle emergency situations effectively. It starts by highlighting the importance of

DOI: 10.4324/9781003529194-13

emergency management in healthcare settings – a fundamental pillar of strong healthcare systems across the globe. Acknowledging this importance means understanding the vulnerabilities and challenges that healthcare institutions face – from calamities to outbreaks and technological interruptions. Grasping these principles empowers healthcare leaders with the expertise and abilities needed to meticulously plan for emergencies and respond to them with foresight.

Keeping up with the trends and advancements is crucial for staying relevant and effective in healthcare emergency management practices. Having a finger on the pulse of emergency management trends and preparedness tools is key as they constantly evolve due to advancements and shifts driven by real-world experiences from global emergencies. Healthcare leaders and emergency managers who welcome these changes are in a position to foresee upcoming obstacles and openings by harnessing resources such as data analysis tools, AI technology, and virtual platforms to boost readiness, response capabilities, and recovery procedures.

As this chapter progresses and unfolds, healthcare leaders are prompted to look at their personal paths and encounters in the area of emergency management. It acts as a nudge towards acknowledging the continuous dedication needed to protect public health and enhance the resilience of healthcare systems amid unpredictable situations. By incorporating insights gained from experiences, mastery of fundamental principles, and embracing new ideas and approaches, healthcare leaders can pave a way ahead that bolsters their organizations' capacity to safeguard and support their communities when faced with challenging circumstances.

Healthcare emergency management goes beyond occurrences – it requires a constant and evolving dedication that calls for continual investment and adjustment over time. It is crucial for healthcare leaders to stay alert and proactive in preparing for and addressing threats that may arise, including natural disasters, health emergencies, as well as technological interruptions. An essential aspect of this dedication is fostering a strong organizational culture within your healthcare facilities that values readiness, flexibility, and taking proactive measures in the face of potential emergencies. Healthcare leaders empower their teams to confidently and competently navigate crises by integrating these principles into the core of their organizations.

The ability to bounce back culturally goes beyond being prepared individually to include working together to make sure everyone is involved. From front-line workers to top management, everyone must be on the same page when it comes to protecting patient care and community welfare. It is crucial to learn from what has happened and be open to new ideas. Looking back at how emergencies were handled in the past helps healthcare leaders spot what worked well and where there is room for growth, leading to improvements in emergency response tactics. Incorporating technological innovations, like AI-powered predictive analytics and virtual platforms, empowers healthcare institutions with the necessary resources to enhance decision-making processes and effectively manage resources and communication in times of crisis.

This message encourages healthcare executives to focus on developing resilience within their organizations as a priority task. By promoting a mindset of readiness and adjusting approaches to address changing obstacles while utilizing solutions, healthcare establishments can efficiently carry out their duty of protecting public health and sustaining business operations amidst unpredictability. This publication emphasizes the responsibility of healthcare leaders in directing their teams to make significant choices and guarantee the security and welfare of patients, employees, and the local community. Leadership in healthcare during emergencies is crucial to ensure that healthcare institutions are ready to handle crises, like natural disasters and public health emergencies, effectively. Healthcare leaders have roles that include planning strategically, allocating resources efficiently, communicating effectively, training staff members, taking care of patients, complying with regulations, and showing adaptable leadership during healthcare emergency situations. They start by carrying out risk assessments to pinpoint potential risks and weaknesses while gauging the probability and consequences of emergencies. Leaders engage in planning to create and manage emergency management plans that detail how resources are distributed and communication strategies are implemented in coordination with external partners for an efficient response capability when needed. Resource management plays a role as leaders assign staff members and allocate medical supplies along with equipment and facilities to meet emergency needs while also ensuring responsible budgeting and financial handling for emergency readiness and response. Furthermore, effective communication networks are put in place to swiftly share information with employees, patients, and stakeholders through technologies. Collaborating closely with emergency management organizations and public health agencies at levels – local to national – helps in coordinating efforts and sharing vital information effectively during emergencies and highlights the significance of working together and forming partnerships in responding to crisis situations. Leaders place an emphasis on ensuring that staff members are well prepared through thorough training initiatives and emergency drills that cover both clinical procedures for patient treatment and addressing the mental well-being of healthcare workers. Healthcare administrators supervise the implementation of patient care guidelines to guarantee suitable treatment in emergency situations while also overseeing safety precautions like controlling access and creating evacuation strategies to protect patients, staff members, and facilities. They ensure compliance with regulations by following state and federal laws governing healthcare emergency management along with accreditation requirements. During emergencies, when circumstances are rapidly changing and challenging decisions need to be made to prioritize patient care safety and staff welfare, adaptive leadership plays a crucial role among healthcare leaders. In times of crises like disasters and disease outbreaks, healthcare leaders showcase their ability to pivot and adjust to meet the specific demands of each situation they face. These responsibilities underscore the crucial role healthcare leaders have in getting ready for and handling emergencies to guarantee the strength and uninterrupted delivery of healthcare services. Healthcare leadership during emergency management demands a thinking and flexible strategy where leaders are ready to lead their organizations through intricate challenges, rapidly changing situations, prioritize the safety and well-being of all stakeholders, and ensure that their healthcare systems remain resilient and capable of providing essential care during crises. This book serves as a compelling call to action for healthcare leaders, urging them to translate the knowledge and strategies gained throughout its chapters into actionable initiatives within their healthcare organizations. Armed with insights into risk assessment, strategic planning, resource allocation, and effective communication strategies, leaders are empowered to enhance their emergency management protocols. By implementing these strategies, healthcare organizations can better prepare for and respond to a wide range of emergencies, from natural disasters to public health crises. Central to this call to action is the emphasis on regular preparedness assessments, updates, and training programs. Healthcare leaders must ensure that their teams are continuously equipped with the latest skills and knowledge necessary for effective emergency response. This ongoing commitment not only reinforces organizational readiness but also cultivates a culture of resilience among staff, fostering a proactive approach to handling unforeseen challenges. Moreover, the call to action encourages healthcare leaders to advocate for the prioritization of healthcare emergency management across all levels of their organizations. By championing the importance of preparedness and resilience, leaders can garner the support and resources needed to sustain robust emergency management frameworks. This advocacy extends beyond internal stakeholders to include engagement with external partners, public health agencies, and community organizations, promoting collaboration and coordination in emergency response efforts. In a rapidly evolving healthcare landscape, embracing emerging challenges and innovations is essential. Healthcare leaders are urged to stay abreast of technological advancements, regulatory changes, and best practices in emergency management. By remaining adaptable and proactive, leaders can effectively navigate new challenges and leverage innovations to enhance their organization's emergency preparedness and response capabilities. Ultimately, the call to action resonates with a commitment to continuous improvement and proactive leadership in healthcare emergency management. By heeding these recommendations, healthcare leaders can ensure their organizations are well-equipped to safeguard patient care, protect staff well-being, and maintain operational resilience in the face of emergencies. The dedication and commitment of healthcare leaders stand as a testament to their pivotal role in safeguarding the well-being of patients and communities during crises. From hospital administrators to emergency managers and community stakeholders, these leaders navigate the intricate challenges posed by natural disasters, pandemics, and other emergencies. Their strategic decisions profoundly impact patient care, staff safety, and community health, ensuring hospitals and healthcare facilities are equipped to respond effectively. Recognizing their leadership, we celebrate the proactive initiatives undertaken by healthcare leaders to enhance preparedness and response capabilities. They develop and implement robust emergency management plans, conduct drills, and foster collaboration with local, state, and federal agencies. These efforts strengthen healthcare infrastructure and bolster community resilience, forging partnerships that transcend organizational boundaries to safeguard public health. Gratitude extends to all community emergency managers who work tirelessly alongside healthcare leaders. Together, they ensure a unified response, pooling resources and expertise to confront emergencies collectively. This collaborative spirit exemplifies resilience in emergency management, promoting mutual support and effective coordination across sectors. As healthcare leaders continue navigating evolving challenges and embracing innovative solutions, their dedication remains a cornerstone of preparedness. Emphasizing ongoing training, adaptation to emerging threats, and advocacy for robust emergency preparedness at all levels, we honor their collective contributions. Their leadership reaffirms the importance of safeguarding the health and safety of communities during times of uncertainty and adversity. The conclusion marks a pivotal moment, emphasizing the critical role of leadership, adaptability, and unwavering commitment in healthcare emergency management. At its core, healthcare leaders are not just stewards of their institutions but pioneers shaping the future of healthcare resilience. They stand as guardians of preparedness, ensuring systems can withstand the unforeseen and respond with agility and compassion. In the face of evolving challenges – be it natural disasters, pandemics, or technological disruptions – healthcare leaders embody resilience. Their foresight and strategic planning are essential in safeguarding patient care, securing staff well-being, and fortifying community health. Through their decisions and actions, they pave the way for adaptive responses that transcend immediate crises, laying foundations for sustainable healthcare systems. This leadership extends beyond boardrooms and administrative offices. It resonates in the dedication to continuous improvement, advocating for cutting-edge solutions, and fostering a culture where readiness is ingrained. Each decision made, from resource allocation to collaborative partnerships, shapes the readiness of healthcare ecosystems to face tomorrow's uncertainties. As we look ahead, the commitment to excellence in healthcare emergency management remains paramount. It calls for leaders who embrace innovation, champion inclusivity, and nurture resilience in their teams and communities.

As we conclude this exploration into healthcare emergency management, we urge each of you to take a moment to re-examine your current emergency management programs. The challenges we face today demand nothing short of excellence in preparedness and response. It is crucial to ensure that your organization is equipped with the best possible emergency management program

– one that is robust, adaptable, and visionary. Central to this endeavor is the selection of an exceptional emergency manager. This individual will play a pivotal role in guiding your organization through crises, coordinating resources effectively, and fostering a culture of readiness among your team. Look for someone who not only possesses technical expertise in emergency planning and response but also demonstrates strong leadership qualities, strategic foresight, and the ability to collaborate across disciplines. Your choice of an emergency manager should reflect a commitment to excellence and a dedication to safeguarding the well-being of your patients, staff, and community. This leader will be instrumental in enhancing your organization's resilience and ensuring that you can navigate future challenges with confidence. We encourage you to prioritize this selection process, invest in the necessary resources, and empower your emergency manager to implement cutting-edge strategies that elevate your emergency management program to new heights. Together, we can uphold the highest standards in healthcare emergency preparedness, setting a benchmark for excellence in the field.

Thank you for embarking on this journey of learning and reflection with us. Your dedication to mastering the intricacies of healthcare emergency management is commendable and essential. By investing your time and energy into understanding and implementing these strategies, you are not only enhancing the resilience of your organization but also safeguarding the well-being of the communities you serve. Your commitment to making a difference in times of crisis will not go unnoticed by those you serve. Together, we can all stand united in our mission to ensure that healthcare remains a beacon of stability and care, prepared to face any challenge with diligence and compassion. Thank you for caring deeply about the communities you serve and for your unwavering dedication to excellence in healthcare emergency management.

Chapter 14

Additional Resources and References

Kimberly Bailey

By the end of this chapter, healthcare leaders will have a valuable roadmap for further exploring and diving deeper into the field of healthcare emergency management. It will serve as a comprehensive reference guide for those seeking to expand their expertise, network with like-minded professionals, and continuously improve their healthcare emergency management practices. The chapter will stress the importance of staying informed about the ever-evolving field of healthcare emergency management and encourage healthcare leaders to continually seek out new knowledge, research, and resources to enhance their preparedness efforts.

Chapter 14 serves as a valuable resource guide for healthcare leaders seeking further information and support in the field of healthcare emergency management. This chapter provides a curated list of additional and essential resources, references, and organizations that can help healthcare leaders expand their knowledge, improve their preparedness efforts, and stay informed about the latest developments in the field.

Key Resources

This list provides a broad spectrum of resources that healthcare leaders can utilize for further information, training, and support in the field of healthcare emergency management.

1. **Books and Publications**
   - *Crisis Standards of Care: A Systems Framework for Catastrophic Disaster Response* by Institute of Medicine
   - A guide on how to develop and implement crisis standards of care during disasters.
2. **Journals and Research Papers**
   - *Journal of Emergency Management*
   - Covers a wide range of topics related to emergency management, including healthcare preparedness.

DOI: 10.4324/9781003529194-14

- *Prehospital and Disaster Medicine*
- Focuses on the intersection of prehospital care and disaster management, with articles relevant to healthcare professionals.
- *American Journal of Disaster Medicine*
- Research on disaster medicine with a focus on healthcare response and resilience.
- *Journal of Healthcare Risk Management*
- Includes articles on managing risks within healthcare settings, including emergency preparedness.

3. **Websites and Online Portals**
   - **Federal Emergency Management Agency (FEMA)**
   - https://www.fema.gov
   - Provides tools, training, and resources for emergency management across various sectors, including healthcare.
   - **U.S. Department of Health & Human Services (HHS) – ASPR TRACIE**
   - https://asprtracie.hhs.gov/
   - Technical Resources, Assistance Center, and Information Exchange for healthcare preparedness.
   - **Centers for Disease Control and Prevention (CDC) Emergency Preparedness and Response**
   - https://www.cdc.gov/cpr/index.htm
   - Resources and guidelines for healthcare emergency preparedness.
   - **National Incident Management System (NIMS)**
   - https://www.fema.gov/national-incident-management-system
   - Provides a consistent nationwide approach for emergency management at all levels of government.
4. **Professional Organizations**
   - **International Association of Emergency Managers (IAEM)**
   - https://www.iaem.org
   - Offers professional development, certification, and networking opportunities for emergency management professionals.
   - **Association of Healthcare Emergency Preparedness Professionals (AHEPP)**
   - https://www.ahepp.org
   - Focused on advancing healthcare emergency preparedness through education, networking, and best practices.
   - **American College of Healthcare Executives (ACHE)**
   - https://www.ache.org
   - Offers leadership training and resources for healthcare executives, including emergency preparedness.
5. **Government Agencies and Regulations**
   - **Centers for Medicare & Medicaid Services (CMS) – Emergency Preparedness Rule**
   - https://www.cms.gov/Medicare/Provider-Enrollment-and-Certification/SurveyCertEmergPrep
   - Regulatory guidelines for healthcare providers on emergency preparedness.
   - **U.S. Department of Health & Human Services (HHS) – Office of the Assistant Secretary for Preparedness and Response (ASPR)**
   - https://www.phe.gov/about/aspr/pages/default.aspx

   - Focuses on healthcare emergency preparedness and response, including pandemic response and bioterrorism.
   - **State and Local Emergency Management Agencies**
   - Contact information can be found through state and local government websites.
6. **Academic and Research Centers**
   - **Johns Hopkins Center for Health Security**
   - https://www.centerforhealthsecurity.org/
   - Research and policy analysis on health security, public health preparedness, and emergency response.
   - **Harvard T.H. Chan School of Public Health – Emergency Preparedness Research, Evaluation & Practice (EPREP)**
   - https://www.hsph.harvard.edu/eprep/
   - Research and training in public health emergency preparedness and response.
   - **University of North Carolina – Gillings School of Global Public Health**
   - https://sph.unc.edu/
   - Programs and research initiatives focused on public health preparedness and disaster management.
7. **Technology and Software Providers**

Here is the list of companies in alphabetical order:

- **Alastar**
- https://www.alastar.com
- Software for emergency management, including situational awareness and common operating picture tools.
- **ArcGIS for Emergency Management**
- https://www.esri.com/en-us/industries/emergency-management/overview
- A geographic information system (GIS) platform by Esri used for mapping, situational awareness, and analysis during emergencies.
- **CommandCentral by Motorola Solutions**
- https://www.motorolasolutions.com/en_us/products/command-center-software.html
- A suite of tools for situational awareness, incident management, and real-time intelligence for public safety agencies.
- **Crisis Track**
- https://www.crisistrack.com
- A disaster management software specializing in damage assessment, situational awareness, and resource management.
- **D4H Incident Management**
- https://www.d4h.com/products/incident-management
- An all-in-one software platform for emergency management including incident management, situational awareness, resource management, and communication.
- **DisasterLAN (DLAN)**
- https://www.bodhtree.com/dlan-emergency-management/
- A web-based emergency management software for incident management, resource tracking, and situational awareness.
- **Everbridge**
- https://www.everbridge.com

- An emergency communication and mass notification system with situational awareness tools.
- **OpsCenter**
- https://www.nc4.com/solutions/opscenter/
- Emergency operations management software providing situational awareness and coordination tools.
- **Palantir Foundry**
- https://www.palantir.com
- A data integration and analysis platform for situational awareness and common operating picture.
- **ReadyOp**
- https://www.readyop.com
- Platform for communication, coordination, and patient tracking in healthcare emergencies.
- **Veoci**
- https://veoci.com
- A cloud-based emergency management and collaboration platform supporting incident management, situational awareness, and emergency operations.
- **WebEOC**
- https://www.juvare.com/webeoc/
- Crisis information management software providing real-time situational awareness and resource management capabilities.

8. **Non-Governmental Organizations (NGOs)**

These organizations offer a range of resources, expertise, and support services that can be crucial for healthcare leaders involved in emergency management and preparedness.

- **American Red Cross**
- https://www.redcross.org
- Provides disaster relief, health and safety training, and emergency preparedness resources.
- **Direct Relief**
- https://www.directrelief.org
- Provides medical assistance and supplies to improve health outcomes in emergencies and disasters.
- **International Federation of Red Cross and Red Crescent Societies (IFRC)**
- https://www.ifrc.org
- Coordinates international disaster relief and promotes humanitarian activities globally.
- **Mercy Corps**
- https://www.mercycorps.org
- Focuses on disaster response and recovery, along with long-term development and resilience-building.
- **Partners In Health (PIH)**
- https://www.pih.org
- Provides healthcare services and supports emergency health responses in underserved regions worldwide.
- **Project HOPE**
- https://www.projecthope.org

- Delivers medical and humanitarian relief in emergencies and provides health education and training.
- **ShelterBox**
- https://www.shelterbox.org
- Specializes in providing emergency shelter and tools for families affected by disaster.
- **The Global Fund**
- https://www.theglobalfund.org
- Supports health programs in low- and middle-income countries, focusing on diseases like HIV/AIDS, tuberculosis, and malaria.
- **The World Health Organization (WHO) Foundation**
- https://www.who.foundation
- Supports the World Health Organization's emergency response efforts and global health initiatives.
- **World Vision**
- https://www.worldvision.org
- Provides emergency relief, development programs, and advocacy to improve the well-being of children and communities in crisis.

9. **Training and Certification Programs**

    1. ***Infectious Disease Training***
        - **American Red Cross**
        - https://www.redcross.org
        - Provides disaster relief, health and safety training, and emergency preparedness resources.
        - **Association for Professionals in Infection Control and Epidemiology (APIC)**
        - https://www.apic.org
        - Offers courses and certifications related to infection prevention and control in healthcare settings.
        - **Centers for Disease Control and Prevention (CDC)**
        - https://www.cdc.gov/cpr/ep/
        - Provides online courses and webinars on infectious disease management.
        - **National Infection Prevention and Control Training Program (NIPCTP)**
        - https://www.nih.gov/research-training/clinical-research/national-infection-prevention-control-training-program
        - Provides training resources and certification for infection prevention and control.
    2. ***Radiological Training***
        - **International Atomic Energy Agency (IAEA)**
        - https://www.iaea.org/topics/emergency-preparedness-and-response
        - Provides international training resources and workshops on radiological emergency response.
        - **National Radiological Emergency Preparedness (NREP) Program – NRC**
        - https://www.nrc.gov/about-nrc/emergency-preparedness/radiological-emergency-preparedness.html
        - Offers training and guidance on radiological emergency preparedness and response.
        - **Radiological Emergency Preparedness Program (REPP) – FEMA**
        - https://www.fema.gov/emergency-managers/practitioners/radiological
        - Provides training and resources for radiological emergency preparedness.

3. ***Mass Casualty Incident (MCI) Training***
   - **Centers for Domestic Preparedness (CDP)**
   - https://cdp.dhs.gov
   - Offers training for emergency responders, including mass casualty incidents and other specialized scenarios.
   - **Emergency Management Institute (EMI) – FEMA**
   - https://training.fema.gov/
   - Provides various courses and certifications related to mass casualty incidents and emergency management.
   - **Federal Emergency Management Agency (FEMA)**
   - https://www.fema.gov/emergency-managers/nims/incident-management
   - Offers courses on incident management, including mass casualty incidents and the National Incident Management System (NIMS).
   - **National Fire Protection Association (NFPA)**
   - https://www.nfpa.org
   - Provides training and certification for mass casualty incidents and emergency management.
   - **Office of the Assistant Secretary for Preparedness and Response (ASPR) – HHS**
   - https://aspr.hhs.gov/
   - Provides training and resources related to healthcare emergency preparedness and response.
4. ***Hazardous Materials (HazMat) Training***
   - **Department of Transportation (DOT)**
   - https://www.phmsa.dot.gov/hazmat/hazmat-training
   - Provides training on hazardous materials transportation and emergency response.
   - **National Fire Academy (NFA) – FEMA**
   - https://www.usfa.fema.gov/training/nfa/
   - Offers specialized training in hazardous materials response and management.
   - **Occupational Safety and Health Administration (OSHA)**
   - https://www.osha.gov/hazmat
   - Provides training resources and certification for handling hazardous materials, including the Hazardous Waste Operations and Emergency Response (HAZWOPER) standard.
5. ***On-Site Training Programs***
   - **Emergency Medical Services (EMS) Training Programs**
   - https://www.nremt.org/
   - Offers certifications and training programs for emergency medical services, including mass casualty and hazardous materials response.
   - **International Association of Emergency Managers (IAEM)**
   - https://www.iaem.org
   - Offers training and certification in emergency management, including on-site exercises and simulations.
   - **The National Academies of Sciences, Engineering, and Medicine**
   - https://www.nationalacademies.org
   - Provides reports and recommendations on emergency preparedness and management, including on-site training resources.

Index